LOUIS KOSSUTH AND
YOUNG AMERICA

Kossuth, about 1849.

LOUIS KOSSUTH AND
YOUNG AMERICA

A STUDY OF SECTIONALISM

AND FOREIGN POLICY

1848-1852

DONALD S. SPENCER

UNIVERSITY OF MISSOURI PRESS

COLUMBIA & LONDON, 1977

Copyright © 1977 by The Curators of the University of Missouri
University of Missouri, Columbia, Missouri 65201
Library of Congress Catalog Card Number 77-2123
Printed and bound in the United States of America
All rights reserved

CIP and permissions on last page.

The leaders of the Hungarian rebellion being escorted to Turkey in August 1849, after their defeat by the Austrian and Russian armies.

After they were transported from their imprisonment in Turkey
by the *U.S.S. Mississippi*, Kossuth and his entourage arrived
at Southampton, England, on the *Madrid* in October 1851.

PREFACE

I hope that this book tells three stories.

First and most obviously it is an account of Louis Kossuth's visit to the United States between December 1851, and July 1852. That tour, although today largely forgotten, was one of the most sensational events of a sensation-ridden era of American history. Kossuth—a rebel and statesman, but also a showman of almost comic proportions—barnstormed through the United States during those months, pleading for American aid for his dead revolution; the nation's response sometimes approached hysteria. This is a story that deserves extended treatment, not only for its intrinsic interest but also because it contributes to our understanding of America at midcentury.

Second, I have sought to chronicle the foreign policy debates of 1848–1852. Seldom during the nineteenth century did the American people pause to examine the philosophical dimensions of their relations with the outside world. They did so during those years; and the result was a series of profound contributions to the nation's intellectual tradition. Diplomatic historians habitually classify the approaches to foreign policy as either "idealistic" or "realistic." In the debates about Kossuth and the issues he symbolized, both approaches won expression from premise to conclusion. Because those debates so often were couched in abstract terms, they possess significance that transcends their specific time and place.

And finally, this is yet another story of the nation dividing. It is one conclusion of this book—not unique, certainly, but not previously amplified in a case study of foreign policy—that by midcentury most Northerners and most Southerners looked at every public question from different and usually antagonistic perspectives. So completely had slavery contaminated the nation's politics, in fact, that radicals from both sides of the Mason-Dixon line could plausibly define every public question as a corollary of the slavery issue; and thus defined, every public question further divided the North from the South. The inevitable result was a tangle of grating sectional tensions, each anchored to slavery, but each also transcending that specific subject in scope. As William Seward observed, "Every question, political, civil, or ecclesiastical, brings up slavery as an incident, and the incident supplants the principal question. We hear of nothing but slavery, and we can talk of nothing but slavery."

Let me point out, perhaps unnecessarily, that I did not set about to find sectional implications in the Kossuth episode. I had neither studied nor taught the era of sectionalism when I completed the early drafts of this book, although I have since assumed both duties. As a diplomatic historian, I had expected—perhaps naively—that I could complete my work without being bothered by the domestic issues of the day. That easy course, I later discovered, was impossible. America's smoldering sectional confrontation intruded itself into every element of my subject.

Some debts can be acknowledged but not repaid. Norman A. Graebner of the University of Virginia supervised my study of diplomatic history for three years. He is a most remarkable teacher, and his influence on the intellectual framework of this book is obvious. William Shade of Lehigh University and Dan Jordan of Virginia Commonwealth University saved me from a variety of errors, as did the anonymous readers who evaluated the manuscript for the University of Missouri Press. I am, of course, responsible for those mistakes of fact and interpretation that remain. I wish most of all to thank Sue Spencer, whose patience and encouragement have made this project more tolerable than it otherwise would have been; it is to her that I dedicate this book.

D.S.S.
March 1976

CONTENTS

Preface, vii

I. Prologue: A City Gone Mad, 1

II. Origins and Meaning of Young America, 11

III. Young America Focuses on Louis Kossuth, 29

IV. "Intervention for Non-Intervention," 49

V. The Abolitionist Defection, 65

VI. Washington: The Whigs, 83

VII. Washington: The South Says No, 95

VIII. Washington: The Young Americans, 107

IX. The Western Tour, 121

X. The Collapse of Interventionism, 135

XI. The Final Weeks, 153

XII. "The Sober Second Thought," 169

XIII. Young America and the Diplomacy of Symbolism, 177

Bibliography, 185   Index, 197

List of Illustrations

Kossuth, about 1849, ii

Hungarian rebels being escorted to Turkey, v

The *Madrid* in Southampton, vi

Kossuth leaving Southampton, xii

Kossuth reception at Southampton mayor's home, 5

Arrival at Castle Garden, New York City, 7

Torchlight parade past the Irving House, 9

Lewis Cass, 18

Mayne Reid, 23

Zachary Taylor, 25

Hungarian revolutionaries in battle, 29

Battle between Hungarian revolutionaries and Austrians, 31

Daniel Webster, 41

Henry Foote, 45

Kossuth's appearance in Central Park, 46

"Hungary Fund" certificates, 60

John Parker Hale, 72

Millard Fillmore, 85

Henry Winter Davis, 132

Pierre Soulé, 138

LOUIS KOSSUTH AND
YOUNG AMERICA

Southampton citizens bade Kossuth farewell as he left for the United States.

I.

PROLOGUE:
A CITY GONE MAD

Louis Kossuth was ill. Through most of fourteen days, vicious westerly gales and violent headseas had convulsed the North Atlantic, heaving the Cunard Liner *Humboldt* and its hapless voyagers back and forth across frigid waves. For Kossuth, who had precious little salt-water flowing in his landlocked Hungarian veins, the churning motion of the ship was agonizing, making it impossible for him to eat or sleep. Yet the distinguished passenger seemed cheerful as the *Humboldt* approached America's shores this December 1851, for he anticipated in the New World an early reversal of the misfortunes that had visited him in the Old.[1]

I.

Hardship had plagued the Magyar patriot for more than two years—at least since August 1849. In that month a massive force of Russian and Austrian soldiers had crushed his nation's infant revolution, restoring Hapsburg authority east of Vienna. As events foreshadowed certain defeat, Kossuth had ignored the pledge he had made to the Hungarian people in the first days of the rebellion: "Should the revolution fail, I will be the first one to suffer, and it will matter very little, whether I expiate my acts on the gallows, under the guillotine or by a bullet."[2] Instead, however, he had abdicated leadership of the struggle in favor of his ranking general and had fled to Turkey, leaving his wife

1. *The New York Times*, 5, 6 December 1851; *The New York Herald*, 6–8 December 1851; Francis Pulszky and Theresa Pulszky, *White, Red, Black: Sketches of American Society in the United States During the Visit of their Guests*, 1:10, 13.

2. *Louis Kossuth, As He Was Known to His Contemporaries*, p. 30.

I

and children and the shattered remnants of his army behind to face the victors' retribution. Hundreds, perhaps thousands of patriots died before Austrian firing squads, and many more were cast into prison. Madame Theresa Kossuth had been more fortunate. Hunted and with a price on her head, she had eluded Austrian agents for five harrowing months— disguised as a chambermaid more than once—before she too managed to escape across the Dardanelles.[3]

But exile had brought only compounded misery. While Kossuth was proclaiming loudly his martyrdom to the cause of Continental liberty, some of his former comrades in revolution were hinting that he was a coward and that he had bungled his homeland into submission.[4] Even more alarming were his prospects for safety in the future. The Turkish sultan had had Kossuth and his twelve hundred fellow exiles arrested, although he had not thrown them into a dungeon, as Kossuth liked to pretend. Russia and Austria were demanding his extradition, obviously intending to execute him, and the sultan seemed to promise permanent protection only if the Hungarians converted to Islam.[5] When the United States offered asylum to the defeated rebels and sent the *U.S.S. Mississippi* to escort them to the New World, they were delivered finally from the grim choice between death and religious dishonor.

Even among his rescuers Kossuth could not escape controversy. George Perkins Marsh, the brilliant linguist and diplomat who was then

3. For Kossuth's own account of these events, see "Letter to the People of the United States of North America," 27 March 1851, reprinted widely in American newspapers; see, for example, *National Era*, 23 October 1851. Madame Kossuth's account of her escape is related in Pulszky, *White, Red, Black*, 1:4–35.

4. See the sentiments expressed by Casimir Batthianyi, Kossuth's Minister of Foreign Affairs, and of Prince Esterhazy, in *The Times* of London, 1 December 1851 and 30 December 1851. Both men's letters are reprinted in Jánossy Dénes, ed., *A Kossuth-Emigráció Angliában és Amerikában, 1851–1852*, 1:86–93, 158–71; both letters are also quoted extensively in review of W. H. Stiles, *Austria in 1848– 49* (New York, 1852), in *North American Review*, 75 (September 1852): 458n.

5. *Kossuth in New England: A Full Account of the Hungarian Governor's Visit to Massachusetts; with His Speeches, and the Addresses That Were Made to Him, carefully revised and corrected*, pp. 20–22. For a longer discussion of Kossuth in Turkey, see John H. Komlos, *Louis Kossuth in America, 1851–1852*, pp. 33–49.

America's minister-resident at Constantinople, had supplied the Hungarians generous grants of food and money—often from his own anemic pocketbook—and still they complained of their living conditions. Marsh pronounced Kossuth an ingrate, who "never had the decency to utter a word of thankfulness" for the Americans' charity.[6] Furthermore, Marsh did not trust the Magyar. When the *Mississippi* arrived to take aboard its cargo of refugees, Marsh dispatched a note to its captain, John C. Long, warning that Kossuth might jump ship anywhere and that he would grasp any opportunity to reignite his dead revolution, even at the cost of American neutrality. Prudence therefore dictated that the *Mississippi* should "touch as few ports as possible, and remain as short a period at them, as is possible" on the journey home.[7]

Kossuth was furious when he learned the limits of his new leash and accused the Americans of operating a floating prison; he avowed that had he known the conditions of his trip to the United States before his release, he would have stayed in Turkey.[8] Bickering led to an open feud, and within two weeks after boarding the *Mississippi* on 10 September, Kossuth had offended every American with whom he had come into contact—and a few with whom he had not. "The devil seems to possess this gentleman," complained Charles W. Morgan, the commander of American naval forces in the Mediterranean. "He is utterly ungovernable. . . . He is like a firebrand."[9]

At every port of call Kossuth tried to harangue the local population

6. Marsh to Solomon Foot, 26 April 1852, quoted in David Lowenthal, *George Perkins Marsh, Versatile Vermonter*, p. 128; Marsh to Charles Drake, 3 August 1850, in *Life and Letters of George Perkins Marsh*, ed. Caroline Crane Marsh, 1:177–79; Marsh to Secretary of State, 14 March 1850, Records of the Department of State, Record Group 59, National Archives Microfilm Publications, M46, Role 14 (hereafter cited as RG 59, NAMP, with appropriate number); U.S. Congress, Senate, *Senate Documents*, 31st Cong., 1st sess., 10, no. 43, pp. 1–3.

7. Marsh to Long, 6 September 1851, U.S. Congress, Senate, *Executive Documents*, 32d Cong., 1st sess., 8, no. 78, p. 49. See also, Lowenthal, *Marsh*, p. 128.

8. Kossuth to John L. Hodge, U.S. Consul at Marseilles, 30 September 1851, Records of the Department of State, RG 59, NAMP, T220, Role 5; U.S. Congress, Senate, *Executive Documents*, 32d Cong. 1st sess., 8, no. 78, pp. 12–13.

9. Morgan to Hodge, 23 September 1851, ibid., p. 2.

about his dead revolution. And the Americans, anxious to protect the reputation of their flag in friendly ports, attempted to restrain him. By the time the ship reached Marseilles, Kossuth was heartily fed up with his hosts. He issued a "demand" that the French government allow him to cross its territory en route to England, where he said he would remain three weeks before rejoining the *Mississippi* at Gibraltar.[10] After a delay of thirty hours (which Kossuth peevishly described as three days[11]), officials in Paris refused permission, undoubtedly because they feared the exile would incite new violence in a nation itself just recovering from an aborted revolution.

Kossuth was beside himself with rage. He threatened to appeal over the head of Louis Napoleon directly to the French people, and then made good his threat by publishing his correspondence with the French authorities, together with an inflammatory commentary on that correspondence, in *Les Peuples*, a radical newspaper in the city.[12] Immediately the French government asked the Americans to keep him on board until he left port. The Americans agreed. Kossuth repeated his accusations about a prison ship, and vowed to leave the *Mississippi* at Gibraltar or "wherever you please."[13] He also promised bitterly that the American people would hear of the offensive conduct of their agents in Europe.[14]

At Gibraltar, after a chilly but civil exchange of bread and butter notes, Kossuth departed for England, where he toured triumphantly

10. De Suleau, Prefet des Bouches du Rhone, to Hodge; Kossuth to De Suleau, 27 September 1851, ibid., pp. 17, 18–19.

11. Kossuth to Hodge, 30 September 1851, ibid., p. 13.

12. Text contained in Hodge's notes, ibid., p. 17; see also Louis Kossuth, *Memories of My Exile*, p. 89.

13. Kossuth to Hodge, 30 September 1851, Records of the Department of State, RG 59, NAMP, T220, Role 5; U.S. Congress, Senate, *Executive Documents*, 32d Cong., 1st sess., 8, no. 78, p. 14; Hodge to Secretary of State Webster, 14 October 1851, ibid., p. 9.

14. Kossuth to Hodge, 30 September 1851, ibid., p. 14. Kossuth never carried out this threat. In fact, he tried manfully to deny that any disagreements had occurred; Louis Kossuth, *Select Speeches of Kossuth. Condensed and Abridged, with Kossuth's Express Sanction*, ed., Francis W. Newman, p. 292. Captain Long's extended recollections of the episode were later printed in *Morning Courier and New York Enquirer*, 15 February, 1852.

The mayor of Southampton, Richard Andrews,
offered his home to Kossuth during the visit.

for three weeks before booking passage on the *Humboldt*. Except for
the short interlude in Britain, Europe had not been kind to the exiled
rebel. But on 5 December, as the *Humboldt* slid into Pier 4 at Staten
Island, he was certain that his misfortunes were behind him.

II.

It was, reported *The New York Times*, "such a scene as the world
seldom beholds."[15]

After pausing a day at Staten Island to allow the city to make last-
minute preparations for its welcome, Kossuth crossed onto Manhattan

15. *The New York Times*, 8 December 1851; Kossuth agreed with this
judgment, almost verbatim; Kossuth, *Memories of My Exile*, p. xiv.

5

Island on Saturday, 6 December. Already the city was hysterical at news of his arrival. Before he could board the steamer *Vanderbilt* for the brief passage across the bay, the Richmond Guards, originally invited merely to add color to the festivities, had to repel mobs of well-wishers. And throughout an hour-long excursion around the harbor, merchant ships and shore batteries fired an unbroken series of deafening salutes. As the *Vanderbilt* approached the Bowery, an immense throng of citizens shouted their nation's welcome.[16] "All the tide of history seemed to beat around her keel," recalled one man.[17]

When Kossuth stepped ashore, New Yorkers saw for the first time their long-idolized hero. With neatly trimmed beard, high forehead, sallow complexion and sad, mellow blue eyes buried beneath bushy eyebrows, he seemed more fitted for quiet contemplation than heroic action. Indeed, his total appearance belied his martial reputation. He was frail, and so slight of stature that the tip of his ceremonial sword trailed him a step behind, skipping along the ground in comic fashion. But to those who stood before him, his image seemed to confirm their previous expectations. In their eyes he was dignity itself, standing erect, solemn, imperious. His tiny frame was partially augmented by a heavy black coat and by a tall felt hat crowned with a feather. Many observers claimed to recognize that boiling just below the surface of his placid demeanor was an intensity befitting a martyred rebel.[18]

Jubilant cheering erupted at this first appearance of the nation's

16. *The New York Herald*, 8 December 1851.

17. Charles Goepp, *E Pluribus Unum: A Political Tract on Kossuth and America*, p. 23.

18. *The New York Herald*, 8 December 1851; *The New York Times*, 6 December 1851; Joseph Neilson, *Memories of Rufus Choate, with Some Considerations of His Studies, Methods, and Opinions, and of His Style as a Speaker and Writer*, p. 147; Nathan Sargent, *Public Men and Events from the Commencement of Mr. Monroe's Administration, in 1817, to the Close of Mr. Fillmore's Administration, in 1853*, 2:383; George Sewall Boutwell, *Reminiscences of Sixty Years in Public Affairs*, 1:206; Henry W. DuPuy, *Kossuth and His Generals*, p. 404; Henry E. Chapin to Helen Kemper, 6 March 1852, quoted in Charles Amory Blinn to Historical and Philosophical Society of Ohio, Cincinnati, 4 May 1949, from the Collections of the Cincinnati Historical Society.

guest. Quickly Kossuth bowed to the people and was ushered inside Castle Garden to be greeted by Mayor Ambrose C. Kingsland. As he entered the building, pandemonium reigned. Ten thousand people were crushed inside its squat, rounded walls, and as a band struck up "Hail to the Chief" the foundations seemed to vibrate under the weight of shouts and stamping feet. Police circulated through the hall, begging the people to restore quiet, but they would not. No one, probably not even Kossuth himself, could hear the mayor's brief address.[19]

Kossuth's reply was drowned under even more hysterical noise. "Oh, it is impossible, Mister Mayor," he shouted in Kingsland's ear after trying twice to begin his speech. "I will give my notes to the press. I can't be heard." But the people implored him to continue, and he tried once

After his arrival in New York at Castle Garden, pandemonium reigned, and crowds lined the street along his parade route between the Bowery and Central Park.

19. This paragraph, as well as the three which follow it, is based on newspaper accounts, primarily *The New York Times*, 6 December 1851, and *The New York Herald*, 8 December 1851.

more. This time his words incited the mob to action. Cheering wildly, they pushed toward the speaker's platform, grabbing at the Hungarian and his entourage. Madame Kossuth, visibly alarmed by this tidal wave of human flesh, wished to leave. Hastily, the dignitaries slipped through a rear door—but not before a woman clipped away a piece of Kossuth's coat as a momento of this remarkable day.

Outside Castle Garden the mob continued to grow. Brooklyn was a ghost town, its shops closed, its houses empty. On the New Jersey shore citizens stood in line for hours, hoping to squeeze onto a ferry, and the lines grew longer as the day passed. Perhaps a quarter million people lined Broadway between the Bowery and Central Park, all waiting for Kossuth's procession to make its way. His approach toward any point was a signal for frenzied pushing and screaming. His own carriage was stalled at one point for two hours at the hub of one ring of admirers. Troops in the procession had to break ranks more than once to restore order among the frantic citizens, and at least one man was killed and a woman hospitalized in the mad shuffle of onlookers.

On every building along the parade route were signs of welcome and of moral support. Amid the thousands of Hungarian tricolors hung signs reading, "U.S. to Russia: Mind Your Own Business," and even more ominous statements of national intent: "His Visit Reminds Us of Our Neglected Duty to Freedom and the People of Europe," and "GRATITUDE! As the People of the United States Were Assisted by Valor and Treasure from Abroad, Our Government Should Be the First to Interfere Abroad in Favor of the Holy Principles of Progress." Everywhere there were portraits of Kossuth, sometimes flanked by likenesses of Washington and Lafayette, the twin symbols of America's own revolution and the relationship of Europe to it. Beneath the banners stood hoards of idolizing citizens, grasping to touch his hand, shouting their hopes that he would one day return to his native Hungary as a hero and as a conqueror.

By day's end, Kossuth was exhausted. As he lounged in the elegantly refurnished apartments provided by the city at the Irving House and listened to the muffled sounds of torchlight parades marching past his

After his zealous welcome to New York, Kossuth watched torchlight parades in his honor from his window at Irving House.

windows, he knew that he owned the keys to America's conscience. His mission, he also understood, was to translate the nation's sympathy into economic and military support for the European rebels, for he had not yet abandoned his hopes for an independent Hungary. "Let me hope that before I leave the United States," he had tried to tell his hosts before being cheered into silence at Castle Garden, "that the generosity of the people will give me material proofs that those sentiments which I have had the honor to hear from you, are the sentiments of the people of the whole country, and that they have so firmly decided to be as good in deeds and acts as in words and sympathy."[20]

Success would depend less on the realities of Eastern Europe than on the mood of the American people.

20. *The New York Times*, 6 December 1851.

II.

ORIGINS AND MEANING
OF YOUNG AMERICA

It is a commonplace to speak of the birth, adolescence, maturity, and old age of civilizations. Indeed, one philosophy, rendered respectable by Oswald Spengler's philosophy of history, is premised on this metaphorical fantasy. In this scheme of things, every great civilization enjoys a dynamic spring, a powerful summer, and a wise, autumnal middle age before hobbling into an endless winter of cultural senility.[1]

Decades before Spengler's birth, Americans of the 1840s recognized a popularized version of this same cosmology. "Nations, like men, have their seasons of infancy, manly vigor and decreptitude," Edwin De Leon told a gathering of student literary societies at South Carolina College in December 1845, and there were few Americans who would have disagreed with him. Nor would they have denied his corollary: the United States was "in the first flush of exulting manhood," prepared by talent, energy, and virtue to dwarf the outmoded, obsolete institutions prevalent among the monarchies of Europe. In De Leon's mind, the term *Young America* characterized his nation's generational consciousness.[2]

I.

Few slogans could have symbolized the age so well. At home, the self-conscious, awkward democracy of the 1820s and thirties had grown pompous. This age's faith in the common man presupposed, of course, faith in Man and confidence that he was moving toward perfection; by the 1840s the cult of perfectability reigned almost unchallenged in the

1. Oswald Spengler, *The Decline of the West*, trans., Charles Francis Atkinson; Spengler summarized his thesis briefly in *Man and Technics: A Contribution to a Philosophy of Life*, trans., Charles Francis Atkinson, pp. 90–104.
2. Edwin De Leon, *The Positions and Duties of Young America*, p. 25.

popular mind. "As Americans, we should have respect . . . for the great principles of PROGRESS," one western journal stated, and Charles Hawley agreed, "The day of universal light and liberty is approaching with the certainty of a comet to the sun."[3]

A sense of expectancy gripped those who, believing that they had discovered the single obstacle to man's perfection, created a committee to supervise its elimination. Abolitionism, temperance and universal public education were among dozens of causes whose advocates sought to speed the United States along the road to utopia. And existing alongside these broad movements were a host of more eccentric, less durable ones—phrenology, inalienable homesteads, Sunday mails, the dietary reforms of Dr. Graham and his therapeutic crackers—which had sprung from the same basic impulses. "Such is the *expansive tendency* of the American genius," declared even the conservative Whig *Scioto Gazette* in Ohio, "that one might as well preach moderation to a herd of buffaloes at full speed, as to stay [its] onward progress."[4]

Foreign policy during this "Age of Boundlessness" was incredibly successful.[5] The Republic of Texas had entered the Union as a single state; American armies had crushed Mexico so convincingly that expansionists could seriously debate the wisdom of annexing that country entirely;[6] new provinces stretched a thousand miles from New Mexico to Juan de Fuca Straits. In four years the United States had won

3. Quoted in Arthur A. Ekirch, Jr., *The Idea of Progress in America, 1815–1860*, pp. 56, 57.

4. *The Daily Scioto* (Ohio) *Gazette*, 10 October 1849. For extended discussions of this subject, see Ekirch, *Idea of Progress*; George M. Fredrickson, *The Inner Civil War: Northern Intellectuals and the Crisis of the Union*, chapter 1; Michael Fellman, *The Unbounded Frame: Freedom and Community in Nineteenth Century American Utopianism*, Introduction and chapters 1–5; Alice Felt Tyler, *Freedom's Ferment: Phases of American Social History from the Colonial Period to the Outbreak of the Civil War*, passim; and John Higham's brilliant essay, *From Boundlessness to Consolidation: The Transformation of American Culture, 1848–1860*.

5. The term is John Higham's, ibid., p. 13.

6. Frederick Merk, *Manifest Destiny and Mission in American History: A Reinterpretation*, chapter 5; J. D. F. Fuller, *The Movement for the Acquisition of All Mexico: 1846–1848*.

lands greater in extent than those of the Louisiana Purchase; and for the first time since independence there were no territorial disputes with neighboring states.

Swaggering, evangelical Americanism marked the country's mood, and the slogan "manifest destiny" embodied its ambitions in the New World: perpetual expansion, exported democracy, the sovereignty of the United States over two continents. "It is clear to all men of sober discernment," wrote James Gordon Bennett in the classic statement of that emotion, that the United States "must soon embrace the whole hemisphere, from the icy wilderness of the North to the most prolific regions of the smiling and prolific South."[7] A speech by James Monroe, delivered twenty years earlier and then virtually forgotten, was resurrected by James K. Polk and renamed the Monroe Doctrine, giving this new expansiveness the same sanction of antiquity that a nouveau riche speculator finds in his genealogical search for a pedigree and coat of arms.

But some Young Americans were convinced that this hemisphere could not contain their country's restless energy; they recklessly spoke of imposing their will on Europe as well. Belief that the New World possessed a special mandate to reform the institutions of Europe was not new in the 1840s, of course; it had existed among the first English settlers in Massachusetts during the seventeenth century. But the special conditions of the forties had transformed the nature of that mission from a quiet and relatively benign sense of superiority into an active, almost belligerent commitment to spread the principles of Americanism far beyond the borders of the United States. "It is the province, the mission, aye, the destiny of my country to become a propagandist of its own principles and institutions, until the language of history shall inscribe upon every throne on earth, 'FUIT,' " declared one congressman in 1849.[8] And journalists, boasting that America's power "goes on, spread-

7. *New York Herald*, 25 September 1845. It was John L. O'Sullivan, in the pages of his *New York Morning News* and *United States Democratic Review*, who coined and popularized the term; see Julius Pratt, "The Origins of 'Manifest Destiny.' "

8. Alexander Buel's speech in *Congressional Globe*, 31st Cong., 1st sess., *Appendix*, p. 144.

ing and growing," concluded that "upon us above all others, in the wisdom of providence, seems to devolve the grand, the sacred duty of hastening [monarchy's] downfall."[9] Bennett, whose *New York Herald* was the spearhead of this burgeoning Americanism, began exporting translations of his principal editorials; and his correspondent in Milan recommended that he create a European edition of the *Herald*, with headquarters in Paris: "The pure, lofty and sublime principles of republicanism, of which our nation affords the only tolerable sample in the world's history would have been brought before the people of Europe, and no limits could have been fixed to the influence that would have been put forth."[10]

Both at home and abroad, Americans were brash, impulsive, cocksure. Whether facing the challenge of world leadership—to become, in Ralph Waldo Emerson's phrase, the "leading nation"—or confronting social injustice at home—as George Henry Evans demanded in his radical newspaper *Young America!*—few Americans doubted their eventual success.[11] It was within this climate of social and political millennialism that on 19 March 1848, word of the French Revolution reached the United States. And it was the coincidence of these forces —mission, nationalism, progress, and European revolution—that gave definition and life to Young America's crusade.

II.

Revolution swept across Europe in 1848. Beginning in France, and spreading quickly to Germany, Italy, and the Hapsburg Empire, popular uprisings demanded constitutional governments and threatened to engulf the established patterns of society and government whether or not their rulers yielded. Explosive riots symbolized the discontent almost

9. "Gossip of the Month," *United States Democratic Review* 22 (January 1848):86–87.

10. *New York Herald*, 20 February 1848.

11. Edward W. Emerson, ed., *The Complete Works of Ralph Waldo Emerson in Six Volumes*, 1:387–88; *Young America!*, 1844–49.

everywhere. Rebels constructed fifteen hundred barricades in the city of Paris; in Berlin, citizens fought soldiers after failing to alter the status quo peacefully. Even England did not escape entirely, for there militant Chartists plotted rebellion until informers betrayed their cause. The Old World was stumbling from one crisis to the next, seemingly incapable either of maintaining order or of creating a new, functional equilibrium.

News of the first fighting in Paris evoked an outpouring of jubilation in the United States. Torchlight parades, public meetings, and long lists of congratulatory resolutions testified to the buoyancy of the American response. The war with Mexico was not yet officially over, but so enflamed was the Young American mentality that one editor demanded that congressmen "quit the exhausted topic of our Mexican affairs, and turn their attention to a new field"—intervention in behalf of republicanism in Europe.[12] The Detroit *Free Press*, even then the most influential Democratic newspaper in Michigan, inserted the "Marseilles Hymn of Liberty" on its masthead and drew parallels between the insurrection in Paris and America's own revolution;[13] Horace Greeley's *New York Tribune* reported with obvious approval one prediction that the movement would spread "until all Europe is one great and splendid Republic . . . and we shall all be citizens of the world."[14] But such optimism was not universal. Bennett, warning that the Old World faced a half century of war betwen despotism and liberty, called upon Congress to create a naval academy, build twenty large steamships, and prepare to fight alongside the French rebels.[15]

In Washington, Sen. William Allen, Democratic chairman of the Foreign Relations Committee, introduced a resolution congratulating the French "upon their success in their recent efforts to consolidate liberty, by embodying its principles in a republican form of govern-

12. *New York Herald*, 20 March 1848.
13. Detroit *Free Press*, 8 April, 24 May 1848.
14. *The New York Tribune*, 4 April 1848; Henry Blumenthal, *A Reappraisal of Franco-American Relations, 1830–1871*, p. 10.
15. *New York Herald*, 20, 21 March 1848.

ment."[16] Critics, skeptical of the French people's capacity for popular government and unconvinced that liberal institutions are the inevitable result of social change, dismissed the proposal as premature. Allen had offered his resolution only ten days after the first unofficial newspaper reports of rebellion had arrived—before the exact nature of the movement had become clear. A self-constituted provisional regime was functioning as France's only government, and would continue to do so until a national assembly met two months later.

John C. Calhoun, the most vocal critic of the resolution, was as convinced as his colleagues that "the old monarchies on the continent of Europe are about coming to an end. The intelligence and progress of the age have outgrown them."[17] But the elimination of monarchy, he warned, did not mean that France inevitably would adopt the American system of government. "They have decreed a republic," he told his colleagues, "but it remains for them to establish a republic." Calhoun, for one, doubted that they could do it.[18]

Supporters of the resolution ridiculed such caution. "When parental love first looks upon the young infant, does it refrain from thanking God till the child has grown to manhood?" asked John Parker Hale, the abolitionist senator from New Hampshire. The spirit of the age and the example of the United States had ordained the rebels' success; Americans should celebrate that fact by welcoming the rebirth of liberty on the Continent.[19]

Sen. Lewis Cass had for years encouraged the extension of American political institutions to other nations;[20] it was inevitable, therefore, that he would support Allen's proposition. "We believe that our congratu-

16. 30 March 1848, *Congressional Globe*, 30th Cong., 1st sess., p. 567.

17. Calhoun to James E. Calhoun, his son, 15 April 1848, in James Franklin Jameson, ed., *Correspondence of John C. Calhoun, Annual Report of the American Historical Association for the Year 1899*, 2:749.

18. *Congressional Globe*, 30th Cong., 1st sess., p. 568; Jameson, *Correspondence of Calhoun*, p. 746ff.

19. *Congressional Globe*, 30th Cong., 1st sess., *Appendix*, p. 456.

20. See, for example, Lewis Cass, *Address . . . Before the Association of the Alumni of Hamilton College*, pp. 5–7.

lations at this time will not only be acceptable [to the French people], but useful to the great cause of freedom throughout the world," he advised his countrymen. "We cannot halt in our course, and withhold our congratulations without . . . announcing to the world that the struggle in which they were engaged will terminate unfortunately."[21] Exactly what relationship he saw between the resolution and a possible political or military confrontation three thousand miles away he did not say. But in the mind of this Young American, the opinion of the American people was so powerful that without a simple congratulation from them, the cause of freedom would perish from the Continent of Europe.

Even the iron-willed Calhoun could not defy such wild rhetoric. When the resolution appeared for a vote, he withdrew from the chamber and allowed the message to pass unanimously with thirty-two affirmative votes;[22] four days later, the House of Representatives adopted the same text, 174 to 2.[23]

But Calhoun's warning had been prophetic, for the debates in the Senate very nearly outlived the democratic experiments in Europe. In early summer, a new wave of industrial rioting in Paris frightened cautious elements of the French bourgeoisie and rural poor, and it became increasingly clear that the French people were not prepared to reconcile the substance of freedom with their longing for order. The magic name "Napoleon" began to circulate among those who feared anarchy, and knowledgeable Americans perceived that the infant French republic would not succeed. Even the aggressively expansionistic *United States Democratic Review* regretted Congress's precipitous action:

At least we might have delayed our official greetings until there was some stability to furnish the subject of the congratulation. The recent insurrection and dictatorship puts our chief legislative body, Congress, in rather an unpleasant position, and it must heartily wish that it had listened to the deprecating voice of that astute statesman, JOHN C. CALHOUN, whose

21. *Congressional Globe*, 30th Cong., 1st sess., *Appendix*, p. 465.
22. *Congressional Globe*, 30th Cong., 1st sess., p. 569.
23. Ibid., pp. 603–4.

democracy is undoubted, when he begged that there might be a little delay in the proffer of fraternal sympathy.[24]

But despite this embarrassing setback, the supporters of evangelical Americanism had achieved a significant victory: they had committed the United States Congress to a concept of foreign policy that was based on ideology, public opinion, and European involvement. Furthermore, during the course of these debates, a leader of the interventionist movement had emerged. Ironically, the spokesman for Young America was to be the ancient senator from Michigan, Lewis Cass.

Lewis Cass, self-righteous senator from Michigan, was the most prominent proponent of the interventionist movement.

III.

In 1825 Lewis Cass and Gov. William Clark of Missouri concluded a treaty with several Indian tribes. After formally signing the pact, Cass seized the liquor customarily given the Indians after such ceremonies, delivered a sharp speech about the evils of strong drink, and, ignoring

24. "Gossip of the Month," *United States Democratic Review* 23 (August 1848):189.

the shouted protests of the assembled chiefs, poured the liquor on the ground. This act manifested, as one of his more admiring biographers has written, "his life-long hatred of intemperance."[25]

Such open displays of self-righteousness were not uncommon with Cass; indeed, he was at times insufferably moralistic. As in his treatment of the Indians' firewater, he seldom paused to consider the consequences of his acts. But in the heady atmosphere of the 1840s, empty gestures sometimes represented virtue, and could pay handsome political dividends. Cass's quixotic personality placed him in the vanguard of the Young America movement during the foreign policy debates of 1848–1852.

In 1848 Cass could look back on a distinguished career. He had emerged from the War of 1812 with an admirable reputation, although that service also left him with a blustering Anglophobia he would never fully shed. In following years he had served most credibly as governor of Michigan Territory, where he developed skill in dealing with the Indians, despite a rather negative view of their prospects.[26] He had been secretary of war under Andrew Jackson for six years following the Peggy Eaton shake-up in the cabinet, had served a brief, stormy tenure as minister to France, had won appointment to the Senate in 1845, and, finally, in 1848, had been rewarded with the Democratic party's nomination for the presidency.[27]

Despite nearly four decades of public service, Cass had never developed a realistic understanding of international affairs. In his mind, diplomacy rested on three fundamentally romantic assumptions. First, he declared that the community of Christian nations was bound together in "one great political family." He believed that public opinion directed this "family." That force "pours forth," he once declared, "is borne,

25. W. L. G. Smith, *The Life and Times of Lewis Cass*, p. 155; Louis Martin Sears, "Lewis Cass," ed., Allen Johnson, *Dictionary of American Biography* (New York, 1929), 3:563.

26. Lewis Cass, "Removal of the Indians," pp. 64–67.

27. There has still been no perceptive biography of Cass. Studies of his career include Smith, *Life and Times*; Frank B. Woodford, *Lewis Cass: The Last Jeffersonian*; and Willis Frederick Dunbar, *Lewis Cass*.

through the civilized world, pronouncing the judgment of the present day, and anticipating that of posterity." His confidence in that elusive abstraction, international public opinion, was total:

> There are none so high as to be beyond its censure—none so low as not to be encouraged by its approbation. The frontiers of a country may be armed at its approach. But it will pass them. It may be checked, but it cannot be stopped. It is stronger than the bayonet, more vigilant than the suspicions of despotism.

The senator's third thesis was a corollary of the second. If public opinion determined the course of nations, then in any conflict over a moral issue a simple appeal to the common sense of mankind could resolve the problem: words could replace guns as the weapons of war, and great victories could be won without cost.[28]

Nor did Cass offer these tenets as merely academic arguments, for he had a disturbing tendency to read moral absolutes into every conflict between nations. The Monroe Doctrine was not, in his mind, a state policy; it was an "everlasting principle."[29] The Anglo-American rivalry for ports on the Pacific during the 1840s was not a confrontation of commercial interests; it was a moral crusade by Americans to halt Britain's "march toward world domination."[30] He was so committed to the concept of the power of public opinion as the arbiter of international morality that while in Paris he had appealed to the French people to reverse their government's ratification of a controversial treaty to which the United States was not even a party. That this appeal forced his recall did not impress him; he and his authorized biographer bragged about it for years.[31]

Other qualities further inhibited Cass's understanding of diplomatic

28. *Congressional Globe*, 31st Cong., 1st sess., *Appendix*, pp. 54–55; the quotations are from Cass's revised version of his speech, which was published in the Washington, D.C., *Daily Union*, 9 January 1850.

29. Norman A. Graebner, ed., *Ideas and Diplomacy*, p. 216.

30. Woodford, *Lewis Cass*, p. 233.

31. *United States Democratic Review* 23 (October 1848):293; Smith, *Life and Times*, pp. 403–27.

affairs. By 1848 he was sixty-seven years old. He had grown ponderous; his eyelids sagged, enormous jowls hung limply from his cheeks. His mind, always inflexible, had grown brittle with age. His irrational hatred for England had become so all consuming, for example, that even sympathetic senators greeted his speeches on the subject with sarcastic laughter.[32] Furthermore, as the presidential nominee of his party, Cass necessarily weighed heavily the political implications of his statements on foreign policy. As Lee Benson and his students have indicated, Democrats had for years appealed successfully to immigrant voting groups, and by 1848 Germans and Irishmen constituted a potent voting bloc, particularly in Cass's own Northwest.[33] Sentiment, habit, and interest dovetailed in the Michigan senator's mind, therefore, to demand a platform encompassing Young America's principles.

Similar considerations made other men his allies. The rampant Americanism of the Old Northwest had produced a phalanx of like-minded Democrats. There was Stephen Douglas, fresh from the House of Representatives, and now ready to launch a national career on the Young America platform; Edward Hannegan, until 1849 the hard-drinking junior senator from Indiana; William Allen, whose chairmanship of the Senate Foreign Relations Committee provided a forum for evangelical resolutions of support for European rebels; and I. P. Walker of Wisconsin, Sidney Breese of Illinois, and Jesse D. Bright of Indiana, all of whom would align themselves with Cass throughout the next three years.

But if western Democrats claimed Young America as their own, they had no monopoly on its ideology. Fundamentally, Young America was nothing more than an emotional reaffirmation of America's system of society and government, and an unthinking willingness to allow

32. Lewis Einstein, "Lewis Cass," ed., Samuel Flagg Bemis, *The American Secretaries of State and Their Diplomacy*, 6:299.

33. In the decade before 1850 alone, more than a million Germans and Irish immigrated to the United States. For information on the Democratic appeal to immigrant groups, see Lee Benson, *The Concept of Jacksonian Democracy: New York as a Test Case*; Ronald P. Formisano, *The Birth of Mass Political Parties: Michigan, 1827–1861*, chapters 5, 9.

that feeling to interfere with the conduct of the nation's foreign policy. It did not challenge the vital interests of either major party; it raised no question of the extension of slavery, no prospect of a Wilmot Proviso. It implied merely that public opinion should, and could, replace realpolitik as the basis of international relations. It was an ideology that could appeal to most Americans, and it did. Two months before Lewis Cass proclaimed public opinion to be "stronger than the bayonet," Daniel Webster, the conservative Whig senator from Massachusetts, paid it even greater homage, at a gathering in the State House in Boston:

> Gentlemen, there is something on earth greater than arbitrary or despotic power. The lightning has its power, and the whirlwind has its power, and the earthquake has its power; but there is something among men more capable of shaking despotic thrones than lightning, whirlwind, or earthquake, and that is, the excited and aroused indignation of the whole civilized world.[34]

The principles of Young America appealed, with varying degrees of intensity, to Free-Soilers, abolitionists, pacifists, and members of scores of other reform movements as well. After 1848, these principles would mushroom, until by December 1851, they would dominate the thinking of the overwhelming majority of Americans throughout the Northern states and of a sizable portion of those in the South as well.

IV.

Events in Hungary captured the nation's interest in August 1849, for it was there and then that the last act of the midcentury revolutions was unfolding. Louis Kossuth, an eloquent and colorful Magyar nationalist, was leading his people in a rebellion against Hapsburg rule, and for Magyar supremacy over other cultural groups at home. Americans understood little of the ethnic rivalries of Austria-Hungary. Their preconceptions of the spirit of this Age of Progress transformed Kossuth's

34. Daniel Webster, Address to the Festival of the Sons of New Hampshire, 7 November 1849, *Works of Daniel Webster*, 2:514.

war from a confrontation over ethnic values into a proud crusade for liberty and republicanism.

Every ship from Europe brought optimistic accounts of Kossuth's prospects for success, and newspapers of every political persuasion reprinted them eagerly. Citizens cheered the efforts of their fellows to aid the Hungarian cause. The entire nation followed, for example, the exploits of Lt. Mayne Reid, the novelist-turned-soldier whose service in the Mexican War had won him a reputation for gallantry. When news of fighting emerged from Hungary, Reid quickly raised a company of men in New York, contacted Kossuth's agents, and enlisted in the rebel army.[35] In Richmond, Virginia, Robert Tyler, son of the former president, announced that he too would raise troops to join the cause.[36] In Little Rock, Arkansas, a branch of the Central Southern Association to Promote the Cause of Liberty in Europe asked its members to con-

Mayne Reid, gallant novelist-turned-soldier in the Mexican War, raised a company of men in New York, hoping to fight for Hungary.

35. *The Liberator* (Boston), 7 December 1849; *Scioto Gazette*, 29 August 1849; *The Oquawka Spectator* (Illinois), 5 September 1849; *Albany Argus* (New York), 25 August 1849; *Appleton's Cyclopaedia of American Biography*, 5:215. The war was over before Reid could reach the battlefield.

36. *The Pennsylvanian*, quoted in *The Liberator*, 7 December 1849.

tribute ten cents each month for supplies for Kossuth's men, while the citizens of Washington County, Maine, satisfied the dictates of conscience by renaming a village after the Magyar hero.[37]

The American people had learned no caution from their ill-timed welcome of the still-born French republic a year earlier. On the contrary, they seemed convinced that Kossuth would win his battles if the United States government would only will them to be won. "We have no doubt," announced Gamaliel Bailey's weekly, *The National Era*, "that the timely interposition of the United States and Great Britain in the recognition of the Government of . . . Hungary . . . would have caused the Czar to hesitate before attempting to enslave Hungary."[38] In Philadelphia, former Vice-President George M. Dallas chaired a Hungarian sympathy meeting that called on President Zachary Taylor to recognize the rebel government, apparently confident that diplomatic relations with the United States would insure the regime's survival; in Newark, Chief Justice Hornblower of the New Jersey Supreme Court presided at a similar gathering that voted to mail its minutes directly to Kossuth, "with a handsome flag." In Wilmington, Delaware, citizens appointed a standing committee of prominent men to coordinate efforts toward official recognition, and in Cincinnati and Louisville, mass meetings declared the same goal. On the Illinois prairie, one-term Whig Congressman Abraham Lincoln authored resolutions for a public meeting in Springfield, imploring the administration to recognize the independence of "Your struggling brethern" at the earliest practicable moment, "consistent with our amicable relations with the government against which they are contending." Even the conservative New York daily, *The Courier and Enquirer*, demanded that the president couple immediate recognition with vigorous protests in Vienna.[39]

Actually, Taylor already had done as much as he reasonably could

37. *The Liberator*, 31 August 1849; Carl Wittke, *Refugees of Revolution*, pp. 96–97.

38. *National Era* (Washington), 16 August 1849.

39. *The Liberator*, 7 December 1849; *Scioto Gazette*, 29 August 1849; Roy P. Basler, ed., *The Collected Works of Abraham Lincoln*, 2:115–16; *Baltimore American and Commercial Daily Advertiser* (Maryland), 30, 31 August 1849.

to satisfy these demands, for he too had yielded to the spirit of Young America. On 18 June, nearly two months before Kossuth had captured the public's imagination, the Whig president had appointed A. Dudley Mann as a special emissary to the rebel authorities. He hoped, he told Mann, that the United States could be the first nation to establish formal ties with the new nation. Taylor even authorized Mann to judge for himself the political and military situation and to grant preliminary recognition if circumstances warranted.[40] That this was the first and perhaps only occasion in American history that a president delegated such sweeping powers indicates the depth of this Whig administration's desire to precede every other country in embracing Hungary's cause.[41] Even Secretary of State John M. Clayton's official instructions to the new appointee dripped revolutionary fervor:

As president, Zachary Taylor hoped the United States would be the first country to officially recognize the new Hungarian republic, when it succeeded.

40. Secretary of State to A. Dudley Mann, 18 June 1849, National Archives, Records of the Department of State, Special Missions, 1:266–75; also contained in U.S. Congress, Senate, *Senate Documents*, 31st Cong., 1st sess., 10, no. 43, pp. 3–6.
41. John Bassett Moore, "Kossuth: A Sketch of a Revolutionist" (June 1895): 264.

To the contemplation of the American Statesman, Hungary, at this time, offers the interesting spectacle of a great people rising superior to the enormous oppression, which has so long weighed her down; and she exhibits, at the same time, the determination, and the power, (we hope,) to assert and maintain her separate and equal station among the powers of the Earth.[42]

Clayton chose to explain his desire for early recognition by alluding to the commercial advantages to be reaped from a Hungary led by the grateful Kossuth, but this was almost certainly a rationalization: the United States already had penetrated Austrian markets, and no one seems to have cared to calculate the financial implications of premature recognition.

Mann rejoiced at news of his assignment. "I shall desire no joy of a more boundless nature during my pilgrimage through life," he gushed to Clayton in accepting his duties, "than to be enabled to report to you that 'Hungary has established her independence on a permanent foundation; that I saw the infant Hercules strangle the mighty serpent.' "[43] In his mind, the struggle would determine nothing less than the future of western civilization. "The question whether continental Europe shall be under Cossack or republican rule hereafter will, in all probability, be definitively decided on the plains and in the passes of Hungary."[44] Mann's sympathy had elevated the civil war into an ideological crusade of global proportions.

Mann left his post at Paris almost immediately, and at every stop he

42. Secretary of State to Mann, National Archives, Records of the Department of State, Special Missions, 1:266–75.

43. Mann to Secretary of State, 13 July 1849. Mann's correspondence was informally classified by President Taylor, and for more than fifty years remained unpublished. In 1909, when Eugene Pivany was researching his brief *Webster and Kossuth: A Discourse on the Relations of Daniel Webster and Louis Kossuth*, he complained that the government's refusal to publish the letters was "incomprehensible" (p. 8), in view of the age and insensitivity of the documents; they were finally published in 1909, U.S. Congress, Senate, *Senate Documents*, 61st Cong., 2d sess., 58, no. 279.

44. Ibid. See also Mann to Secretary of State, 8 August, 27 September 1849, ibid.

penned detailed summaries of the military situation. He never reached Kossuth's headquarters. While he waited in Vienna for a favorable moment to act, the rebels' prospects deteriorated severely. Czar Nicholas, alarmed by the presence of an unstable government near his western border and worried by its possible effect on neighboring peoples, dispatched nearly two hundred thousand men to aid his Hapsburg ally. The ragged rebel forces were hopelessly inferior to the combined enemy armies. By late August Kossuth had fled to asylum in Turkey, and days later the Hungarian armies defied his parting utterances by surrendering to avoid annihilation.

As these events developed, Mann's ardor for the revolution cooled dramatically. A few weeks earlier he had hailed Kossuth as the savior of republican virtue in Europe; by 9 September he was wondering aloud if Kossuth had absconded with the crown jewels.[45] And in an almost comic reversal of sentiments, he began congratulating himself and his superiors for adhering to America's traditional policy of noninvolvement in European affairs. "How salutary to our best interests—to our tranquility and security—our established policy with respect to the concerns of foreign states," he lectured Clayton in one dispatch. "Without an honest observance of it, what unprofitable difficulties may we not have been involved in on account of one or another of the abortive revolutionary movements in Europe?" Suddenly, Mann was ridiculing those "demogogical influences" that sought to lure the United States into European quarrels and was boasting that he, Clayton, and Taylor were influenced "by reason, instead of passion."[46]

But if Mann could abandon his evangelical diplomatic philosophy with the flick of a pen, most Americans could not. The explosive mixture of mission, power, and urgency, created by the circumstances of the 1840s and ignited by the outbreak of revolution in Europe, was cemented too firmly to the predominant thinking of the nation.

45. U.S. Congress, Senate, *Senate Documents*, 61st Cong., 2d sess., 58, no. 279.
46. Ibid.

III.

YOUNG AMERICA
FOCUSES ON LOUIS KOSSUTH

News of Hungary's defeat shocked the American people. Throughout late August and early September the nation's daily newspapers had printed optimistic accounts of the struggle, detailing Kossuth's magnificent speeches and his generals' brilliant tactical victories. So confident were these stories that even as late as 5 September, the Baltimore *American* was crediting rumors that an envoy from Hungary had arrived in Washington and that the United States was preparing to extend to him full diplomatic status. But that same day this rumor collapsed, along with any hope for Hungary's cause; a late telegraphic report from a ship that had just reached Canada stated, "The Hungarians have been defeated at all points . . . complete rout of the Magyars . . . 60,000 roubles

Reports during the summer of 1849 indicated that the Hungarian revolutionaries were easily defeating the Austrian army.

on Kossuth's head, dead or alive . . . for the time, darkness broods over the lately illumined plains of Hungary."[1]

Americans had accepted with sullen contempt the internal collapse of the French revolution of 1848, for that might have demonstrated merely the unfitness of the Gallic race for enlightened self-government. But Hungary's was a different case. There it seemed that a proud and noble people had proven themselves capable of creating a liberal political order that would have succeeded but for the massive infusion of foreign troops. Together, the Hapsburgs and their Romanoff allies had arrested the march of progress, and Young Americans could not forgive that act.

I.

"Public opinion is so enraged against Austria," reported that nation's chargé d'affaires, Chevalier G. J. Hülsemann, to his superiors in Vienna, "that scarcely an editor admits anything favorable to her."[2] Indeed, the press was mobilizing itself for a campaign of invective against the "butchery," the "execrable, hideous" barbarities of "the fiends who are nicknamed rulers in Austria."[3]

Political figures echoed the press's indignation. For example, Daniel Webster, in one Boston speech, condemned the czar of Russia for his role in Hungary's defeat and warned him not to seek Kossuth's extradition for trial and execution. If he did, "the whole world will be the tribunal to try him, and he must appear before it, and hold up his hand, and plead, and abide its judgment."[4] Webster's listeners, convinced that popular opinion could complete its work, cheered wildly, never asking who would carry out the sentence.

1. Baltimore *American and Commercial Daily Advertiser*, 25 August–7 September 1849; *The Albany* (New York) *Argus*, 7 September 1849.

2. Quoted in Merle Eugene Curti, "Austria and the United States, 1848–1852: A Study in Diplomatic History," *Smith College Studies in History* 11 (April 1926): 159–60.

3. *National Era*, 22 November 1849; Baltimore *American and Commercial Daily Advertiser*, 6 September 1849.

4. Webster's address to the Festival of the Sons of New Hampshire, *Works of Daniel Webster*, 2:514.

The Hungarian army was reportedly victorious in this battle during the summer of 1849.

Some statesmen were interested in a more practical form of punishment. As early as 16 July, former President John Tyler—the very symbol of the Southern wing of Jeffersonian thought—called for vigorous federal action. The United States should lodge forceful protests in Vienna, he advised, and if the Hapsburgs did not bow to America's will, the president should withdraw his representative there and expel the Austrian minister in Washington. No less forceful action would do, for Tyler was as convinced as the rest of his countrymen: "The fate of centuries is involved in the contest."[5]

Nothing came of Tyler's proposition while Hungary seemed likely to win its independence. But on Christmas Eve, after Kossuth's flight and in the first days of a new session of Congress, Lewis Cass resurrected the idea in a motion to the Senate: "Resolved, That the Committee on Foreign Relations be instructed to inquire into the expediency of sus-

5. John Tyler to Robert Tyler, 16 July 1849, in Lyon G. Tyler, *The Letters and Times of the Tylers*, 2:491–92.

pending diplomatic relations with Austria."[6] Cass justified his proposal in purely ideological terms: Austria had offended the moral sense of the American people and deserved to be isolated from the community of Christian nations. The condemnation by the United States might not affect the Hapsburgs immediately, he admitted in one speech, "Whatever we may do or say, the immediate march of Austria will be onward in the course of despotism." But if Americans could spark similar protests in other capitals, then the moral authority of all mankind would shatter the forces of tyranny: "Its bulwarks will be shaken by the rushing of mighty winds—by the voice of the world, wherever its indignant expression is not restrained by the kindred sympathies of arbitrary power."[7]

It was Henry Clay who rose to defend the nation's conservative diplomatic tradition. It was ironic that he should lead these debates, for much of his early career had revolved around the very principles Cass was now asserting. In March 1818, the Kentuckian, then Speaker of the House of Representatives, had demanded that his government recognize the insurgent regimes in Latin America, and four years later he had championed the cause of Greece in its war for independence from Turkey. In neither case had he paused to consider the limited interests of the United States. Indeed, he had seemed willing to sacrifice the nation's interests in order to win recognition for the Latin American republics, for at the time Clay proposed that action, Secretary of State John Quincy Adams was negotiating with Spain for title to Florida, and premature recognition might have scuttled those talks. But considerations of narrow interest had mattered less to Clay than the need for "justice" toward the rebels and the prospect of an alliance of republican states to serve as a "counterpoise" to the monarchies of the Holy Alliance.[8] In the two decades after 1820, Clay had drifted away from his

6. *Congressional Globe*, 31st Cong., 1st sess., *Appendix*, p. 54.
7. Ibid., p. 55.
8. For an extended discussion of Clay's position, see Randolph Bluford Campbell, "Henry Clay and the Emerging Nations of Latin America, 1815–1829," chapters III, VI.

early identification of diplomacy with ideology and had come to distrust any implication of evangelical fervor in the conduct of foreign policy. In its place he had substituted an interpretation based on the economic and strategic interests of the country—an approach strictly within the intellectual tradition of the founding fathers.

In debates over the move to suspend relations with Austria, Cass and his fellow Young Americans sought to embarrass Clay by claiming to expect his support and sought to prove they were entitled to his backing by quoting long passages from his speeches on Greek and Latin independence.[9] But Clay responded with a devastating assault on the logic of Young America. It was the very nature of Cass's proposal that disturbed him, its "want of sympathy between the premises and conclusion," its refusal to balance its goals with the means at hand to achieve them. He recalled the enormities of Austrian despotism as described by Cass himself: the mass executions, the leveling of entire towns, the imposition of a police state on a once-free nation. How should the United States respond to such needless cruelty, if it were in fact to respond? "Why, the natural conclusion would be to declare war immediately against Austria," he told his colleagues. It would be absurd to simply act on Cass's resolution and recall "a little chargé d'affaires that we happen to have in Vienna." Such an act would be a mere gesture: it would not affect the Hapsburgs, but it would punish the American people by depriving them of commercial and diplomatic protection in a foreign capital.

But Clay objected to more than Young America's inability to resolve an obvious imbalance between its objectives and its competency to achieve them. He was more concerned with the movement's easy assumption that it had a moral duty to judge the virtue of governments in foreign states. "Where, then, is the limit?" he asked Cass. "You may extend it to religion. You may extend it to the inquisition. Have we not an equal right to say to Spain, unless you abolish the inquisition, we will suspend diplomatic intercourse with you?" To adopt ideology as the basis for national policy, the Kentuckian concluded, would be to "de-

9. *Congressional Globe*, 31st Cong., 1st sess., pp. 44–46, 103–4.

33

nationalize nation after nation, according as how their conduct may be found to correspond with our notion and judgment of what is right and proper in the administration of human affairs."[10]

Precedent was on Clay's side, for never had the United States departed from Jefferson's decision in 1793 to recognize de facto governments, regardless of their ideological positions. Indeed, most knowledgeable Americans must have understood that the withdrawal of diplomatic agents was ordinarily a prelude to war. But despite these facts, and despite Clay's vigorous and reasoned attack on Cass's notions of foreign policy, the movement for suspension of diplomatic ties with Austria made ominous progress. In Pennsylvania, the legislature instructed its appointees in the Senate to vote for the resolution, and Sen. Daniel S. Dickinson of New York introduced four petitions from his constituents —one signed by the poet and newsman William Cullen Bryant—each advising the Senate to adopt the Cass proposal.[11]

Cass's original proposition never appeared for a vote; it seems to have gotten lost in the shuffle of compromise measures for which the year was famous. But on 16 April, the Senate did consider a significantly more drastic measure. Whereas Cass's resolution had proposed only a study of the advisability of suspending relations, his proposal on 16 April was to bypass the Committee on Foreign Relations altogether by stripping an appropriations bill of all funds for the legation in Vienna. Even this stronger measure failed by only eleven votes, 28 to 17. Northwestern Democrats were unanimous in its favor, of course; senators from that section consistently supported Young American policies. But they accounted for only seven affirmative votes. Joining them were five senators from the slave states, two from New England, two from the Middle Atlantic region, and one Northwestern Free-Soiler, Salmon P. Chase of Ohio.[12]

There was not a single Whig vote in favor, but the reason was

10. *Congressional Globe,* 31st Cong., 1st sess., pp. 114–15.

11. U.S. Congress, Senate, *Journal of the Senate,* 31st Cong., 1st sess., pp. 56, 66, 94, 465.

12. *Congressional Globe,* 31st Cong., 1st sess., p. 746.

nonideological. Only a few weeks earlier, Zachary Taylor had appointed James Watson Webb, the perennial Whig spoilsman and vigorously partisan editor of the New York *Courier and Enquirer*, as his new chargé d'affaires in Austria. Webb had been less than enthusiastic about Kossuth's revolution, but that fact had played no role in his appointment: he had legitimate claims on the federal patronage, and among those who had recommended him for the post was Simeon Draper, a New York Whig politician who eventually would head Kossuth's national fundraising drive.[13]

But Webb had enemies in the Democratic party, and he had not improved his standing with them after his appointment. Hounded by creditors and harassed by a vindictive former father-in-law, Webb had sailed for Europe as soon as he had received notice of his appointment—without waiting for the necessary Senate confirmation.[14] Cass denied positively that his motion was aimed at eliminating Webb's position, and he was probably telling the truth. The principles contained in his proposal corresponded precisely with his philosophy of international morality. In addition, he had been a close friend of the publisher for twenty years or more.[15] But despite Cass's disavowals of partisan motives, both Whigs and Democrats continuously brought up Webb's hasty departure.[16] In the minds of many senators, therefore, a vote in favor of suspension would constitute censure of a presidential appointee and, not incidentally, of an influential party spokesman. Only this political consideration could explain why every Whig voted against the resolution—even William Seward, who would become one of Kossuth's most forceful and tenacious defenders.[17]

If Cass had not yet thought of taking advantage of the ideological

13. Memorandum, apparently not in Clayton's hand, 1 June 1849, John M. Clayton papers; Central Hungarian Committee, Simeon Draper, Chairman, to potential donors, 22 February 1852, John Hartwell Cocke papers, University of Virginia.

14. James R. Crouthamel, *James Watson Webb: A Biography*, p. 112.

15. Ibid., p. 55; *Congressional Globe*, 31st Cong., 1st sess., *Appendix*, p. 58.

16. *Congressional Globe*, 31st Cong., 1st sess., pp. 103–6, *Appendix*, p. 46.

17. For Seward's attitude, see chapter 10.

implications he could draw from the Whigs' refusal to support him, some of his colleagues had. The explosive emotions aroused by the Hungarian cause had made that almost inevitable. Alexander Buel, the Michigan Democratic congressman, asserted without proof (and without truth) that by not granting immediate recognition when war had first erupted, "the President and his Cabinet departed from the settled policy of the country."[18] And Thomas Ritchie's *Union*, the organ of the national party in the capital, declared that Taylor and his allies, by refusing to support Cass's original resolution, had proven themselves a "MONARCHICAL PARTY," who "desire that our government shall continue to shake hands with the degraded homicide government of Europe."[19] Surprisingly, there were few such charges. By and large, Young Americans focused directly on the Old World villains.

II.

Partisan rhetoric notwithstanding, the administration was doing what it could to alleviate the condition of Kossuth and his fellow exiles. Anticipating by nearly a month an identical Democratic proposal, Secretary of State John M. Clayton directed George Perkins Marsh, the American minister at Constantinople, to intercede with the sultan in Kossuth's behalf, obtain his freedom under American auspices, and send him to the United States aboard a ship from the Mediterranean fleet.[20]

Taylor's humanitarian offer was not accepted. Simultaneously, Austria and Russia were demanding the rebels' return for trial on charges of treason. The sultan had refused to cooperate in what would certainly be a mass execution but had parried the Austrian demand with a promise to intern the most prominent Hungarians for at least a year. Although

18. *Congressional Globe*, 31st Cong., 1st sess., *Appendix*, p. 146.

19. Washington *Daily Union*, 9, 11 January 1850.

20. *Journal of the Senate*, 31st Cong., 1st sess., pp. 179, 180; Clayton to Marsh, 12 January 1850, Records of the Department of State, Record Group 59, National Archives Microfilm Publications, M77, Role 162 (hereafter cited as RG 59, NAMP, with appropriate role number); U.S. Congress, Senate, *Senate Documents*, 31st Cong., 1st sess., 10, no. 43, p. 13.

the Hapsburgs had refused to agree to this compromise, the sultan felt honor bound to fulfill his spurned offer. He therefore transferred Kossuth and twelve hundred other refugees to a makeshift camp in the nation's interior and undertook to support them from his country's feeble resources.[21] He had rescinded his demand that the Magyars convert to Islam,[22] but he had insured that they would not renew their revolutionary careers for at least a year.

III.

If some Democrats pretended that the Whigs were too friendly toward the Old World monarchs, Austria's chargé d'affaires in Washington, Chevalier G. J. Hülsemann, held the opposite impression. Although Hülsemann was confident that after twelve years in the United States he could distinguish between national policy and political claptrap, he consistently classified sincere statements of opinion as mere partisan maneuvering for advantage in domestic affairs. He had concluded, for example, that Lewis Cass had been playing for votes when he had proposed that the United States suspend relations with the Hapsburgs, and he would eventually level a simlar charge at the Whig secretary of state, Daniel Webster.[23]

But even this tendency did not prevent Hülsemann from expressing alarm at the expansive tendency of the young republic. On the contrary, he recognized that Americans were often serious when they spoke of

21. Marsh to Secretary of State, 14, 25 March 1850, Records of the Department State, RG 59, NAMP, M46, Role 14; U.S. Congress, Senate, *Senate Documents*, 31st Cong., 1st sess., 10, no. 43, pp. 1–4. An editorial error in publishing these documents resulted in incorrect page numbers for these letters; they comprise the last four pages of document no. 43.

22. Louis Kossuth, *Select Speeches of Kossuth. Condensed and Abridged, with Kossuth's Express Sanction*, p. 153.

23. Merle Eugene Curti, "Austria and the United States, 1848–1852: A Study in Diplomatic History," *Smith College Studies in History*, pp. 155, 157, 185. Curti's is the only work yet done based on Austrian diplomatic archives. Although my conclusions do not match Curti's, I have relied heavily on his research in the following two pages.

intruding upon the affairs of Europe. Even a year before Kossuth had undertaken his war for independence, Hülsemann had warned his government to avoid any interference with American ambitions in the western hemisphere, because he feared that the United States might welcome a precedent for intervening in behalf of future revolutions in Europe.[24] Because of Hülsemann's warning Viennese officials would soon become anxious that negotiations between the United States and Portugal for an American naval station at Lisbon foreshadowed exactly that type of interference.[25]

Hülsemann's understanding of his hosts' ambitions made his position during and after the Hungarian revolution particularly difficult. He was forced to walk a diplomatic tightrope, on the one side to avoid allowing hostile American officials to embarrass his government, and on the other, preventing at least an informal rupture with Washington. A. Dudley Mann's mission to Vienna made it impossible for him to do both.

Despite Mann's elaborate precautions for secrecy, the Austrian minister of foreign affairs, Prince Felix Schwarzenberg, had obtained a copy of his confidential instructions to monitor the progress of the Hungarian civil war some time before November 1849.[26] As long as the instructions remained at least nominally a secret, Schwarzenberg wisely chose to ignore them. Controversy with the United States over an unperformed affront would have served the interests of neither nation. Furthermore, it was clear that in any exchange the United States could reply with a demand to know exactly how the Austrian government had come into possession of a confidential American state paper.[27] Twice during December 1849 Hülsemann debated with Secretary of State Clayton about the propriety of American conduct, but neither time did he venture to put his protests in writing.

24. Ibid., p. 144.
25. Ibid.
26. Ibid., p. 154.
27. Clayton to Webster, 12 January 1851, in C. H. Van Tyne, ed., *The Letters of Daniel Webster*, pp. 452–54.

But on 18 March of the new year, President Taylor sent the Senate a copy of his instructions for the mission, deleting only a potentially embarrassing reference to the "iron rule" of Austria within the empire[28]— an omission that indicates that the statement was an accurate reflection of administration attitudes, not a demogogic appeal for popular support. Publication of the correspondence infuriated the Austrian government, and Schwarzenberg, with Russia's encouragement, ordered Hülsemann to lodge a vigorous formal protest. On 30 September, after a five-month delay caused by textual changes and by Zachary Taylor's sudden death on 9 July, Hülsemann handed his government's tardy protest to the new secretary of state, Daniel Webster.

The message was more than a routine complaint. Indeed, beneath a thoroughly transparent coating of diplomatic aplomb, it was a vicious series of calculated insults. Hülsemann called former Secretary of State Clayton a liar for disguising, in previous conversations, the real purpose of the mission; he quoted directly the very phrase Taylor had edited out of the published instructions, virtually daring the Americans to make an issue of the Austrian espionage; and he hinted sharply that the Hungarian civil war was hardly unique. Indeed, Hülsemann warned, "All countries are obliged at some period or other, to struggle against internal difficulties; all forms of government are exposed to such disagreeable episodes; the United States have had some experience in this recently. Civil War is a possible occurrence everywhere." Americans might soon regret their interference, he concluded pointedly, for "the encouragement which is given to the spirit of insurrection and of disorder most frequently falls back upon those who seek to aid it in its developments."[29] In those months following the bitterly divisive debates that surrounded

28. Secretary of State to A. Dudley Mann, 18 June 1849, National Archives, Records of the Department of State, Special Missions, 1:266–75; compare this text with that transmitted to the Senate, U.S. Congress, Senate, *Senate Documents*, 31st Cong., 1st sess., 10, no. 43, pp. 3–6; see also Schwarzenberg to Hülsemann, 6 November 1849, in Van Tyne, ed., *Letters of Webster*, p. 456; Fillmore to Webster, 16 January [1851] ibid., p. 457.

29. Hülsemann's letter is contained in *Works of Daniel Webster*, 6:488–90; Daniel Webster, *Writings and Speeches of Daniel Webster*, 12:162–64.

the Compromise of 1850, no one could mistake Hülsemann's meaning. If Austria deserved an apology from the United States—and it did—its insulting note was hardly the means by which to get it.

The people, Congress, and the national honor demanded a spirited reply. After trying unsuccessfully to persuade Hülsemann to withdraw the note, Webster began to compose a suitable response. The result, three months in the writing, was one of the most sensational documents ever penned by an American secretary of state. In that famous letter Webster rejected Austria's right to contest the nature, substance, or rhetoric of confidential correspondence between a president and his appointees. Furthermore, he ridiculed Hülsemann's suggestion that the administration had no right to investigate, for its own purposes, the prospects of a foreign people's establishing an independent government.

But the significance of the letter was not its technical defense of American policy. It was the bombastic tone in which the letter was written. Webster lectured Hülsemann about the new significance of the United States within the world order. "The power of this republic, at the present moment," he boasted, "is spread over a region one of the richest and most fertile on the globe, and of an extent in comparison with which the possessions of the house of Hapsburg are but a patch of the earth's surface." In population, commerce, and maritime power, the United States was—or soon would be—superior to the Austrian empire. Republican institutions, Webster avowed, had made possible his nation's stunning development during the more than six decades since independence. And it was this example of unparalleled progress and liberty, he repeated no fewer than five times, that had inspired the Hungarians to rebel. How could Americans ignore a revolution patterned after their own?[30]

Webster had done little more than reply in kind to the Austrian note, an act justified by the offensive language employed by that government. Some historians, as well as the members of the contemporary dip-

30. Webster to Hülsemann, 21 December 1850, Records of the Department of State, RG 59, NAMP, M99, Role 27; *Works of Webster*, 6:491–505.

lomatic corps, occasionally have dismissed the American response as a document intended primarily for domestic purposes—as the first volley in Webster's 1852 presidential campaign.[31] But in confidential letters to political allies, the secretary of state described his motives in entirely different terms. "I have given a good deal of labor to its preparation," he told President Millard Fillmore on 18 November, "but still am not satisfied with it. I hope you will alter and amend freely. It is an important occasion and furnishes an opportunity of exhibiting the temper and spirit in which the foreign relations are to be carried on tempore Fillmore."[32] He was even more specific in his correspondence with George

Although Daniel Webster was privately entirely committed to the ideals of Kossuth and Young America, as secretary of state his position was much more judicious.

31. For a recent example of this interpretation, see Robert F. Dalzell, Jr., *Daniel Webster and the Trial of American Nationalism, 1843–1852*, p. 226. This same interpretation, with a twist, is contained in Kenneth E. Shewmaker, "Daniel Webster and the Politics of Foreign Policy, 1850–1852."

32. Webster to Fillmore, 18 November 1850, quoted in John Bach McMaster, *A History of the People of the United States, from the Revolution to the Civil War*, 8:147n. This letter, which McMaster discovered in the collections of the Buffalo and Erie County Historical Society, is no longer there; Memorandum for Record, Arthur Detmers, research assistant of that society, to author, 9 April 1973.

Ticknor: "If you say that my Hülsemann letter is boastful and rough, I shall own the soft impeachment," he reported. "My excuse is twofold: 1. I thought it well enough to speak out, and tell the people of Europe who and what we are, and awaken them to a just sense of the unparalleled growth of this country. 2. I wished to write a paper which should touch the national pride, and make a man feel *sheepish* and *silly* who should speak of disunion."[33]

Nor did other knowledgeable contemporaries recognize Webster's letter as predominantly political in nature. John M. Clayton, a fellow Whig and Webster's predecessor at the Department of State, congratulated his successor for his spirited defense of American institutions and closed by wishing him "many more such victories over the Agents of Despotism."[34] In the Senate, Stephen Douglas, a potential rival to Webster for the presidency in 1852, ultimately insured that ten thousand copies of the letter would be printed for circulation throughout the nation. Indeed, the only objection to the resolution to print was voiced by Henry Clay, Webster's fellow Whig.[35] If the secretary of state had written the letter solely to further his own presidential ambitions, some of the most influential Democratic politicians in Washington either did not recognize his aims or were willing to help win them.

It would be a mistake, of course, to insist that there were no political implications in Webster's rhetoric. In a republic, all important issues are inherently political. But Webster's response to Hülsemann primarily sought to impress upon Europe the reality of the United States' emerging power, and to voice official support for liberal revolutionaries who were struggling against Old World monarchs. It was, therefore, representative of the Young America movement and of Webster's commitment to its principles.

33. Webster to Ticknor, 16 January 1851, *Writings and Speeches of Webster*, 16:586.

34. Eugene Pivany, *Webster and Kossuth: A Discourse on the Relations of Daniel Webster and Louis Kossuth*, pp. 13–14; Clayton to Webster, 12 January 1851, Webster, *Letters of Webster*, p. 454.

35. *Congressional Globe*, 32d Cong., 1st sess., pp. 586–90.

IV.

"Hero worship is one of the many sweet dreams of youth," recalled one American about the 1840s and fifties."[36] After Kossuth's defeat in Hungary, many Young Americans looked to him as the focus of interest in and hopes for the regeneration of the Old World. Kossuth helped fan that interest by addressing an open letter from Turkey to "the People of the United States of North America," in which he begged for American arms and insisted that "a shot fired by an English or an American vessel from the Adriatic would be like the trumpet at the city of Jericho."[37] He also opened a private correspondence with Lewis Cass, in which he praised the Michigan senator's fiery speeches in favor of Hungarian liberty.[38]

So convinced was the nation of Kossuth's virtue that it became hazardous to attack him publicly or to question his dedication to those principles Americans claimed as their own. Francis Bowen, the historian and editor of the *North American Review*, contended in January 1850 and after that the Hungarian revolution had been little more than a "war of races," in which Kossuth and other "arrogant, cruel and tyrannical" Magyars had sought unsuccessfully to subjugate the various ethnic minorities within their borders. Furthermore, Bowen ridiculed "those who believe that the spirit of propagandism is the essence of republican institutions" and characterized Kossuth's American supporters as a pack of "infidel socialists, mostly refugees from Europe, who had obtained command of a few penny newspapers."[39] Bowen already had won ap-

36. Alexander K. McClure, *Colonel Alexander K. McClure's Recollections of Half a Century*, p. 192.

37. Kossuth, "Address to the people of the United States of North America," 27 March 1850, reprinted in various American newspapers; see, for example, *National Era*, 23 October 1851; *The New York Times*, 20 October 1851; *Living Age* 31 (15 November 1851):319–25.

38. W. L. G. Smith, *The Life and Times of Lewis Cass*, p. 642.

39. [Francis Bowen], "The War of Races in Hungary," *North American Review* 70 (January 1850):121; "The Rebellion Against the Magyars," ibid., 72 (1851):238–40.

pointment to the distinguished McLean chair in history at Harvard when he began his attacks against Kossuth. When the first of them appeared in print, the university's board of overseers revoked his appointment.[40] To challenge the premises of Young America had become an exercise for martyrs, even within the community of scholars.

V.

On 17 February 1851, Sen. Henry S. Foote of Mississippi introduced a joint resolution, which called upon the president to obtain Kossuth's release and to transport him to the United States in a national ship. Within the next two weeks both houses of Congress endorsed the resolution.[41] Kossuth's year of internment had elapsed during the early weeks of 1851, and Turkey, anxious to be rid of its expensive guests, granted the American request almost immediately. The Austrians could do little more than complain. Finally, in their frustration, the authorities in Vienna tried Kossuth in absentia on charges of treason. On 10 September 1851, the day he boarded the *U. S. S. Mississippi*, the Austrians hung him in effigy.[42]

In the United States, the long-awaited release sparked renewed enthusiasm for the Hungarian cause. The Detroit *Free Press* called for a

40. *National Cyclopaedia of American Biography*, 11:452; Arthur A. Ekirch, Jr., *The Idea of Progress in America, 1815–1860*, p. 59.

41. *Congressional Globe*, 31st Cong., 2d sess., pp. 580, 710, 777, 779, 816. Some sources contend, without satisfactory evidence, that the invitation to Kossuth originated with William Correy and other Young Americans in Cincinnati; see, for example, Siert Riepma, "Young America," p. 89; John W. Oliver, "Louis Kossuth's Appeal to the Middle West," p. 483; Benjamin Tefft, *Hungary and Kossuth*, pp. 7–8; Andor M. Leffler, "Kossuth Comes to Cleveland," pp. 243–44. This explanation seems inadequate; the idea had originated in Congress as the natural culmination of a series of debates in 1849 and early 1850, and was first broached by Pierre Soulé of Louisiana; *Congressional Globe*, 31st Cong., 1st sess., p. 293. The Taylor administration had similar thoughts at the same time; see above, chapter 3, part 2. If Correy and his fellow Young Americans in Ohio wanted Kossuth released, so did many other Americans in both political parties.

42. Hülsemann to Webster, 30 September 1851, in Webster, *Letters of Webster*, p. 489.

Sen. Henry Foote of Mississippi remained intensely loyal to Kossuth and the Hungarian cause after almost all other Southern politicians had abandoned it.

national crusade in Europe to revive Kossuth's struggle. "An American force in the battlefield of Europe, raising the standard of universal democracy, would call forth every people of the continent," it pledged, paraphrasing an earlier statement by the *London Leader*. "Floating in that field, 'the star spangled banner' would strike terror and despair to the hearts of old Despotism, conscious of its doom. Its very coming would be victory."[43] Tammany Hall, the Democratic voice of New York's immigrant population, condemned the traditional American policy of neutrality toward foreign conflicts; its members cheered wildly when William Correy of Cincinnati told them, "The question for us to settle is, whether we can or ought to allow republicanism to be destroyed." The people of the United States were demanding a new foreign policy, he declared—a crusade founded on the slogan, "Emancipation for Mankind."[44] Even the Washington *Daily Union*, which seldom endorsed a principle not acceptable to both the Northern and Southern wings of

43. Detroit *Free Press*, 10 October 1851; see also, *London Leader*, quoted in *The New York Times*, 1 October 1851.

44. The proceedings at Tammany Hall and the entire text of Correy's speech are contained in *The New York Herald*, 23 October 1851.

the Democratic party, pronounced Correy's sentiments sound and told its readers that the United States had the power to enforce its will on the Old World tyrants.[45] Charles Sumner—a professed pacifist in 1851—leaned in the direction of interventionism when he told one Boston audience, "No people, for the sake of any seeming expediency, can afford to sacrifice a principle of justice or a sentiment of humanity, and thus to peril the everlasting verdict of History."[46] So universal was pro-Hungarian sentiment that Daniel Webster felt certain that the issue would sweep into national office a "warlike administration," reflecting the nation's new "zeal . . . for intervention in other states."[47]

Kossuth's attempt to speak to crowds in Central Park on the day of his arrival in the United States was overwhelmed by cheering.

45. Washington *Daily Union*, 29 October 1851.
46. Charles Sumner's address, 27 October 1851, in *Charles Sumner: His Complete Works*, 3:169.
47. Webster to Abbot Lawrence, 29 December 1851, in Webster, *Letters of Webster*, p. 508.

By the first days of December, newspapers wrote of little but Kossuth's immiment arrival; in one issue, *The New York Times* devoted twelve full columns to the story.[48] Guns were implanted at Castle Garden in New York to announce his arrival in the city. And Edson B. Olds of Ohio notified Congress that he would introduce legislation granting Kossuth honorary citizenship—a gesture previously accorded only Lafayette.[49] It was in this atmosphere that at two o'clock in the morning, 5 December, Kossuth arrived in the United States.

48. *The New York Times*, 3 December 1851.
49. *Congressional Globe*, 32d Cong., 1st sess., p. 21.

IV.

"INTERVENTION FOR NON-INTERVENTION"

New York's nearly hysterical welcome in the days after 6 December was a toast to a new citizen as well as a reaffirmation of hope in the future of republicanism in the Old World. Most Americans assumed that Kossuth had come to the United States to stay; he would take up land in the West and, as one newspaper put it, "end his days in philosophical retirement."[1] An advance guard of the defeated army had already landed in northwestern Iowa, thanks to the generosity of W. W. Corcoran, the Washington, D.C., philanthropist, and had established homesteads on lands given them through a congressional resolution introduced by William Seward, the New York Whig.[2] Josef Brick, a spokesman for the immigrants, had assured the nation that Kossuth would join them soon after his arrival.[3] And if he preferred another section of the country, he would have a choice of sites, including a plantation near Andrew Jackson's Hermitage, already subscribed and paid for by sympathizers in Nashville, Tennessee.[4]

Such benefactors were not yet aware of Kossuth's purposes in coming to the United States. He had no wish to become an American, even less a farmer. He wanted American help in renewing his war for independence. And basing his logic on the perfectly plausible assumption that Americans meant what they had said in countless resolutions, essays, and congressional debates, he was certain that he would win that aid.

The revelation of Kossuth's purpose surprised many of his hosts.

1. *Daily Scioto* (Ohio) *Gazette*, 18 October 1851. This was a common assumption; see John H. Komlos, *Louis Kossuth in America, 1851–1852*, pp. 43–46.
2. *National Era*, 24 April, 18 September, 13 November 1851; *Congressional Globe*, 31st Cong., 1st sess., pp. 128, 233.
3. *National Era*, 18 September 1851.
4. Ibid., 16 October 1851; *Daily Scioto Gazette*, 18 October 1851.

"Is n't [*sic*] there a story somewhere of a man uncaging, as he thought, a spaniel, and finding it to be a lion?" asked Orville Dewey, the nationally prominent Unitarian preacher, less than a week after Kossuth's arrival. "We thought we had released and were bringing over a simple, harmless, inoffensive, heart-broken emigrant, who would be glad to settle, and find rest, and behold, we have on our hands a world-disturbing propagandist, a loud pleader for justice and freedom, who does not want to settle, but to fight."[5] In the first days after his arrival Kossuth made clear his continued interest in revolutionizing Europe; and in the face of his unprecedented popularity, there were few men prepared to challenge his demands for American aid.

I.

The portraits of Kossuth and Washington that hung outside the Magyar's windows at Irving House betrayed more than a hint of irony. So did the constant references to Kossuth as "the Washington of Hungarian liberty." The nation's emotional welcome had convinced Kossuth that he commanded the allegiance of the American people. Now his principal fear was the dead hand of the past. Only Washington's Farewell Address, and the prestige conservatives could marshal behind the tradition it represented, he believed, could thwart his scheme to drag the United States into the vortex of European politics.

Washington had published his famous valedictory in September 1796. In that portion of the address devoted to foreign policy he had counseled his countrymen to balance carefully their interests and their commitments overseas. Specifically he had advised them to avoid any policy based on sentiment, "that illusion of an imaginary common interest." Perhaps recalling his own bitter experiences in 1793, when the nation had clamored for an alliance with republican France, he warned that an emotional attachment to any nation gave "ambitious, corrupted or deluded citizens . . . facility to betray or sacrifice the in-

5. Orville Dewey to Reverend Henry W. Bellows, 11 December 1851, in Mary E. Dewey, ed., *Autobiography and Letters of Orville Dewey, D.D.*, p. 223.

terests of their country" on the altar of misplaced idealism. Above all, he concluded, the United States should maintain a cautious distance from purely European quarrels.[6] The first president could not have condemned Kossuth's program more specifically if he had predicted his name.

Washington's analysis did not, of course, bind his successors, and no historian has yet discovered an instance in which a later administration resolved a dilemma by referring to the first president's pronouncement. But so precisely had Washington defined the nation's semipermanent interests that the Farewell Address had become the polestar of American diplomacy, and its title a short-hand description of the nation's cautious and self-interested policy toward Europe. Since 1796 eleven chief executives had proclaimed their allegiance to its precepts. Indeed, the substance of the address was as ingrained in American values as the Constitution itself. But by 1851 it was easy to confuse the substance of the address with the mystique that surrounded it. Among most Americans, in fact, the doctrinal myth of the farewell seemed to constitute a protective covering for its actual text: its ideas were easier to attack than its name. To convince Americans to intervene in Europe, Kossuth would first have to penetrate that outer shell.[7]

The specter of so formidable an adversary must have haunted Kossuth. His first nonceremonial act in the New World was to request a copy of the address, along with a set of Jared Sparks's eleven-volume edition of Washington's writings.[8] For a week afterward, he and his staff closeted themselves with those documents in their few free hours, preparing a definitive attack against the address and admitting publicly that the fate of his entire mission depended upon the success or failure of that attack.[9] On 11 December, when the city honored him with a municipal dinner, Kossuth seized that opportunity to deliver his speech.

6. James D. Richardson, ed., *Messages and Papers of the Presidents*, 1:221–23.

7. For an incisive discussion of the mythology of doctrines in American history and diplomacy, see William Graham Sumner's "War," in Albert Galloway Keller and Maurice R. Davies, eds., *Essays of William Graham Sumner*, 1:169–73.

8. *The New York Times*, 6 December 1851.

9. Quoted, ibid., 12 December 1851.

It was a hard-hitting lecture. He began by sneering at his hosts' childlike, "religious attachment" to the judgments of their first president; he derided them for hiding behind the obsolete aprons of their founding fathers; and, while conceding that Washington's advice had been wise for a young and defenseless people unschooled in the realities of world politics, he nevertheless censured them for failing to recognize that they were no longer innocent enough—or weak enough—to justify a self-imposed isolation from Europe. "Is the dress which well-suited the child still convenient to the full grown man, nay the *giant*, which you are?" he demanded.

The spectacle of the United States refusing to act its age was not simply ludicrous, he contended; it was an absolute menace to the nation's continued existence. If the United States persisted much longer in its fetish for nonintervention in European politics, it would dissolve into a mere shell of its potential greatness, and its citizens would soon "see this country degraded to the rotting vegetation of a Paraguay, or the mummy existence of Japan and China." "In a word, this glorious Republic . . . must feel resolved to be a *power* on earth—a power among the nations; or else . . . be doomed to continual decay, and soon cease to be great, glorious and free." Kossuth had postulated a new physical law of nations: if they did not exercise their powers, and keep them honed by constant conflict, those powers would atrophy like so many unused muscles. Posing as a nation healer, Kossuth had in effect prescribed boxing as the only cure for premature senility. He even invoked Washington's own words to support his thesis. After quoting the first president's famous letter to Lafayette, in which he predicted that the United States would be a power on earth when its institutions were "settled and matured," the Magyar lashed out at his audience. "I confidently ask you gentlemen are your institutions settled and matured, or are they not?"

Having thus disposed of the reverence to the first president's pronouncements, Kossuth pounced on the fifth. The Monroe Doctrine too had contained wisdom—for its day. But Monroe had argued on the basis that the Old and New worlds were entirely independent pockets of humanity, isolated by the great distance between them. Such an interpretation was no longer tenable, Kossuth contended. "Since the development of your Fulton's glorious invention distance is blotted out of the dictionary." Furthermore, the United States' internal expansion had made ludicrous any reference to isolation from Europe, for New York was actually closer to London than to San Francisco. The lesson Kossuth wished to impart was not that the United States should abandon the Monroe Doctrine; rather it should be extended—to the very gates of St. Petersburg! Technology and the raw energy of the American frontiersman had decreed an end to America's innocence. The 1850s demanded a vigorous foreign policy, committed to liberalism, democracy, and the global struggle against Russian tyranny.

Kossuth closed his speech by recommending four steps that the United States should take immediately. First, President Fillmore should notify the czar that another act of aggression against Hungary "would not be regarded indifferently by the people of the United States." This was the genesis of "Intervention for Non-Intervention," a slogan the Magyar would employ repeatedly in the months that followed. Although it was couched in the form of a pleasantly phrased paradox, that slogan embodied a simple idea: that the United States must abandon its policy of nonintervention in order to defend the principle of nonintervention. Americans must stop any nation from interfering with the internal affairs of a neighboring state.

Second, Kossuth advised his audience that the American navy should patrol the Mediterranean in order to protect key trade routes from Russian interference. Third, the United States should recognize Hungary's independence, although he did not suggest where an American minister might reside. And, fourth, overcoming the "tortuous humiliation" of asking for money (an embarrassment he would find easier to dispel in the following weeks), he pleaded for funds to continue his struggle. He offered to accept loans, he said, but he preferred "free, gratuitous subscriptions," and he suggested helpfully that committees be organized to solicit such gifts.[10] It was, in sum, an audacious performance. For three hours he had lectured, insulted, and harangued United States citizens and their foreign policy before many of the most important men in New York city.[11] Then he had asked them to give him money and to persuade their government to intervene in favor of his dead revolution.

Only one man tried to reply to Kossuth's speech, James Watson Webb, who was still disgruntled over the Senate's refusal to confirm him as chargé d'affaires to Austria. With curious logic, he blamed his disappointment on Kossuth's popularity. The municipal dinner offered Webb a splendid opportunity to repay an old, and, to Kossuth, inadvertent, insult. Webb's effort to answer the speech was, according to George Templeton Strong, "the most impudent act—the occasion considered—of the Colonel's impudent life." Apparently the audience agreed. When the publisher began to read the speech he had prepared, he was "coughed down" by the hostile audience.[12]

II.

"He is the master of the art of stump oratory," remarked George Templeton Strong a day before Kossuth arrived in New York. "But I recollect no instances in history where a great work has been done by platform or dinner-table oratory, or much farthered thereby."[13]

Strong had underestimated the power of Kossuth's eloquence. When he spoke, his listeners sat enraptured, almost mesmerized by the flow of words. It was one characteristic all men noticed, regardless of their attitude toward his mission. "What suggestive power lies in his supernaturally beautiful voice!" admitted one of his bitterest enemies.

10. The text of Kossuth's address is contained in *The New York Times*, 12 December 1851.

11. John Bach McMaster, *A History of the People of the United States from the Revolution to the Civil War*, 8:151.

12. Allan Nevins and Milton Halsey Thomas, eds., *The Diary of George Templeton Strong: The Turbulent Fifties, 1850–1859*, p. 77. For a more detailed account of this incident, see Komlos, *Kossuth in America*, p. 86.

13. Ibid., p. 75.

"Against his magic, like Ulysses, we have to tie ourselves to the mast, so that unknowingly we do not run after him."[14] Men were often so taken by his persuasive delivery that they analyzed his style in minute detail in order to find the basis of its power. *The Daily Picayune*, in New Orleans, found an answer in the Latin construction of his sentences, the product of his early training in that language; one man credited his colorful use of archaic words; another, the quaint accent with which he spoke English.[15]

Kossuth invited attention to his talent as a speaker, even spreading the romantic rumor that he had taught himself English while locked in an Austrian dungeon after being arrested for printing political tracts. For the first twelve months of his confinement, he related, he had been denied the use of any books. During the final two years, however, he was allowed to read books not related to politics. He had asked his jailors for a volume of Shakespeare, an English grammar, and a copy of Johnson's dictionary. Without knowing a single word, he had begun to study *The Tempest*, devoting two weeks to the first page. With the help of this intensive introduction to Shakespeare, he said, he eventually mastered the language. Contemporaries believed the story.[16]

Kossuth relied on rhetoric in other ways. In nearly every public statement, even when speaking to visiting delegations of admirers, he managed to quote some piece of history or a flattering anecdote that referred to his audience's hometown or to the organization they represented. His preparation for these seemingly off-hand remarks was intense. Three members of his party—General Klapka, Count Francis

14. Gabor Egressy, quoted in Andor M. Leffler, "The Kossuth Episode in America," p. 95.

15. *The Daily* (New Orleans) *Picayune*, 11 January 1852; Eugene Pivany, *Webster and Kossuth: A Discourse on the Relations of Daniel Webster and Louis Kossuth*, pp. 5–6; Robert Winthrop, "The Obligations and Responsibilities of Educated Men . . . ," in *Addresses and Speeches on Various Occasions*, 2:28.

16. Louis Kossuth, *Select Speeches of Kossuth*, p. 201; *Picayune*, 15 January 1852; Winthrop, "Tongue and Pen," p. 28; and Pivany, *Webster and Kossuth*, pp. 5–6, was repeating the story as fact as late as 1909.

Pulszky and Pulszky's wife, Theresa—spent much of their time poring over local histories and biographies, marking those passages that might be useful in speeches.[17] Almost never did this practice fail to captivate his American audiences.

III.

Kossuth devoted the days after his speech to cajoling the citizens of the Empire City. His time was always in demand. He lectured the Bar Association about international law, the fourth estate on the meaning of freedom of the press. He even described to the city's most prominent matrons the esteem in which his countrymen held their mothers. But mostly he asked for money, and for assurances that the United States would help him when he led his people in a new rebellion against Hapsburg authority.[18]

The nation's response had so far been encouraging. The president had sent his son, Millard Fillmore, Jr., to New York to invite Kossuth to visit the nation's capital. Newspapers were continuing to speak favorably of "Intervention for Non-Intervention." And delegations from across the Atlantic seaboard still pressed for appointments to meet the nation's guest and pledge their support to him.[19] Many otherwise apolitical citizens were swept away in the Hungarian excitement. Reverend William Ware, for example, was known to his friends as "calm as a philosopher, usually, wise as a judge, possessed in full measure of the very Ware moderation and wisdom." But in these first days of Kossuth's visit he took a "tremendous lurch" into the Young America campaign,

17. George S. Boutwell, *Reminiscences of Sixty Years in Public Affairs*, 1:206–7.

18. *The New York Herald*, 13 December 1851; *The New York Times*, 13 December 1851; *National Era*, 25 December 1851; *The New York Tribune*, 6–20 December 1851; Kossuth, *Select Speeches*, pp. 74–91, 107–24; Phineas Camp Headley, *The Life of Louis Kossuth . . . Including . . . His Principal Speeches*, pp. 446–52.

19. *The New York Times*, 9 December 1851; *National Era*, 25 December 1851.

thus earning the gentle derision—and surprise—of at least one less impressionable friend.[20]

Kossuth's emotional appeal for funds already had taken effect. The city's Whig Central Committee gave him a thousand dollars.[21] Henry Ward Beecher's fashionable Plymouth Church of Brooklyn collected ten times that amount by charging admission to hear the hero speak.[22] The city's Bar Association, self-consciously aware that it was assuming the role of a *"revolutionary committee"* by "raising funds towards an insurrection in a friendly state," nevertheless anticipated that it could donate $15,000, the net profit from its reception for Kossuth on 19 December.[23] And complementing these huge collections were the uncounted smaller donations, comprising only a few dollars each, which had begun to pour into the Magyar's headquarters. Even if these contributions were drastically overestimated, they dwarfed the $11,593.92 which Kossuth's lieutenants announced that they had received by the last week of December.[24] Since the city was paying the expenses of his entire entourage, it is impossible to determine exactly what happened to that money.

In addition to this cash income, admirers had donated a number of items for which a fair market value had not yet been determined. For example, Henry C. O'Reilly, the president of the Atlantic and Pacific Telegraph Company, had given the Hungarians the deed to five hundred acres of land. Others had sent books, maps, "several beautifully worked purses," three gold rings, a number of portraits of various prominent men, "and other things from different people."[25] One gift excited par-

20. Dewey, *Autobiography and Letters*, p. 224.
21. McMaster, *History of the United States*, 8:151; *New York Tribune*, 22 December 1851; Leffler, "Kossuth Episode," p. 198.
22. *The Liberator*, 26 December 1851; Carl Wittke, *Refugees of Revolution*, p. 96; William C. Beecher and Samuel Scoville, *A Biography of Rev. Henry Ward Beecher*, pp. 256–57.
23. Strong, *Diary*, p. 77.
24. *The* (London) *Times*, 6 January 1852.
25. Ibid.; see also Kossuth to O'Reilly, 20 December 1851, O'Reilly papers, Rochester Historical Society, cited in Leffler, "Kossuth Episode," p. 65; O'Reilly to Kossuth, 2 January 1852, in Jánossey Dénes, ed., *A Kossuth-Emigráció Angliában és Amerikában, 1851–1852*, 1:266–67.

ticular interest. Andrew Jackson Donelson, once private secretary to his namesake and now an editor of the party's national organ, *The Union*, a prominent Democratic politician in his own right, had donated for auction the former president's famed "Bunker Hill Casket," containing bullets from the battles at Bunker Hill and New Orleans, together with locks of hair from Jefferson and Jackson. Donelson stipulated only that the casket's new owner never allow it to leave the United States.[26] No records exist detailing the income Kossuth derived from the auction of these and other items, but the amount must have been several thousand dollars.

Of more significance on the national level was the creation of the Central Hungarian Committee, under the leadership of Simeon Draper, Theodore Sedgwick, Oscar W. Sturdevant, and John L. O'Sullivan. With Draper, a Whig of the progressive "Sewardite" faction,[27] as chairman of the committee, and the Democratic expansionist O'Sullivan as secretary, the committee represented both political parties and brought to the movement a legitimate image of non-partisan concern. The Central Committee became immediately the vehicle for Kossuth's national fund raising drive.[28]

"Hungary bonds" formed the basis of the committee's efforts. These certificates, issued in denominations of one, five, ten, fifty, and one hundred dollars, promised repayment when (not "if") Kossuth was safely returned to the governorship of an independent Hungary. Each bond bore the portrait of the Magyar chieftain, and he personally autographed all fifty- and one-hundred-dollar certificates. The committee flooded the country with letters to locally prominent men, asking each to peddle the bonds to friends and promising each agent a ten percent commission on his sales, payable, of course, in bonds.[29]

26. Memorandum, 15 December 1851, Andrew Jackson Donelson Papers, 16, Library of Congress; *The* (London) *Times*, 6 January 1852.

27. *The New York Tribune*, 5 June 1852.

28. *The New York Times*, 9 December 1851; *National Era*, 25 December 1851.

29. Draper to potential donors, Cocke papers. Kossuth also promised Hungary's salt mines as collateral; Komlos, *Kossuth in America*, p. 154.

The committee also passed along suggestions for alternate ways of raising cash. In some areas, they reported, the ladies ("God bless them!") had solicited contributions from their friends and from the neighborhood children. Elsewhere, sympathizers had organized rummage sales of "fancy articles, jewelry, books, engravings, &c.," and had transmitted the proceeds to the Hungarian Liberty Fund in New York. In addition to their promises of repayment, the committee assured its correspondents that all contributors would have their names recorded in an honored place in the archives of the future Republic of Hungary.[30]

Kossuth and his allies were tapping every available source for contributions. But the sudden explosion of Young American sentiments—raised to new intensity by the hero's presence in the city—had lured other, less altruistic figures into the business of satisfying the public's preoccupation with the Hungarians and their burgeoning American crusade.

IV.

John Nicholas Genin was one of those Americans now forgotten through no fault of their own. Genin was a hat salesman by trade and a publicity hound by avocation. In 1850, he had wrangled an estimated eighty thousand dollars in free publicity for his shop by buying the first ticket to Jenny Lind's American singing debut. The ticket had cost him $225. Another time he offered to build, at his own expense, a bridge across the Hudson River. The city fathers declined Genin's bizarre (and well-publicized) offer, as he probably knew they would. But later, when the city decided to build its own bridge, it used Genin's original plans. Perhaps coincidentally, the span touched Manhattan almost directly across the street from Genin's haberdashery. Whether he was designing a distinctive cap to complement Amelia Bloomer's newfangled pants or dedicating a museum to immortalize famous hats of the past, everything Genin touched seemed to turn to newsprint—and ultimately to profits.[31]

30. Ibid.
31. *Appleton's Cyclopaedia of American Biography*, 2:624–25.

"Hungary Fund" certificates were sold to raise revenue for the renewed revolution. Fifty- and one-hundred-dollar certificates were personally signed by Kossuth.

It was not surprising, therefore, that Genin anticipated the Hungarian craze. First he offered to contribute one thousand dollars to the cause if other prominent businessmen would pledge the same amount.[32] The proposal excited little popular interest, for other men had been making similar offers for months. Genin then tried a different tack. Pulling together a pile of hideous and unmarketable black felt hats that had been gathering dust in his warehouse, Genin put his staff to work modifying their shape. First they sewed the left side of the brim to the crown, and then they added a shiny feather. The result was a fair likeness to Kossuth's own distinctive headpiece.[33]

When the *Humboldt* paused briefly at Sandy Hook before continuing into New York harbor, Genin climbed aboard and distributed his creations among Kossuth's ragged companions, and the Hungarians, apparently mistaking Genin's advertisements for gifts, wore them proudly in their Saturday afternoon procession down Broadway. Almost immediately the arbiters of high fashion decreed that these "Kossuth hats"

32. Genin's letter to Mayor Ambrose J. Kingsland reprinted, *The New York Times*, 8 October 1851.

33. *Appleton's Cyclopaedia*, 2:624–25.

were "all the go," and the style became a symbol of republican sentiment.[34] Genin not only sold his remaining stock of that style, but also
placed huge orders from hastily retooled factories nearby. Eventually,
an estimated half-million dollars would be spent on these hats, and the
association of hat manufacturers would present Genin with a silver service worth twelve hundred dollars in appreciation for his ingenuity.[35]
Competitors could only try to overtake his sales advantage by assuring
the public that their Kossuth hats were constructed by genuine Hungarian ladies.[36]

Critics of the Kossuth mania caught the humor of this idolizing
trade war. "Perhaps a reform in the hats of America will flow from the
preachings of the illustrious Magyar," George Templeton Strong recorded in his diary. "I doubt the likelihood of any other lasting result
from his mission."[37]

Genin's success in exploiting the Hungarian fever was unique only
in its magnitude. Throughout the city, the carnival atmosphere had
invited other merchants to reinforce the public mood. Fishmongers
hawked their wares as "Kossuth oysters";[38] someone opened a "Kossuth
Restaurant" on Broadway; A. Joel and Company, jewelers, advertised
Kossuth miniatures, and E. Anthony was selling the same item "very
cheap." Professional copyists offered to write memorials to the nation's
guest; button salesmen reported a variety of items expressing sympathy
for the European rebels; flag makers boasted a large inventory of Hungarian tricolors; and Kossuth marches and dances suddenly appeared in
theaters throughout the city.[39]

Several photographers advertised that they would soon sell exclusive

34. Ibid.; *The New York Herald*, 10 December 1851; Alexander K. McClure,
Colonel Alexander K. McClure's Recollections of Half a Century, p. 200.

35. *Appleton's Cyclopaedia*, 2:624–25.

36. *The New York Tribune*, 5 December 1851.

37. Strong, *Diary*, p. 79.

38. *The New York Herald*, 13 December 1851.

39. *The New York Tribune*, 4, 5 December 1851; *The New York Herald*, 12
December 1851; Leffler, "Kossuth Episode," chapter 2, contains other examples of
such exploitation.

poses of the noble Magyar, apparently unaware that Kossuth already had granted exclusive commercial rights to his likeness to Walter Gould, a young artist from Fredericksburg, Maryland.[40] But one enterprising photographer nevertheless managed to get the hero's picture, and advertised, "*Kossuth Taken*—What the Austrians could not do, Root & Co. . . . have done, for on Friday they succeeded in capturing the illustrious hero in his carriage on Staten Island."[41] Even the manufacturers of rat poison found ways to capitalize on Kossuth's popularity:

> Kossuth's coming, so they say;
> He's a lion in his way
> And made tyranny his prey;
> But for bugs and such as they
> Our old Lyon is O.K.
> Rats and mice, too, he can slay.[42]

But exploitation of the Magyar's fame was not confined to the commercial community. It was an honor when the American Bible Society, declaring Kossuth "a true friend of the Bible," elected him a vice-president. But some churchmen, perhaps attempting to boost sagging attendance, sought to capitalize on his name. A man calling himself The Prophet of the Highest announced that he would preach on "The Mission of Kossuth." And a Baptist pastor elsewhere in the city, speaking from the text, "Behold he cometh with clouds and every eye shall see him," pronounced Kossuth's arrival in the Empire City as the prelude to the second coming of Christ.[43]

But the people did not seem to care that their emotions were being exploited doubly—by the Magyar and the American commercial com-

---

40. *The New York Tribune*, 5, 8 December 1851; *National Era*, 9 October 1851.

41. *The New York Tribune*, 11 December 1851.

42. Ibid., 23 October 1851; Leffler, "Kossuth Episode," pp. 66–67.

43. *The New York Times*, 6 December 1851; Wittke, *Refugees of Revolution*, p. 97; *Daily Union*, 24 December 1851; *The New York Tribune*, 15 December 1851; Leffler, "Kossuth Episode," p. 105.

munity. They gobbled up enormous quantities of memorabilia—spending money, Kossuth might have lamented, that could have gone into his own war chest.

V.

New York had been kind to Kossuth. His visit had been so successful, in fact, that by late December he had announced that he would also tour Philadelphia, Baltimore, Washington, "and probably Cincinnati."[44] His decision to visit Cincinnati had presumably been a tortuous one, for he made it known to the press that he felt some distaste for that city's sobriquet, Queen City of the West. "It is too monarchical a name for the great leader of republicanism in Europe, and apostle of freedom everywhere," remarked *The Times* of London with subtle sarcasm.[45] But the profits he had reaped in New York and the prospect of repeating that success among Cincinnati's large and sympathetic German population persuaded him to accept that city's invitation.

Only a few critics in New York had dared to challenge the frenzy of Young American sentiment. James Watson Webb's *Courier and Enquirer* had, of course, rained abuse on the nation's guest, scoring him as the champion of "*Kings, Lords, and Commons,* and the aristocratic institutions of the Magyar nobles," and challenging anyone to document his professed republicanism.[46] And at the Bar Association dinner on 18 December, Webb's crony, "Judge" William Duer, had tried to debate Kossuth before the crowd shouted him down.[47] But Kossuth's opponents

44. *The* (London) *Times,* 6 January 1852.

45. Ibid., 2 January 1852. Kossuth's sensitivity on this subject was widely accepted as genuine. When Kossuth later visited Cincinnati, the mayor apologized for the nickname, saying, "Notwithstanding *you* may properly object . . . we cannot believe in using it here, that we compromise any principles of Republicanism in applying it to a city like ours." *Daily Enquirer* (Cincinnati), 12 February 1852.

46. Quoted in *The New York Times,* 4 December 1851.

47. *The* (London) *Times,* 2 January 1852; "Miscellany," *The Democratic Review* 30 (January 1852):92.

were relatively insignificant, for they spoke only for themselves. The near unanimity of the city would brook no isolated dissenters. "The Czar himself does not exercise a more unrelenting despotism over his subjects than that which has been enforced upon the people of this city by the worshippers of Kossuth during his short stay among us," reported the correspondent of Washington's neutral *Union*. "No one, whoever he may be or whatever his talents or character, has been suffered to dissent from any of the principles he has put forth, or their application even, but all have been required to bow down and worship, and cry amen to all that has been demanded by the Great Magyar."[48]

But even before the *Union* published that dispatch, this near unanimity had been shattered. The Garrisonian wing of the abolitionist movement—once among Kossuth's warmest admirers—already had identified their erstwhile hero as a friend of the slavery forces.

48. *Daily Union*, 24 December 1851.

V.

THE ABOLITIONIST DEFECTION

Slavery owned the soul of American politics during the 1850s. When men gathered for serious conversation in any section of the country they spoke of expansion, or trade, or the prospects for foreign war; but inevitably these subjects, and every other social and political problem facing the Union, blurred into and out of the reality of black slavery. Even traditionally diplomatic terms such as *non-intervention, non-intercourse,* and *balance of power* were losing their international connotation and were more likely to headline a sectional dispute than a European crisis.[1] Slavery was functioning as a prism on American society, dispersing national issues into sectional issues, national loyalties into regional ones.

A small but dedicated corps of idealists, concentrated in New England, had long since vowed to tolerate no more compromise and no more delays: they wanted immediate emancipation of the slaves, and they condemned any politician who refused to echo their demands. In other Northern states, growing numbers were pledging to eradicate the "Great National Sin," or at least to prevent its further extension. And in the South, where planters once had felt sufficiently secure to debate among themselves the wisdom and morality of human bondage, the burdens of Yankee condemnation had led them to close ranks and to threaten to quit the Union rather than yield to Northern political pressure. Even the Compromise Acts of 1850, devised by Henry Clay and rammed through both houses of Congress by working alliances between moderates and radicals in each section, had not quieted the agitation over slavery. While Southern senators were declaring the compromise

1. See, for example, *Charleston* (South Carolina) *Telegraph*, quoted in *National Era*, 6 September 1849; *National Era*, 24 January 1849; 13 June 1850; 5 September 1850; 7 August 1851.

to be a "definitive adjustment and settlement" of the problem,[2] abolitionists and Free-Soilers throughout the North were redoubling their
efforts to eliminate slavery from the American continent.

Louis Kossuth understood the significance of this smoldering deadlock, and he had resolved even before landing at Staten Island that he
would maintain a strict neutrality in the explosive national debate.[3] To
do otherwise, he understood, would shatter his prospects for a broad
American commitment to European reform. But ultimately Kossuth became a victim of the slavery question: extremists in both sections of the
United States were prepared to judge the Hungarian cause only in terms
of their own domestic struggle. And in the superheated atmosphere of
sectionalism during the 1850s, even Kossuth's professed neutrality was
a partisan issue.

I.

Radical abolitionists had watched with intense sympathy as the
defeated Magyar fled first to Turkey and then toward the United States.
They were humanitarians of a passionate breed, and in their minds
Kossuth symbolized the global contest between despotism and the
rights of man. These New England firebrands had inherited the inflexi-
bility, if not the theology, of their Puritan ancestors, and their moral code
demanded an absolute commitment to righteous action. Few mortals
could endure their detailed scrutiny, but Kossuth, they believed, was one
who could. He had scorned compromise and expediency, and had waged
a futile war against the two great tyrants of Eastern Europe. That he had
failed did not pale his greatness. On the contrary, it had confirmed him as
a martyr to the cause of liberty. While the success of his revolution had
remained a possibility, abolitionists had dismissed him as an immoral
military chieftain; only after his crushing defeat did the Garrisonians
adopt him as a hero.[4]

2. *Congressional Globe*, 32d Cong., 1st sess., p. 12.
3. Andor M. Leffler, "The Kossuth Episode in America," pp. 137–38; *The
New York Times*, 31 October 1851.
4. For the radicals' early view of Kossuth see William Lloyd Garrison, "Pa-

Long before Kossuth was released by the Turkish sultan, therefore, the radicals had developed a keen sense of fraternity with him, for they could identify his frustrations with their own. Like him they believed they were prophets of freedom, and they too had watched helplessly as their nation yielded to the dictates of a corrupt and degraded oligarchy. So perfect was the presumed kinship, in fact, that as early as August 1849, abolitionists were celebrating the exiled rebel as "the William Lloyd Garrison of Hungarian liberty."[5] Garrison, the most vocal and uncompromising advocate of immediate emancipation, had three decades earlier pondered joining the Greeks in their war for independence against Turkey.[6] To prove that his convictions toward European revolutions had not changed, he promptly reprinted the double-edged compliment in his weekly newspaper, *The Liberator.*[7]

But the radicals seemed bewildered by the hysterical reaction of most Americans to Kossuth's cause. For decades abolitionists had championed the principle of universal liberty, and their countrymen had dismissed them as deranged fanatics. Now, after 1848, a European rebel was voicing identical abstractions and was gathering applause from every section of the country. There was something terribly illogical about this national outpouring of pity, they believed. In Arkansas, sympathizers were passing resolutions and contributing money for Hungarian liberty, while slaves rattled their chains outside the door; in Pennsylvania, dough-faced politicians were chairing Hungary committees; in New York, New Jersey, and New Orleans, men who had hailed the Compromise Acts of 1850 were now echoing the Magyar's lofty principles and declaring him the greatest man of his or any age.[8]

"National hypocrisy," the radicals complained sullenly.[9] The spec-

triotism and Christianity—Kossuth and Jesus," excerpts of which are contained in Wendell Phillips Garrison, *William Lloyd Garrison, 1805–1879,* 3:340–41.

5. J. B. Syme, "Joseph Kossuth, the Student Chieftain of Republican Hungary," in *Burritt's Christian Citizen* (Worcester, Massachusetts)," 11 August 1849.

6. Louis Filler, *The Crusade Against Slavery, 1830–1860,* p. 56.

7. *The Liberator,* 31 August 1849.

8. Ibid., 7 December 1849; Carl Wittke, *Refugees of Revolution,* pp. 96–97.

9. *The Liberator,* 7 December 1849.

tacle of slaveholders and compromisers daring to endorse the principle of liberty seemed to the Garrisonians a two-faced exercise in conscious self-deception. Kossuth had fought for freedom, they believed, but most Americans had helped pass laws forbidding it. Frederick Douglass, himself a former slave and now an important figure in the antislavery crusade, fumed that for Kossuth to satisfy the American people, "he must cease to be Kossuth." Obviously referring to the Fugitive Slave Law, the most grating element of the new compromise package, Douglass advised the exile that to harmonize himself with this nation's avowed ideals, "he must own himself a rebel, a traitor, a base fugitive, turn his back upon this country, give himself up into the hands of his Austrian master and repent of ever having run away."[10] Henry C. Wright, *The Liberator's* itinerant correspondent, expressed even greater disgust. This nation's character was so polluted, he worried, that the Hungarian would lose his integrity if he dared even to visit the United States. "Kossuth," he chanted: "Tell him of American slavery! Save Him! Save Him! 'HERE LIES KOSSUTH—THE AMERICAN SLAVEHOLDER'— must be his epitaph if he touches our shores. Friends of freedom in Europe and America—to the rescue!"[11]

To impress upon their countrymen the absurdity of the Kossuth mania, many abolitionists reduced their arguments to a set of simple analogies. Hungary represented the badgered, victimized American slave, and the Hapsburgs were cast as foreign equivalents of the Southern aristocracy. Thus, in Charles Sumner's words, Kossuth had escaped not tyranny but "the house of bondage"; his forthcoming arrival in the United States would bring not asylum but "emancipation."[12] And other abolitionists described the emperor in Vienna as speaking habitually of "*his* Government, and *his* Imperial city, and *his* people, as a planter talks of *his* slaves."[13] Abolitionists pushed the analogy in their propaganda

10. *Frederick Douglass's Paper* (Rochester, New York), 20 November 1851.
11. *The Liberator*, 7 November 1851.
12. "Sympathy for the Rights of Man Everywhere," 27 October 1851, in *Charles Sumner: His Complete Works*, 3:169; *National Era*, 16 November 1848.
13. Ibid.

campaigns. "Help the American Kossuths," or, alternatively, "Austrianism in Pennsylvania" appeared in headlines of antislavery journals.[14]

In Washington, Gamaliel Bailey and John Greenleaf Whittier, two transplanted New Englanders, mounted an extended propaganda campaign around this same approach. In their reform-minded weekly, *The National Era*, they began comparing the sad experiences of Americans traveling in Austria with the hazards of journeying into the Southern United States. Bailey told, for example, the stories of the Reverend Charles L. Brace and Nathan Bird Watson. Reverend Brace had been detained in Austria for possessing revolutionary tracts and other documents linking him to the anti-Hapsburg movement. But Watson, a Yankee tourist, had been terrorized by vigilantes in Warrenton, Georgia, simply because he was assumed to oppose slavery and because he had visited "suspicious Negro houses."[15] On another occasion Bailey admitted that Americans were experiencing some trouble having their passports revised in Vienna but exclaimed that in South Carolina, Yankees were being tarred and feathered. "We all grow very indignant at the unfriendly conduct of Austria," he told his readers in one article, "but that South Carolina should lynch an American citizen for opinion's sake is deemed a matter of course."[16]

Other critics of slavery—Horace Mann, Henry Ward Beecher, Elihu Burritt, and a host of less famous thinkers—repeated the analogy, and always its implication was clear: Americans were as corrupt as the Austrian monarchs, and they had no business expressing sympathy for the cause of reform in Europe unless they chose to champion necessary reforms in the United States as well.[17] Indeed, with half the nation own-

14. *Frederick Douglass's Paper*, 13 November, 25 December 1851.

15. *National Era*, 31 July 1851.

16. Ibid., 11 September 1851. See also, Charles L. Brace, *Hungary in 1851, with an Experience of the Austrian Police*.

17. Mann's speech at Worcester, Massachusetts, 16 September 1851, is quoted in *Frederick Douglass's Paper*, 30 October 1851; Henry Ward Beecher's contribution, originally printed in *The New York Independent* in October 1851, was reprinted widely; see also *Burritt's Christian Citizen*, 25 August 1849; *Frederick Douglass's Paper*, 23 October, 20 November 1851.

ing slaves and the other half looking the other way, radicals wondered aloud who could "properly" welcome Kossuth when he arrived in the New World. John Greenleaf Whittier put the question most directly: "Who will receive him?" he asked, "Who will be freedom's mouthpiece?" Among the Garrisonians the answer was unanimous: Kossuth was their own particular hero, for they alone could match his abiding devotion to free institutions; professions of support by any other factions were "hypocritical and hollow."[18]

Despite their cynical attitude toward the popular frenzy, most radicals were delighted when Kossuth and his entourage embarked on the last leg of their journey to America. True, Kossuth had warned while he was still in England that he would take no stand on the slavery question, and that statement disturbed some abolitionists;[19] but he had also congratulated the British for repealing slave laws in the West Indies, and the abolitionists could find reason to hope that Kossuth would speak out after he arrived. Betraying more hope than objective judgment, the Garrisonian clique seemed to be erecting a dreamy, improbable scenario for the Magyar's visit: he would see firsthand the corruption that pervaded the ruling slavocracy and its Yankee fellow travelers, and he would damn it as rigorously as he had damned Austrian tyranny three years earlier; with his popularity at a fever pitch in all sections of the country he would align himself firmly with the abolitionists' cause; and his sudden conversion would spark a precipitous shift in public opinion away from continued compromise and toward a positive program for immediate emancipation. "He will be a Godsend," Frederick Douglass promised his readers. "He stands forth a liberator, and commands the cooperation of the Sons of Freedom everywhere to emancipate the serf and the slave."[20] Nor were such hopes limited to the Garrisonian ex-

18. Garrison, *Garrison*, 3:341–42; *Frederick Douglass's Paper*, 6, 20 November 1851.

19. Lewis Tappan to John Scoble, 26 November 1851, in Annie Heloise Abel and Frank J. Klingberg, eds., *A Sidelight on Anglo-American Relations, 1839–1858*, p. 276.

20. *Frederick Douglass's Paper*, 27 November 1851; *The Baltimore Clipper*,

tremists. Speaking of the more politically minded Free-Soil movement in a letter to his son, Joshua Giddings, himself an abolitionist congressman from Ohio's Western Reserve, employed a revealing, if perhaps unconscious, play on words. "The free soilers intend to make Capitol out of Kossuth," he wrote his son, "and they will do it."[21]

Success for the abolitionist plan depended on Kossuth's future conduct. To insure that their prospective ally would play his role properly, the Garrisonians launched a massive effort to educate him about the true nature of American society. While he was still in England the antislavery forces had placed in his hands two documents, a copy of the Fugitive Slave Law and a copy of Theodore Dwight Weld's controversial tract, *Slavery As It Is*.[22] And in the days immediately before and after the *Humboldt* docked in New York, radical newspapers contained dozens of glowing accounts of Kossuth's movements and spirited appeals for him to speak his mind by denouncing slavery. William Ellery Channing, the Unitarian preacher, pacifist, and literary dean of the antislavery crusade, spoke of Kossuth as himself a "flying slave" and begged him to "take the slave's part" in America as well.[23] Garrison composed a poetic demand on the exile:

> Say slavery is a stain upon our glory,
>> Accursed in Heaven, and by the earth abhorred;
> Show that our soil with Negro blood is gory,
>> And certain are the judgments of the Lord;
> So shall thy name immortal be in story,
> And thy fidelity the world applaud.[24]

Columns describing the horrors of slavery appeared side by side with stories praising Kossuth's conduct in Europe, and a report detailing

December 1851; William G. Allen to Douglass, *Frederick Douglass's Paper*, 1 January 1852.

21. James Brewer Stewart, *Joshua R. Giddings and the Tactics of Radical Politics*, p. 206.

22. Filler, *Crusade Against Slavery*, p. 193.

23. Garrison, *Garrison*, 3:357.

24. Ibid., p. 346; *The Liberator*, 19 December 1851; National Anti-Slavery Bazaar, *The Liberty Bell*, 1852.

the capture of a black fugitive in Boston was headlined, quoting Kossuth's own description of the United States, " 'This free, great and glorious country'!!! An item for Kossuth to read and ponder."[25] Letters from private citizens poured into the Magyar begging him to let his conscience speak.[26] The New England radicals entreated the nation's guest as a political philosopher and as a fellow humanitarian. To maintain his grip on the Garrisonian conscience he would necessarily have to establish once again his credentials as a crusader for reform.

II.

In the United States Senate, John Parker Hale was, as always, playing his own hand. Witty and eloquent, but also indolent and more than once suspected even by his friends of serious moral lapses, Hale did not conform to the image of intense single-mindedness that characterized the popular view of the abolitionist crusade. But it was generally agreed that he was the most dedicated and consistent opponent of slavery

John Parker Hale, senator from New Hampshire, was independent of formal party alliances and single-mindedly opposed to slavery.

25. *The Liberator*, 12 December 1851.
26. *Frederick Douglass's Paper*, 4 December 1851.

in Washington. This distinction, in fact, twice brought him nominations to the presidency, once in 1848 for the Liberty party, and again in 1852 for the dying Free-Soilers. Disowned by the regular Democratic party in his native New Hampshire in 1845, Hale nevertheless lingered on in the Senate without formal party allegiances. This independence allowed him to indulge his almost monomanic preoccupation with the slavery issue.[27]

Hale half-heartedly and impishly subscribed to the politics of disruption. It offended him that public business continued while south of the Mason-Dixon line black men remained slaves, and at irregular intervals he demonstrated his displeasure with "politics as usual" by harassing his colleagues with verbal guerrilla tactics. In the midst of any debate on almost any subject he would win recognition from the chair and, with clever puns and sharp double entendres, twist the debate in midcourse into a discussion of free-soil policy. So adept was he at this strategy that he once transformed a simple discussion over credentials into a brief exchange over the morality of slavery.[28] It was a similar series of verbal exchanges that had led to Henry S. Foote's offer to personally lynch Hale should he ever venture into Mississippi—an episode that gave Foote the nickname "Hangman" among Northern antislavery writers.

More often, however, Hale preferred to disrupt discussions of foreign policy. In 1848, for example, when the infant French Revolution seemed destined to succeed, Senate Young Americans, led by Michigan's Lewis Cass, then the Democratic party's nominee for president, had proposed a resolution congratulating the new authorities in Paris for the victory of their liberal principles. Hale had pretended to endorse the resolution and had delivered an eloquent speech in its support. Then, to the disgust of Cass and his allies, Hale had offered an amendment to the congratulatory message, singling out the French decision to free all slaves in their overseas colonies as the one revolutionary act particularly

27. William A. Robinson, "John Parker Hale," *Dictionary of American Biography*, 8:105–7; for a more extended, and more sympathetic treatment of Hale's career, see Robert H. Sewell, *John P. Hale and the Politics of Abolition*.

28. *Congressional Globe*, 32d Cong., 1st sess., pp. 2–4.

worthy of praise. The reason for his proposal, he explained innocently, was that he wished the French people to "be informed of the object of our sympathy." That he had offered his amendment only to embarrass the resolution's Southern supporters seemed obvious: when his amendment appeared for approval or rejection he did not bother even to register his vote, and it failed by a margin of 28 to 1.[29]

A year later, Cass and his fellow ideologues recommended that the United States sever diplomatic relations with Austria, in protest against that nation's military action against the Hungarian revolution. Hale again claimed to support the idealists. In a long, imaginative speech Hale endorsed the humanitarian principles Cass had employed to defend his proposal; then, quoting those same principles, he extended the proposition to include Russia, then England, then France and Spain— for these nations too had violated the moral sense of mankind in the conduct of foreign relations. Then he applied Cass's ideals to the American South and was poised to launch into a tirade against slavery. But Henry Clay gained the floor and quickly changed the subject. Cass's resolution ultimately failed, and years later he recalled with disgust that Hale's blustering and irrelevant remarks had defeated it.[30]

In December 1851, Hale returned to his guerrilla tactics. The occasion was a mild resolution of welcome to Kossuth, supported by the Fillmore administration, introduced by Henry Foote of Mississippi, and embodying little more than assurances of the Senate's "profound respect" for the Hungarian rebels. Taking the floor for less than two minutes, Hale announced to his colleagues that he welcomed the resolution. But, he added, he noticed that certain Southern congressmen had doubted that Kossuth alone was worthy of the nation's praise. To satisfy these doubts, he said, he was proposing a brief amendment, expressing sympathy not only for Kossuth, but also for the "victims of oppression everywhere." This transparent reference to the slaves evoked sarcastic attacks from both sides of the Mason-Dixon line. Hale was seeking "a

29. Ibid., 30th Cong., 1st sess., pp. 568, 592.
30. Ibid., 31st Cong., 1st sess., pp. 113–14; 31st Cong., 2d sess., p. 36; 32d Cong., 1st sess., p. 25.

74

little contemptible notoriety," charged Henry Foote, "which may perchance serve to call into renewed action those elements of domestic discord, which I suppose every good man in the land hoped might terminate forever." Lewis Cass agreed. "There is not a man within these walls," he suggested, "who does not know what the gentleman means perfectly well. He means to bring up the old question of slavery, and he means by this declaration to defeat the present resolution, for he knows it cannot pass with such an amendment."

Hale denied everything. "Now let no man retort that I am in favor of agitation," he said. "I used to be in favor of it, but I got sick of it." Seizing upon a statement by Henry Foote that there was a global struggle progressing between freedom and slavery, Hale again invoked a double entendre. "Well, I want to enroll myself under the banners of those who are fighting the battle of liberty." The next day Foote, admitting that he found opposition coming from an "unexpected source," withdrew his resolution, and endorsed in its place a compromise and watered-down statement authored by William Seward. Seward's proposition expressed simply a "cordial welcome" to Kossuth and his entourage.[31]

In reporting developments in the Senate, *The New York Times* recognized the pivotal role Hale was playing in diluting support for Kossuth. Indeed, in that paper's opinion Hale ranked equally with the Austrian minister himself as an opponent of the Hungarian cause. The *Times* predicted that when Seward's resolution appeared for debate in the Senate, "we [will] have another and a regular HALE-storm."[32] But Hale did not, as many observers assumed, oppose Kossuth's mission. Like the Garrisonians, he endorsed the abstractions symbolized by the Hungarian revolution but he was also determined that first things should come first. The antislavery forces viewed the abolition of slavery as America's first priority. If they could exploit Kossuth to further that goal they would do it—even if that meant shattering the Magyar's hopes for American aid. Kossuth's principal worth was a tool for domestic reform.

31. Ibid., pp. 21–27, 30–31.
32. *The New York Times*, 5 December 1851.

III.

Kossuth slept late this Friday morning, 12 December. Throughout the week since his arrival he had devoted every day and night to cajoling the citizens of New York, and the task had been an exhausting one. But it was not only the physical exhaustion from constant speechmaking and handshaking that had tired Kossuth. He was also encountering enormous psychological pressure. For a week he had tried to divorce himself from domestic American politics, but the abolitionists would not let him. Kossuth was losing patience with these antislavery crusaders. He had come to the United States for guns and money and men, and he had no intention of jeopardizing his mission with a quixotic attack on American institutions. The radical abolitionists were claiming to welcome him but they were, he understood, on the verge of wrecking his prospects for success. They were twisting his own rhetoric, invoking his catch phrases for freedom, to lure him into a public endorsement of their own ideology. For a week he had managed to dodge or downplay radical appeals for support. But this morning, as he tardily made his way toward the Irving House's large and lavish ballroom, he would confront the slavery issue head-on.

Kossuth's eyes registered visible surprise as he strode through the main entrance, noted the reporter from *The New York Herald*. Standing in the center of the room were more than a dozen black men, waiting patiently to deliver a memorial to their city's guest. Uneasily, Kossuth continued into the room and took his place. The committee's spokesman, a fishmonger named George Downing, who had excited some local interest by dubbing his wares "Kossuth oysters," stepped forward and began reading a prepared statement. "We appear before you," he told Kossuth, "to pay homage to a great principle, which you announce with so much distinctness and uphold with so much power: the principle that a man has a right to the full exercise of his faculties in the land which gave him birth." After wishing Kossuth success in his mission, Downing concluded by denying that the Hungarian revolution was the exclusive property of any country or party or sect; it was, instead, the "common cause of crushed, outraged humanity." The black men did not mention slavery, but they did not need to. The combination of their color and their words would have made the word redundant.

Kossuth could think of no appropriate response. To endorse these sentiments would certainly label him as an abolitionist; to reject them would cast him as a phony reformer and would provoke doubts, in some men's minds, about the seriousness of his concern for liberty in his own country. He therefore chose to make no pertinent response at all. With icy reserve, the Magyar remarked simply that "the time for addresses has passed; and the time for action has come." In only one respect did he treat this delegation as he had all others: he remembered to ask them for money before ushering them unceremoniously to the door.[33]

The interview angered Kossuth, for in his opinion these black men were seeking to embarrass him publicly. Sometime later that same day he determined that similar incidents would not happen in the future. Hastily he scrawled a rambling, clumsy public statement and handed it to the newspaper reporters for immediate publication. Invoking the euphemism "domestic concerns" when he meant to say "slavery," he avowed his intention "not to be mixed up with" any aspect of the sectional struggle. He begged those who claimed to be his friends "to give one proof of their sympathy by avoiding every step which might entangle me into difficulties" while in the United States. The document was nothing less than a formal proclamation of neutrality. But neutrality necessarily implied support for the status quo, and in 1851 the status quo was the South's own program.[34]

IV.

Suddenly Kossuth's crusade in Europe mattered little. His reforms, his revolution, his crushing defeat at the hands of Czar Nicholas's armies

33. *The New York Herald*, 13 December 1851; *The New York Times*, 13 December 1851; *The Liberator*, 18 December 1851.

34. Kossuth's statement was published in its entirety in the New York newspapers, 13 December 1851.

—all the benchmarks of his celebrated career—now seemed to the radical forces only so much "Bunkum."[35] In the metaphysical world of these idealists, rhetoric ranked equally with solid achievement. "I had rather have a great and true man," confided William H. Furness, "than the political liberation of twenty Hungarys."[36] That Kossuth had risked death to liberate his homeland was unimportant if in America he neglected to condemn slavery. Moreover, his backsliding posture had shattered the radicals' dreams of a coup against their corrupted countrymen. For both these reasons, the New England abolitionists within the Garrisonian camp turned against their erstwhile hero in a wild, passionate fury.

Garrison received word of Kossuth's public statement regarding slavery only after composing most of *The Liberator* for 19 December; two and a half of its four pages were devoted to a florid tribute in prose and poetry to the Hungarian cause, and Garrison did not have time to rewrite the entire issue. Instead he simply penned a hasty and sad denouement before putting the paper to press: "Since these lines were written," he told his readers in one place, "Kossuth has made a dishonorable election. He is a trimmer."[37]

In subsequent weeks Garrison lambasted the nation's guest with every insult in his imposing arsenal of invective. Kossuth was "as demented as the renowned Don Quixote," who had been unable to distinguish between giants and windmills. When he praised American liberty, as he constantly did, "it was as if one should go into a notorious house of ill-fame, and praise its polluted inhabitants as the most virtuous of all flesh." He was "criminal" and "cowardly," "slippery," and "selfish"; he was "deaf, dumb and blind" to the dictates of morality. So important was this issue to Garrison that in order to explain the radical position he published one of the two long prose works of his career the following February, "Letter to Louis Kossuth concerning Freedom and Slavery in the U.S." This "letter," more than one hundred pages long,

35. *The Liberator*, 9 January 1852.
36. Furness to Garrison, 30 December 1851, in Garrison, *Garrison*, 3:347.
37. *The Liberator*, 18 December 1851.

systematically refuted Kossuth's public utterances about American liberty and castigated the Magyar as a hypocrite who was prepared to say anything to win the hearts and dollars of American citizens.[38]

Not all critics of the slavery system abandoned Kossuth. Less radical thinkers than Garrison chided the Hungarian for ignoring the pleas of the Southern bondmen,[39] but his single-minded attachment to Hungary did not constitute, in their minds, a satisfactory excuse for censure. "We notice that some of our friends are anxious that he should express himself on the special question of slavery," remarked the Cleveland *True Democrat*. "Why should they be? Is not his life an eloquent defence of freedom?" "He has his own great work to do," the *Hartford Republican* agreed, "Let him do it."[40]

But the radicals were oblivious to such appeals for moderation. One after another they fell into line behind Garrison. Wendell Phillips condemned the Hungarian as a mere nationalist, unburdened by high principles; Channing accused him of accepting a Southern bribe; and H. P. Crozier argued that Kossuth would have been better off dead than as an apologist for slavery. But it was William G. Allen, of McGrawsville, New York, who best summed up the frustrations of the Garrisonian clique. "One word from him to this people would have startled this nation into a sense of propriety never felt before," he wrote Frederick Douglass, "and would have given such an impetus to the cause of freedom as would almost have enabled us to fix the very day when the good time should come." But Kossuth had instead chosen the path of expediency and had thereby forfeited his claim on the radical conscience.[41]

38. Ibid., 9 January 1852, 20 February 1852; William Lloyd Garrison, *Letter to Louis Kossuth concerning Freedom and Slavery in the U.S.*

39. *National Era*, 25 December 1851.

40. Ibid.; Cleveland *True Democrat* and *Hartford Republican*, quoted in *The Liberator*, 9 January 1852.

41. Theodore Calvin Pease, ed., *Speeches, Lectures and Letters by Wendell Phillips*, pp. 40–68; Oscar Sherwin, *Prophet of Liberty: The Life and Times of Wendell Phillips*, pp. 253–57; Irving H. Bartlett, *Wendell Phillips, Brahmin Radical*, p. 160; *The Liberator*, 2 January 1852; *Frederick Douglass's Paper*, 18 December 1851, 1 January 1852.

It was in the backwash of this revelation, perhaps, that the radical forces grasped the true purpose of the Magyar's American tour. In a letter dripping with contempt and disappointment, Edmund Quincy revealed his new understanding of Kossuth's mission. "He did not come here for trumpet processions and snobbish speeches, and bad dinners, and worse wine," he told readers of the *National Anti-Slavery Standard*:

> He came for men and for money, for loans and for bayonets, for an American legion under the Hungarian flag, for an American fleet sweeping the Baltic and thundering at the gates of St. Petersburg. The sympathy for which he asks is that uttered by the cannon's mouth and urged home at the point of a bayonet. Resolutions either by mobs or of Congress are but so much foul breath, unless they stand for these things.[42]

V.

It mattered little that the Garrisonians represented only a tiny fraction of the American people or that they were thoroughly despised, even by many citizens who themselves opposed slavery. What did matter was that the near unanimity of the pro-Kossuth coalition had been shattered. Until the Garrisonians abandoned the cause, there had been no coherent opposition to the Hungarian madness; Kossuth's critics had spoken only for themselves. But after 12 December, the radical antislavery forces provided one focus for that opposition.

Numerically, the Garrisonian defection was insignificant. But those radicals were more important than their numbers would indicate. Occasionally they interfered with Kossuth's progress with political dirty tricks, as when one of their number sent him a letter warning him not to enter Pennsylvania because his ideas about liberty smacked of abolitionism; the letter was signed W. B. Reed, the attorney general of the state. Finally realizing that the note was "a vile and stupid forgery," Kossuth lashed out angrily at those who would make him misstep on the "slippery ground" of domestic politics.[43]

42. *The National Anti-Slavery Standard*, 18 December 1851.
43. Garrison, *Letter to Louis Kossuth*, p. 82.

The radicals' abandonment of Kossuth's crusade had much deeper implications than their ability to disrupt. Symbolically, they were self-proclaimed keepers of the nation's conscience, and that was, after all, the announced target of Kossuth's appeal.

VI.

WASHINGTON: THE WHIGS

Despite the withdrawal of the radical abolitionists from his coalition of supporters, Kossuth's perfectly executed performance in New York could hardly have been more successful. Indeed, he had grown almost arrogant from that city's adulation. When one admirer asked him for an autograph, for example, he refused and remarked irritably that if he yielded just once to such a request he would have "all the people, from the President to the hard workingman" making the same demand.[1] He did not bother even to remind his listener that he could buy an authentic signature for the price of a fifty-dollar Hungary bond.

But if he could win popular adulation in New York, he had to visit Washington, D.C., to restructure his hosts' foreign policy. In late December, therefore, he departed the Empire City and moved deliberately toward the national capital. Throughout the journey he met more idolizing Americans, and at each carefully orchestrated stop he implored them to demonstrate their sympathy with gifts of money and with insistent messages to their national representatives, demanding diplomatic and military action against Russian expansion into Eastern Europe. At one such meeting, a Christmas Eve rally at Independence Hall in Philadelphia, he attracted listeners from as far as one hundred and fifty miles, despite the fact that he had been persuaded to share the platform—and the audience—with dozens of public-school children who delivered orations in honor of the visiting hero.[2]

Even after arriving in Washington, Kossuth found time to ex-

1. Quoted in *Frederick Douglass's Paper* (Rochester, New York), 1 January 1852.

2. Alexander K. McClure, *Colonel Alexander K. McClure's Recollections of Half a Century*, p. 192; P. H. Skinner, *The Welcome of Louis Kossuth to Philadelphia, by the Youth.*

cite the emotions of the American public. Socially prominent families crowded his levees, displaying finery not seen even at presidential receptions.[3] Delegations of local officeholders called to pay their respects. American Indians told him of their sympathy for his program;[4] the city's Jewish community gave him a donation of money, and a painting of Moses with his right hand extended over the head of Washington and his left over Kossuth's;[5] and weeping ladies, emotionally devastated by Kossuth's eloquent description of Hungary's fate, pressed rings into his hand, begging him to sell their gold to renew his crusade against Austrian and Russian tyranny.[6]

But Washington was, above all, a city of politicians. Neither hysterical women nor Indian chiefs could accomplish his purposes there, for what mattered was the attitude of the national government. To win his objectives, Kossuth would first have to persuade the president and Congress to adopt his principle of "Intervention for Non-Intervention."

I.

Millard Fillmore, unlike his predecessor, was totally disinterested in Young America and the crusading spirit it had spawned. His was a political career built on moderation and quiet efficiency. In the endless internecine quarrels of the New York Whig establishment, his most enduring rivalry continued to be with the flamboyant and opportunistic partnership of Thurlow Weed, William H. Seward, and Horace Greeley. And the qualities he claimed to find so distasteful in these men were also the hallmarks of Young America: emotional and melodramatic rhetoric that promised more than its spokesmen could deliver and that excited passions so severely that rational decisionmaking became impossible.[7]

3. Francis P. Blair to Martin Van Buren, 1, 2 January 1852, Van Buren papers, Library of Congress.

4. *The Liberator*, 16 January 1852.

5. *The New York Times*, 1 January 1852.

6. Moncure Daniel Conway, *Autobiography, Memories and Experiences*, I:111.

7. Robert J. Rayback, *Millard Fillmore: Biography of a President*, pp. 210–13, 255–60.

Unlike his predecessor to the
presidency, Millard Fillmore was
totally disinterested in
Young America and its crusading spirit.

More recently Fillmore had encountered these same demagogic
weapons in the campaign to win approval for the Compromise of 1850.
In debates about that set of bills, Southern fire-eaters and self-righteous
Northern Whigs had very nearly destroyed the delicate compromise—
and with it the party and, perhaps, the Union—by demanding more than
they could realistically achieve. The president had no use for such tactics,
for they made a mockery of the political process as he understood it. He
preferred to operate within the realm of the attainable: to balance interests, moderate evils, and inch his party and the nation toward the
realization of practicable as well as desirable goals.[8]

The pattern of Fillmore's statesmanship is revealed precisely in a
single sentence he wrote to Daniel Webster in late 1850, in which he
explained his willingness to enforce the new fugitive slave law. "God
knows that I detest slavery," he told his secretary of state with evident
conviction, "but it is an existing evil, for which we are not responsible,
and we must endure it, and give it such protection as is guaranteed by
the constitution, till we can get rid of it without destroying the last hope

8. Ibid.

85

of free government in the world."[9] It was this fundamental realism—this ability to distinguish between idealistic gestures and genuine progress—that shaped the president's political philosophy.

In matters of foreign policy Fillmore observed the same criterion for action. He had already announced his attitude toward evangelical Americanism when he condemned Narciso López's filibustering expedition against Cuba. "Our true mission is not to propagate our opinions, or impose upon other countries our form of government, by artifice or force," he told the American people; rather, the nation's destiny was "to teach by example, and show by our success, moderation and justice, the blessings of self-government and the advantages of free institutions."[10]

And, he might have added, to pursue her own legitimate interests. For while the nation thundered ovations to Kossuth, gave him money, and demanded that the federal government exert moral or physical power to return him to the governorship of Hungary, Fillmore was devoting his attention to furthering the interests of the United States' commercial fleet in the markets of Asia. He sought shorter routes to the Pacific, first by continuing the nation's pursuit of an interocean canal in Central America and then by cooperating with Stephen Douglas, the Illinois Democrat, in plans for a transcontinental railroad. He asserted new interest in the Hawaiian Islands, for they offered an accessible coaling station for American steamers en route to the Orient. And in the most celebrated act of his presidency, he dispatched Commodore Matthew C. Perry to penetrate the veil of secrecy and isolation that for two centuries had surrounded the Japanese Empire and that had confined its contact with the outside world to one small port visited only by a few favored Dutch captains.[11]

It was not surprising, therefore, that Fillmore, preoccupied with worthwhile and attainable goals in the Far East, could express little in-

9. Fillmore to Webster, 23 October 1850, Daniel Webster, *The Letters of Daniel Webster*, p. 437.

10. James D. Richardson, *Messages and Papers of the Presidents*, 5:116–17.

11. Rayback, *Millard Fillmore*, chapter 16; Richard W. Johannsen, *Stephen A. Douglas*, p. 315.

terest in the pronouncements of Kossuth and his allies. Toward all European rebels he had summed up his policy in his first annual message, on 2 December 1850.

> Among the acknowledged rights of nations is that which each professes of establishing that form of government which it may deem most conducive to the happiness and prosperity of its citizens. . . . The People of the United States claim this right for themselves, and readily concede it to others. Hence it becomes an imperative duty not to interfere in the government or internal policy of other nations and although we may sympathize with the unfortunate or the oppressed everywhere in their fight for freedom, our principles forbid us from taking any part in such foreign contests.[12]

Even as he agreed to invite Kossuth to the United States, and as he watched the nation go mad in support of the Hungarian cause, he refused to say more. But his fundamental policy had not changed. Daniel Webster recorded the administration's position the morning Kossuth arrived in the capital. "I shall treat him with all personal and individual respect, but if he should speak to me of the policy of 'intervention,' I shall 'have ears more deaf than adders.'"[13]

Kossuth might have believed that the nation's response would influence the administration's course. Or, perhaps, he concluded simply that whatever his chances for success he must appeal to the president for aid. Immediately upon his arrival in Washington he met with Webster,[14] and circumstantial evidence indicates that it was Kossuth who introduced the possibility of a personal interview with the president. Fillmore already had advised Congress that it would be responsible for adopting plans for the Magyar's reception to the capital, and after speaking with Kossuth, Webster returned to the White House to learn the president's attitude toward a private meeting.[15]

12. Richardson, *Messages and Papers of the Presidents*, 5:78.
13. Webster to Blatchford, 30 December 1851, Daniel Webster, *Writings and Speeches of Daniel Webster*, 18:501–2.
14. *Daily Union*, 31 December 1851.
15. Richardson, *Messages and Papers of the Presidents*, 5:120; Webster to Fillmore, 30 December 1851, Webster, *Writings and Speeches of Webster*, 18:501.

"If he desires simply an introduction, I will see him," Fillmore later recalled telling his Secretary of State, "but if he wants to make a speech to me, I must most respectfully decline to see him."

"He has promised me not to make a speech," replied Webster.

"Very well, then, I will see him," Fillmore said. At the secretary's suggestion, the interview was scheduled for the following day, New Year's Eve.[16]

Kossuth promptly forgot his pledge. In that conference he delivered a long and florid address to an audience composed only of the president, his cabinet, and Senators Seward and Shields, his Senate-appointed escorts; Lewis Cass, the other official guide, did not attend. Kossuth's unmistakable theme was that the United States already had committed itself to the defense of Hungary by obtaining his freedom, bringing him to the capital, and treating him as a head of state. In what must have been an act of desperation, he tried even to identify the president as an avowed interventionist and misquoted him as proclaiming to the world that "this country cannot remain indifferent when the strong arm of a foreign power is invoked to stifle public sentiment and repress the spirit of freedom in any country."

Fillmore repudiated his guest's claims with frigid reserve. He had announced his attitude toward Europe's difficulties "fully and freely" in his messages to Congress, he replied, and those sentiments were the same "whether speaking to Congress here or to the nation of Europe." If Kossuth could win his revolution without American aid, the president would celebrate a glorious step toward the recognition of human rights in the Old World; "but should that never happen, I can only repeat my welcome to you and your companions here, and pray that God's blessing may rest upon you wherever your lot may be cast."[17] The president then

16. Quoted in an interview with Fillmore, *The New York Herald*, 16 September 1873, reprinted, *Publications of the Buffalo Historical Society: Millard Fillmore Papers*, 2, ed. Frank H. Severance, p. 138.

17. Both statements were reprinted widely in the press, sometimes with partisan additions or deletions; see, for example, *Republic*, 1 January 1852; *The New York Times*, 3 January 1852; "Presidential Courtesies," *The Democratic Review* 30 (January 1852):40–41.

invited Kossuth to dine with him on 6 January, and the Magyar promptly accepted.[18] But these were mere gestures. "Intervention for Non-Intervention" was dead—at least until Millard Fillmore left the White House.

II.

Daniel Webster was less dispassionate than his chief. As much as anyone in the nation, he had helped generate the Hungarian fever, first in 1849 by citing Kossuth's revolution as an object for serious American concern, and subsequently with his celebrated Hülsemann letter. He had not changed his position: he still wished to see republican institutions prevail in Europe, and he still seemed eager to identify himself and the nation with the liberal movements there. However, even as an acknowledged leader among those who championed an evangelical foreign policy, he had never hinted that the United States should inject anything more than "moral force" into the European diplomatic equation.

But Kossuth's arrival in the United States had transformed the nature of Young America. It was no longer a mere symbol of sympathy for the rights of man; nor could one now subscribe with the cheap dues of passionate but essentially meaningless oratory. "The spirit of liberty has to go forth, not only spiritually, but materially, from your glorious country," Kossuth had told his hosts in New York. "I hope the people of the United States will remember, that in the hour of *their* nation's struggle, it received from Europe *more* than kind wishes. It received material aid from others in times past, and it will, doubtless, now impart its mighty agency to achieve the liberty of other lands."[19] He wanted immediate diplomatic and military assistance, and many Americans were echoing his demands. Moreover, they were justifying their pro-

18. Francis Pulszky and Theresa Pulszky, *White, Red, Black: Sketches of American Society in the United States During the Visit of Their Guests*, pp. 178–83; Webster to Fillmore, 30 December 1851, Webster, *Writings and Speeches of Webster*, 18:501.

19. Louis Kossuth, *Selected Speeches of Kossuth. Condensed and Abridged, with Kossuth's Express Sanction*, p. 20.

gram by quoting the same principles of international morality that Webster himself had employed more than once in official and private correspondence.

The secretary of state's dilemma was therefore complete: he had divorced his rhetoric from his commitments as the guardian of American interests abroad. And in the process he had helped to create a crusade that he recognized now seemed certain to devour his political future.[20] To resolve his political and philosophical dilemma, Webster had but two alternatives: he could abandon Kossuth and the principles of intervention, or he could abandon Fillmore, the administration, and the nation's conservative diplomatic tradition. At the congressional banquet for Kossuth on 7 January, he did neither.

Congress's dinner at the National Hotel was an explosive affair. The two hundred and fifty invited guests repeatedly interrupted the series of speakers with applause and shouts of approval; William Seward became a nuisance to his partners at table, cheering boisterously "with hands, feet and voice." But his behavior was not untypical. "The 'Hungarian Whirlwind' certainly carried away everything," recorded the Reverend C. M. Butler, chaplain of the Senate, "and mingled all parties into one confused mass of admirers, prostrate at M. Kossuth's feet."[21] Only a few hours earlier, the House of Representatives had welcomed Kossuth in open session—an honor previously accorded only Lafayette.[22]

At that banquet, Daniel Webster delivered one of the principal addresses, and in it he betrayed the contradictions inherent in his previous statements. Incapable of resolving the immense intellectual gulf between his genuine sympathy for the Hungarians and his rational appreciation for the interests of the United States, the secretary of state retreated to the political and philosophical haven of wishful thinking. He predicted that Austria would eventually recognize that an indepen-

20. Webster to Abbott Lawrence, 29 December 1851, in *Letters of Webster*, p. 508.
21. Quoted in Eugene Pivany, *Webster and Kossuth: A Discourse on the Relations of Daniel Webster and Louis Kossuth*, p. 20.
22. *Congressional Globe*, 32d Cong., 1st sess., p. 225.

dent Hungary would be a blessing to the Hapsburgs, because "the cost of keeping Hungary quiet is not repaid by any benefit derived from Hungarian levies or tributes"; he reminded his audience of the inevitability of progress; he declared that public opinion would soon "animate all minds" and guarantee Kossuth's success. And on the basis of these abstractions he offered the toast, "Hungarian independence, Hungarian control of her own destinies; and Hungary as a distinct nationality among the nations of Europe."[23]

But if it was irrelevant to Kossuth's demands, Webster's speech was nevertheless politically effective. Most observers failed to recognize the shaky, nervous ambivalence of the address. They did not notice Webster's apparent determination to ride out the crusade with cheerful words and little action. On the contrary, they seemed to focus on the closing sentences and ignore all that had gone before. Even the *New York Herald* interpreted the address as an endorsement of the Magyar's crusade, and Greeley's *Tribune* announced that it "exonerated" the secretary of state from responsibility for the administration's "shabby position" toward Kossuth.[24]

Less auspiciously, Hülsemann, the Austrian chargé d'affaires, also emphasized the end of the address. Enraged by such pronouncements from the highest-ranking diplomat in the administration, Hülsemann dispatched a virtual ultimatum directly to the president and then repeated its terms in a personal interview: if Webster continued at the Department of State, Hülsemann would leave his post, thereby suspending official diplomatic relations between the two nations.[25] Fillmore's assurances that Webster had not spoken for the administration did not satisfy the Austrian diplomat; nor did Webster's bizarre explanation,

23. Webster, *Writings and Speeches of Webster*, 13:452ff; Kossuth, *Select Speeches*, pp. 147–51.

24. *New York Herald*, 15 January 1852; *The New York Tribune*, quoted in James S. Pike, *First Blows of the Civil War: The Ten Years of Preliminary Conflict in the United States. From 1850 to 1860. A Contemporaneous Exposition . . .*, p. 100.

25. Hülsemann to Fillmore, 8 January 1852, in Jánossy Dénes, ed., *A Kossuth-Emigráció Angliában és Amerikában, 1851–1852*, 1:324–26.

that Hülsemann had no grounds for complaining since Webster "went to the Dinner in no official capacity, but simply as an individual."[26] Hülsemann first refused to attend White House social functions and then angrily departed the capital to await further instructions from his government. He would not return on a permanent basis for more than a year.[27]

III.

Kossuth could find little comfort in the icy disavowals of Millard Fillmore, only slightly more in the meaningless praise of Daniel Webster. Of those Whig statesmen who could boast national reputations, only Henry Clay remained on the Hungarian's itinerary.

In prestige, Clay surpassed every other living American. Through four decades of the nation's phenomenal growth and maturation, his name had been associated intimately with every party battle and every crisis of the Union. Three times—in 1820, 1833, and 1850—he had championed compromise adjustments to the developing sectional confrontation. If his popular title, "The Great Compromiser," implied little intellectual profundity, it did reveal his image as the country's foremost intersectional politician. Even more than Daniel Webster's strident nationalism, Clay's conciliatory policies of expediency and moderation embodied America's only hope for a future free from dissension and disunion.

Furthermore, Clay was now near death, frail and feeble, and racked by a dry, persistent cough that his doctors could not cure. It had become impossible for him to attend to his duties in the Senate and increasingly

26. Fillmore to Hülsemann, n.d., ibid., 1:339–40; Webster to Charles J. McCurdy, American chargé d'affaires in Vienna, 15 January 1852, in *Writings and Speeches of Webster*, 16:588.

27. Hülsemann to Fillmore, 22 January 1852, in Jánossy, *Kossuth-Emigráció*, 1:400–401; Webster to McCurdy, 15 January 1852, in *Writings and Speeches of Webster*, 16:588; Curti, *Austria and the United States*, pp. 189–91. See also, in this regard, Crampton to Granville, 25 January 1852, in Jánossy, *Kossuth-Emigráció*, 1:416–18.

clear that he would not recover. On 17 December 1851, he had notified the Kentucky general assembly in Frankfort that his four decades of public service had come to an end. Still he lingered on in Washington, determined to spend his remaining months there. It was these last circumstances that had completed the transformation of "Harry of the West," political manipulator, into Henry Clay, elder statesman. "His voice comes to us clothed with all the sanctity the grave can give, with the added knowledge of existing things, which the grave must take away," declared one congressman, himself a onetime political foe of the aged Kentuckian.[28]

If Kossuth could tap the enormous prestige of Henry Clay, his campaign for intervention would gain new influence, for such a coup might rally those Whigs outside the administration who earnestly sympathized with the Hungarian cause. Moreover, in recent years Clay's pronouncements on the nature of American foreign policy had been identical to those of important Southern conservatives, including John C. Calhoun, the symbol of Southern nationalism. Kossuth apparently believed that if Clay enrolled in the Young America crusade, he might bring with him many of those who previously had rejected the evangelical Americanism of the interventionist forces. Looking toward this prospect, Kossuth had spoken of Clay with reverence and respect since his arrival in the United States.[29]

The Magyar called on Clay at his rooms in the National Hotel on 9 January. In the presence of Senators Cass of Michigan and Jones of Tennessee and Congressman Presley Ewing of Kentucky, the two men conferred at some length about the wisdom of American involvement in the Old World's internal troubles. Clay was adamantly opposed to any overt act. After expressing sincere concern for Hungary's future, the Kentuckian added feebly, "for the sake of my country, you must allow me to protest against the policy you propose to her." Isolated from the dangers of European conflicts, the United States had prospered.

28. *Congressional Globe*, 32d Cong., 1st sess., *Appendix*, p. 181; Allan Nevins, *Ordeal of the Union*, 2:31.
29. Kossuth, *Select Speeches*, pp. 57, 144.

But if we should involve ourselves in the tangled web of European politics, in a war in which we could effect nothing, and in that struggle Hungary should go down, and we should go down with her, where then would be the last hope of the friends of freedom throughout the world? Far better is it for ourselves, for Hungary, and for the cause of liberty, that . . . we should keep our lamp burning brightly on this Western shore as a light to all nations, than to hazard its utter extinction, amid the ruins of fallen or falling republics in Europe.

Kossuth tried to counter Clay's analysis. Russia's power had been greatly exaggerated, he claimed. Furthermore, if war did erupt, the United States would not fight alone, for he predicted accurately that Turkey and Russia would soon battle for control of the Crimea and the Dardenelles. Kossuth contended that the Turkish army would defeat the Russians if it were supplemented by American naval protection.

Clay refused to agree. "A dying man, I oppose your doctrine of intervention," he repeated, and then, clutching Kossuth's hand in his own he concluded emotionally, "God bless you and your family! God bless your country! May she yet be free!"[30]

Later, Clay talked with Francis Blair, his former enemy from the days of Andrew Jackson's presidency, and explained the tragic implications of American intervention. Then he turned to Blair's own role in the Hungarian movement. "What shall I say to you Mr. Blair who are carrying the country into a war to fight for a country on the borders of Asia?" he asked.[31] After rescuing the republic three times from internal collapse, Clay seemed convinced that he would live to see it commit suicide in a quixotic war nearly five thousand miles away.

30. Presley Ewing's notes to the meeting were reprinted widely in the newspapers; see, for example, *The Liberator*, 13 February 1852; *Southern Advocate*, 18 February 1852; Macon *Georgia Telegraph*, 24 February 1852. See also Glyndon G. Van Deusen, *The Life of Henry Clay*, pp. 421–22.

31. Francis Blair to Martin Van Buren, 11 January 1852, in Martin Van Buren papers, Library of Congress.

VII.

WASHINGTON:
THE SOUTH SAYS NO

Nor was the national Whig leadership the only important group to condemn Kossuth's crusade during these weeks. Equally damaging to the Magyar's hopes was the emerging consensus among many of the Southern statesmen in Washington that Young America represented a threat to their own institutions and to their understanding of America's role in world politics. During December and January, the lukewarm support of many Southerners of both parties evolved into implacable hostility. And strong bipartisan opposition from throughout the South would make it difficult to win a commitment to Young America from either major party in the coming presidential election.

I.

Protests from some regional historians notwithstanding, there were profound differences between the slaveholding and the nonslaveholding states.[1] Most of the significant distinctions evolved from the practice of slaveholding itself: black slavery made the South's a precapitalist environment. To be sure, there were banks in Southern communities, and cotton played an important role in world commerce. But the South's unique labor system lacked the defining characteristic of capitalism: it forbade a free exchange of goods and services.[2] Openly contemptuous of

1. The latest and perhaps best attempt to minimize the differences is Grady McWhiney, *Southerners and Other Americans*, chapter 1.
2. The presence or absence of capitalism in the slave system has occupied historians in a continuing and somewhat heated debate. Those who argue that it was capitalistic include Stanley Elkins, *Slavery: A Problem in American Institutional and Intellectual Life*, chapter 2, and, more recently, Robert W. Fogel and

the principle of free labor, the South's planter aristocracy relied instead on a semi-feudal, semi-barbaric and wholly anachronistic form of chattel labor. And as Hinton Rowan Helper would soon make clear in his explosive book, *The Impending Crisis of the South*, that section was suffering all the consequences—material and intellectual—of its backwardness.[3]

Materially, Southerners could rival neither the swelling industrialization of the Northeast nor the agricultural advances that Western farmers were undertaking with a passion. Instead they continued to forestall economic progress by uniting capital and labor in the person of the slave. That process had cost them much. In the six decades before 1850 the South's contribution to the national economy had diminished steadily; by 1850 the North's agricultural production alone represented more wealth than the South's total economic output. And still the planter aristocracy clung to ownership of land and labor—those commodities a precapitalist society holds in greatest esteem. Immigration sagged for want of opportunity; cities grew, but only slowly; and economic diversity—the dream of Southern nationalists like William Gregg and J. D. B. De Bow—remained an empty dream, the victim of both an agrarian mentality and an absence of liquid capital.

Intellectually, too, the South was stagnant, or nearly so. If the North was juggling too many ideas for a mature society, the South was producing far too few. Its thinkers had for two decades narrowed the scope of intellectual inquiry to two subjects: defending slavery and preserving their control of the national government. Aside from these essentially

---

Stanley L. Engerman, *Time on the Cross: The Economics of American Negro Slavery*, passim. Those who argue otherwise include Eugene Genovese, whose views are explained most fully in *The Political Economy of Slavery*, and Eric Foner, *Free Soil, Free Labor, Free Men: The Ideology of the Republican Party Before the Civil War*. This debate, while illuminating, seems to lack focus on the meaning of capitalism; by definition, slavery and capitalism are opposites. The contributions of Genovese and Foner lie in their analysis of the significance of that fact, not in their establishing its existence.

3. Hinton Rowan Helper, *The Impending Crisis of the South: How to Meet It.*

practical exercises, the slaveholding states encouraged little creativity. No Emerson, Hawthorne, or Melville emerged from that section. Indeed, the most exhaustive chronicler of American letters found it necessary to treat such minor figures as John Pendleton Kennedy, William Alexander Caruthers, and William Crafts to fill out his treatment of literature in the South.[4] And literacy statistics were a national disgrace: except for Indiana and Illinois, every Northern state could boast rates higher than any in the South, and this despite two important facts: first, census figures considered only the free populations; and second, few of the nation's often illiterate immigrants ever ventured south of the Mason-Dixon line. From almost any point of view save politics, the South represented what may have been the only truly retrogressive society in modern Western history.

The tragedy of all this—and the one fact that divided the two sections irrevocably—was that the articulate members of Southern society did not seem to care. While Northerners were making a fetish of anything new or innovative, many Southern spokesmen seemed proud, almost chauvinistic, about their region's failure to complement the age. "We are an agricultural people; we are a primitive but a civilised people," Sen. Louis T. Wigfall would later declare. "We have no cities—we don't want them. We have no literature—we don't need any yet. . . . We want no manufactures; we desire no trading, no mechanical or manufacturing classes."[5] And the editor of the Huntsville, Alabama, *Southern Advocate* voiced identical convictions when he linked "socialism and progress" as twin threats to the Southern way of life.[6]

Such statements contained no hint of sour grapes, for these men and

4. Vernon Louis Parrington, *Main Currents in American Thought: An Interpretation of American Literature from the Beginnings to 1920*, 2:41–56, 112–14. It was Henry Steele Commager (*The Search for a Usable Past*, p. 26) who observed, "The most familiar of southern symbols came from the North: Harriet Beecher Stowe of New England gave us Uncle Tom and Little Eva and Topsy and Eliza, and it was Stephen Foster of Pittsburg who sentimentalized the Old South, while even 'Dixie' had northern origins."

5. Quoted in Alvy L. King, *Louis T. Wigfall: Southern Fire-eater*, p. 126.

6. Huntsville, Alabama, *Southern Advocate*, 11 February 1852.

others were convinced that the trappings of the modern world were at best a mixed blessing. Independently of Karl Marx, a number of them had concluded that capitalism and its concomitant free labor were fundamentally unstable institutions. Northern society, they believed, would eventually collapse under the weight of radical social experiments.[7] Indeed, many were convinced that the process had already begun with the profusion of "isms" that lately had swept across the North. Abolitionism was the most damnable of these reforms, of course, but it was only symptomatic of many others. Linked to it, according to the fire-eating propagandist George Fitzhugh, were "Free Love and Free Lands, Free Churches, Free Women and Free Negroes . . . No-Marriage, No-Religion, No-Private Property, No-Law and No-Government"—all ideologies aimed to destroy polite society.[8] In his more extreme moments, Fitzhugh could decry the first amendment to the Constitution as anarchistic.[9] Moncure Daniel Conway, a Virginian who had fled to the North early in life to escape the crushing conformity of his native state, recalled that among his former countrymen even public education had been cited as a "dangerous Northern 'ism,'" and other Southerners spoke earnestly of "Bloomerism," "mobism," and even "Jenny Lindism" as ideologies subversive to the fabric of civilization.[10] From this perspective, it is no surprise that at least one Southern editor referred to Yankees as "Round Heads," recalling the Levellers of the English civil war.[11]

7. For a survey of this interpretation see Richard Hofstadter, "John C. Calhoun, Marx of the Master Class," in *The American Political Tradition and the Men Who Made It*; Harvey Wish, *George Fitzhugh: Propagandist of the Old South*, passim. A lesser known exposition of these views appeared in the Natchez *Mississippi Free Trader* during the early months of 1851; most particularly see ibid., 4 June 1851: "In the South Capital and Labor are not antagonistic. Capital is Labor."

8. George Fitzhugh, *Cannibals All! or Slaves Without Masters*, ed., C. Vann Woodward, p. 215.

9. Merrill D. Peterson, *The Jefferson Image in the American Mind*, p. 169; Wish, *Fitzhugh*, pp. 188–89.

10. Moncure Daniel Conway, *Autobiography, Memories and Experiences*, 2:88; Wish, *Fitzhugh*, p. 56; Judge William Russell Smith, quoted in William Garrett, *Reminiscences of Public Men in Alabama, for Thirty Years*, p. 561.

11. Natchez *Mississippi Free Trader*, 29 January 1851.

It would be impossible to prove that these statements reflected a universal attitude in the South, because they quite obviously did not. But every society is known by the ideas it produces. Southerners elected John C. Calhoun and Louis Wigfall to the Senate; they subscribed to the *Southern Advocate*; they bought George Fitzhugh's books and burned Hinton Helper's. Most Southerners, in short, distrusted change and suspected that progress was a subversive, degenerative force. They lacked sympathy for, and even understanding of, the utopian vision of Young America. These convictions in large measure shaped the Southern attitude toward foreign policy.

II.

As Frederick Merk has pointed out, Southerners had never subscribed wholeheartedly to the evangelical Americanism of the 1840s.[12] They were the products, as well as the defenders, of a rigidly regimented social order, an order that could exist only because one segment of the population had monopolized the effective instruments of power—the political, military, and educational institutions—and had mobilized those tools to hold another segment of the population as slaves. Theirs was, by any definition, a despotic society. And even when, after 1830, Southern theoreticians and apologists sought to define their culture as ideal, they could do so only by defending despotism as an abstract good and by emphasizing that fact by purging their section of critics who originated from either caste.[13]

12. Frederick Merk, *Manifest Destiny and Mission in American History: A Reinterpretation*, p. 39 and passim. Expansionism, without the philosophical trappings of Young America, was of course implicit in much Southern thought; see, on this point, C. Stanley Urban, "The Ideology of Southern Imperialism: New Orleans and the Caribbean, 1845–1860," *Louisiana Historical Quarterly* 39 (January 1956), 48–73; Genovese, *Political Economy of Slavery*, pp. 243–49; and Robert E. May, *The Southern Dream of a Caribbean Empire, 1854–1861*. Despite the occasional rhetoric about uplifting and regenerating the peoples of the Caribbean, the South's impulse toward expansion into Latin America lacked the altruism that characterized Young America as defined in Chapter 2.

13. For discussions of various aspects of this same theme, see Clement Eaton,

There was no room in such a scheme for an altruistic foreign policy. While Young Americans were projecting their own optimism, moral fervor, and democratic ideology into their conception of world affairs, the most profound thinkers in the slave states were clinging to the doctrine of realpolitik. Not only was it the traditional American approach to foreign policy, it was also, and perhaps more importantly, the perfect diplomatic equivalent of the domestic social and political order of the South: human action was regulated in both systems by the realities of power. To men bred to the ways of slavery and intellectual tyranny, it was the only rational approach to foreign policy. With few exceptions, those Southerners who spoke about foreign policy during the 1840s and 50s—Joseph Underwood, Jeremiah Clemens, James C. Jones, and others—subscribed to realpolitik. Nor was it coincidence that John C. Calhoun was, until his death in 1850, the nation's most brilliant exponent of "realism" both at home and abroad.[14] Not all Southerners resisted Young America's doctrine, of course; some were among Kossuth's most ardent sympathizers. But throughout December and January, the most articulate spokesmen for that section responded to the Hungarian fever with incomprehension, ridicule, and outright rejection.

First, few Southerners could fathom why Young Americans had chosen to "lick the very dust" from the steps of a man who had achieved nothing of lasting significance—a man who "at most is but the chief of a purely national party, in an extinct revolution, which had no government, in the days of its highest success, that was recognized by any nation in the world."[15] Even more distasteful was the fiction that Kossuth was another Washington. "The man who was the first to shrink at the approach of the tempest he had raised, who abandoned his country, when he still had an army of one hundred and thirty-five thousand men

---

Freedom of Thought in the Old South; Wish, *Fitzhugh*; Peterson, *Jefferson Image*, pp. 165–71.

14. For the attitudes of Underwood, Clemens, and Jones, see pages following, and chapter 10; for the most intelligent treatment of Calhoun as a "realist," see Parrington, *Main Currents*, 2:69–82.

15. Macon *Georgia Telegraph*, 16 December 1851.

at his command . . . is not made of such stuff as Washington," declared Senator Clemens, the Alabama Democrat.[16] Kossuth might deserve pity, most men agreed; but neither his character nor his personal achievements qualified him for anything more.[17] And if one assumed that his cause was sufficiently just and his personal integrity unimpeachable for him to deserve help, there was still no guarantee that the United States could make a difference in his ultimate fate. Many Southerners were convinced, as was Presley Ewing of Kentucky, that it would be a "hopeless task" to "regenerate the old, worn-out, effete institutions of Europe."[18]

Ultimately, however, Southerners were most disturbed by Young America's altruism and by its easy assumption that moral force alone could liberate the Old World. In words tinged with ridicule, the *Macon Telegraph* informed Lewis Cass that his constant references to the "family of nations" might be poetic, but they did not reflect reality: "There is no analogy between the duties which appertain to the members of a family towards each other and those which attach to nations."[19] Unlike people, governments did not respond to the ethical judgments of other governments or to the dictates of any public opinion outside their own borders. Thus, the paper protests of any American government would exercise no influence over the despots of Eastern Europe. "As a mere declaration of opinion it would be idle," advised the *New Orleans Picayune*. "Its only efficacy for restraint would be in the supposed power to enforce it, and the implied engagement to exercise the power when needed."[20]

Senators agreed. "How long is it, after you begin your aid and assistance by words, before you must carry it out in deeds?" asked Underwood, the Kentucky Whig. And Clemens continued, that "an

16. *Congressional Globe*, 32d Cong., 1st sess., *Appendix*, p. 179.

17. See also, in this regard, *Brownlow's Knoxville Whig, and Independent Journal* (Knoxville, Tennessee), 20 December 1851; *Southern Advocate*, 3 December 1851.

18. *Congressional Globe*, 32d Cong., 1st sess., *Appendix*, p. 532.

19. Macon *Georgia Telegraph*, 6 January 1852.

20. This was a theme to which the *Picayune* returned often; see the series of reports on Kossuth in that paper throughout December 1851 and January 1852.

interference begun by threats must be ended by cannonballs and bayonets. It is childish to talk of trammeling the action of Russia by threats uttered on this side of the Atlantic. She would laugh your threats to scorn." "To indulge in the use of threats towards Russia is either to cover ourselves with ridicule or involve the country in war."[21]

To most Southerners all this seemed self-evident: that Kossuth was a coward and a failure; that Young America was yet another manifestation of profound instability in Northern society; and that the only way Americans could influence the behavior of Russia or any potential adversary was through the use or threat of force.

III.

The enormous intellectual gulf between this interpretation of foreign policy and the idealistic approach of the Northern Young Americans further aggravated the distrust between spokesmen for the two sections. Many Northerners suspected that their Southern critics refused to cheer Kossuth only because he was a living symbol of their own sins. "The whole opposition [to Kossuth] comes from the South," reported Horace Mann, the educator and antislavery Whig from Massachusetts. "The avowed opposition is based on the question of 'intervention;' but the real motive is slavery. While they demand that one fugitive shall be fettered and sent home, they cannot bear to see another *feted* and honored. You see the cloven foot."[22] Such a judgment was, of course, anchored to the false premise that Southerners themselves believed that they were sinners.

And many Southerners, incapable of recognizing the sincerity of the Young Americans, claimed to identify a conspiracy against their own section in the agitation for intervention in Europe on the basis that because Young America seemed self-evidently irrational, it must be a new, insidious tactic in the abolitionist crusade. Speaking of interven-

21. *Congressional Globe*, 32d Cong., 1st sess., pp. 25, 53.
22. Horace Mann to Reverend S. J. May, 3 January 1852, quoted in Mary Peabody Mann, *Life of Horace Mann*, p. 356.

tionism, the *Southern Advocate* declared, "This most fatal doctrine for the South should not find a single advocate on her soil. It is a doctrine fraught with ruin and devastation to all her interests. It strikes at the very citadel of her safety—it undermines the very foundations of her security. It is the Wooden Horse."[23]

Other newspapers voiced identical concerns. "We think we can comprehend the motive which induces [the antislavery press] to adopt the cause which M. Kossuth advocates," editorialized the *Baltimore Clipper* in late December:

> They look somewhat further than to its effects on Hungary. They want to get this Government to commit itself to a principle which can hereafter be applied to internal concerns. Their sympathies are not for Hungary, but for the colored race in the United States; and we warn the people of the South against uniting in a policy supported by the Abolition press and designed to affect the institution of slavery in this country.[24]

The *New Orleans Bulletin*, after reminding its readers that Kossuth had won support from William Seward, John Parker Hale, Joshua Giddings, "and the whole abolition party generally," stated the case even more bluntly:

> If we sanction interference, we will be the first who will be interfered with; if we become a consenting party to the project of overthrowing European forms of government, our own institutions will be the first crushed beneath the juggernautic wheels of unlicensed, unconfined radicalism and fierce, relentless and bigoted fanaticism. . . . Of all the people upon the earth's surface, the Southern people are the last to think of, much less attempt to enforce, doctrines of this character.[25]

For those who could not grasp the meaning of these arguments, the Natchez *Mississippi Free Trader* supplied a less abstract hint, a ficticious fugitive slave notice: "One Million Dollars Reward—Ran Away from the subscriber, on the 18th of August, 1849, a likely Magyar fellow,

23. *Southern Advocate*, 25 February 1852.
24. Quoted in *National Era*, 1 January 1852, and in *Frederick Douglass's Paper*, 8 January 1852.
25. Quoted in *Southern Advocate*, 25 February 1852.

named Louis Kossuth.... He pretends to be free, but says he was robbed of his freedom.—Francis Joseph, Emperor of Austria."[26]

Among those prominent Southerners who earlier had yielded to the appeal of Young America, it was this identification of Kossuth with the antislavery crusade that persuaded them to withdraw their already-unenthusiastic support for his movement. Two of the Magyar's warmest sympathizers—Joshua Giddings of Ohio's Western Reserve and Thomas A. Hendricks, the Indiana Democrat—recognized this fact. Indeed, each man set the precise date of that identification at 10 December 1851, when Charles Sumner delivered his maiden address in the Senate.[27] In that address Sumner praised Kossuth, but he said little that other men had not said before.[28] Apparently, Sumner's reputation as the newest addition to the chamber's antislavery vanguard was enough to alienate those Southerners who were not already committed totally to one side or the other.

And as the principles of the hard-line realists came to represent the opinions of larger numbers of Southern politicians, the Washington *Daily Union*—the national organ of the Democratic party—drifted away from its earlier endorsement of Kossuth and assumed a more critical posture that would satisfy the demands of the party's Southern wing. In October and November 1851, that paper had welcomed Tammany Hall's call for intervention in Europe as a new, effective, and legitimate issue in the coming presidential election. But by 9 January 1852, that same paper was declaring that "the whole wisdom and patriotism of our land would rightfully rise up and protest" against any interventionist policy adopted by the federal government.[29]

26. *Mississippi Free Trader*, 25 February 1852, quoting an item from the *London Morning Advertiser*.

27. John W. Holcombe and Hobert M. Skinner, *Life and Public Services of Thomas A. Hendricks, with Selected Speeches and Writings*, pp. 139–40; Joshua Giddings, *History of the Rebellion: Its Authors and Causes*, p. 323.

28. *Congressional Globe*, 32d Cong., 1st sess., pp. 50–51; *Charles Sumner: His Complete Works*, 3:171–79.

29. Washington *Daily Union*, 26, 29 October 1851, 9 January 1852; Siert Riepma, "Young America," pp. 115–16.

Not all Southerners abandoned Kossuth, but those who remained were hardly representative of their section: Pierre Soulé, the transplanted Frenchman who had fled his homeland for reasons similar to Kossuth's and who since had come to dominate Louisiana politics; George Nicholas Sanders, who had fled his native Kentucky for the business and political opportunities of the North; and Henry Foote, the wildly eccentric Mississippian who had become one of Kossuth's most ardent supporters in the Senate. For these men, Young America's principles were more than once at least a semantic embarrassment. When Foote spoke in favor of the Magyar's claims on the American conscience, for example, he had pleaded for support on purely ideological grounds and had invoked the name of liberty to justify Kossuth's cause. "Those who are not with us are against us," he had declared. And then, with ill-chosen words, "Those who are not for freedom are for slavery." To this the impetuous Hale had responded, "Exactly."[30]

IV.

Kossuth recognized that Southerners represented that sectional interest least susceptible to his crusade. In fact, he had consciously sacrificed his early abolitionist support, presumably to pacify suspicious advocates of slavery. And while moving toward the capital in the last days of 1851 he had made even stronger gestures. He had reiterated his disinterest in the antislavery movement and had even endorsed the traditional Southern line of defense, states' rights. He was himself a states' rights man, he quipped in Philadelphia, "even in regard to Hungary." But this contrived remark won him little more than a lonely compliment in the New Orleans *Picayune*.[31] Less auspiciously, it reminded Senator Clemens that Kossuth was also damnable as a secessionist.[32]

On 7 January, when more than fifty Southern congressmen ob-

30. *Congressional Globe*, 32d Cong., 1st sess., p. 23.
31. New Orleans *Picayune*, 9 January 1852.
32. *Congressional Globe*, 32d Cong., 1st sess., *Appendix*, p. 180.

jected to receiving Kossuth in open session,[33] the Magyar was confronted with a vivid reminder that he had not yet dispelled that section's profound suspicion of his program. At the congressional banquet that evening, therefore, he aimed his address directly at his critics from the slave states. His theme, the virtues of a political system based on states' rights, had become familiar fare. But in this speech Kossuth made his strongest appeal yet for Southern support. He seemed even to have mastered that section's political dialect: he referred to the individual American states as "sovereign," to centralization as a "venomous plant"; he even praised the United States for tolerating a system in which each local unit of government could regulate its own "domestic concerns."[34] He could hardly have been more conciliatory had he pledged to cross the Potomac and buy a dozen slaves.

Yet, ironically, Kossuth's appeal had not yet confronted the primary objections of his most sophisticated Southern critics. Few Southerners had ever identified Kossuth as an abolitionist.[35] What concerned them were two related but entirely separate matters: first, that support for Kossuth marked a departure from traditional American foreign policy and toward a policy based on wholly alien values devised by Northern radicals; and second, that "interventionism" represented a dangerous abstraction that could be applied, some time in the future, against the Southern states. It therefore mattered little what Kossuth thought about slavery. What mattered to prudent Southerners was who supported his crusade, and why.

33. U.S. Congress, House of Representatives, *Journal of the House of Representatives*, 32d Cong., 1st sess., pp. 166–68.

34. Louis Kossuth, *Select Speeches of Kossuth. Condensed and Abridged, with Kossuth's Express Sanction*, pp. 137–46.

35. The closest any seem to have come was in a quotation from the *Washington Republic*, quoted in *Southern Advocate*, 25 February 1852: "The Kossuthisms about 'the great heart of universal humanity' are but selections from the abolitionists' vocabulary."

VIII.

WASHINGTON:
THE YOUNG AMERICANS

That the three most prestigious statesmen in the Whig party had refused to endorse the principle of "Intervention for Non-Intervention" meant inevitably that the slogan would play an important role in the approaching presidential campaign. Even as important Whigs, abolitionists, and Southerners disavowed Kossuth's claims on the American conscience, the interventionist forces were continuing to attract new advocates, and were discovering that those who already subscribed to the Hungarian cause were growing more insistent in their demands for federal action. To those figures in the Democratic party who championed the doctrines of Young America, this support represented an important constituency. Kossuth had become, in the words of one New York paper, "a trump card skillfully played, which may win the White House."[1]

I.

"The [Kossuth] fever is . . . abating," Daniel Webster reported as early as 29 December. "It has met cooling influences from sober minds, North and South."[2] The secretary of state's analysis was little more than wishful thinking, for although Kossuth had failed to capture the imagination or support of either the Fillmore administration or of a significant number of important Southern politicians, he continued to win converts in both the North and West. Indeed, some men who previously had

1. William Eliot Griffis, *Millard Fillmore: Constructive Statesman*, p. 81; *The New York Herald*, 15 January 1852.
2. Webster to Abbott Lawrence, 29 December 1851, Daniel Webster, *The Letters of Daniel Webster*, p. 508.

ridiculed any suggestion of American intervention in the affairs of Europe had, by the early weeks of the new year, reversed their positions completely. Perhaps the most influential of these new spokesmen was Gamaliel Bailey, whose *National Era* was, along with Horace Greeley's New York *Tribune*, among the most widely respected reformist newspapers in the nation.

Bailey had for years sympathized with Kossuth.[3] But at the same time he had consistently rejected out of hand any hint that the United States possessed a moral obligation to fight for Hungarian freedom. As late as 20 November, in fact, he had declared, "The first duty . . . of the American Union is to preserve its own Republicanism, to keep its fires ever burning like the sacred fire of the vestal virgins."[4] Such rhetoric was an almost perfect anticipation of Henry Clay's own advice. But during December, while the Senate debated whether or not to welcome the Magyar to the New World, Bailey had made a series of sensational discoveries, the most important of which associated the bloc of slave-state congressmen with the Austrian minister in a conspiracy to discredit the nation's guest. His evidence was hardly conclusive: Hülsemann allegedly had been heard advising a Southern representative to vote against the joint resolution of welcome, and during debates on the measure, ministers of several other Continental powers had been recognized sitting behind a clump of Southern senators.[5] But by Christmas this notion of a league of despots encompassing two hemispheres had led Bailey to endorse the Magyar's demand for aid, provided only that that aid stop short of a declaration of war against Russia.[6]

And even this restriction disappeared after Kossuth brought his crusade to Washington. "Love thy Neighbor as thyself," Bailey was proclaiming by late February. "This is the fundamental *principle* of Intervention." He advised his readers to consult their Bibles for evidence

3. See, for example, the series of poems in his honor in *National Era*, 8 November 1849; 15, 29 August, 24 October 1850; 4, 11 December 1851.
4. Ibid., 20 November 1851.
5. Ibid., 11 December 1851.
6. Ibid., 25 December 1851.

of their international obligations, particularly Luke 10: 30–37—the story of the Good Samaritan. "The Apostles were Interventionists," he was now insisting; "—the fathers of the Church were Interventionists—philanthropists and reformers, all who have written, spoken or acted so as to elevate Humanity, have been Interventionists." Indeed, all good citizens must favor Kossuth's cause, for "Intervention in behalf of Freedom, Justice and Humanity is the maxim of Democracy; Non-Intervention, except to limit them, is the demand of Slavery."[7]

Elsewhere Young America was continuing to make progress. Philadelphians, in the wake of Kossuth's visit to their city, organized a new series of public meetings and fund-raising drives, to which William Seward subscribed the first fifty dollars.[8] On 7 January the Maine legislature adopted a series of resolutions, the fourth of which expressed their state's "earnest desire that the General Government of the United States may exert an influence, in some wise and proper manner" to insure that Russia never again intervene in a republican revolution.[9] A day later the Massachusetts General Court invited the Magyar to visit their state, and a week after that Gov. James Boutwell declared in Boston that the federal government should assert its right to interfere in favor of any republican or constitutional regime, whenever and wherever it might be threatened by a European monarch.[10]

Cassius M. Clay, the Kentucky abolitionist, divorced himself from the Garrisonians on matters of foreign policy by sending Kossuth a check for one hundred dollars and attaching to it a note that declared, "I am for committing myself—committing the people—committing the United States Government—and all free people, against the despotic 'intervention' of tyrants—by word—by protest—by arms!"[11] And Samuel Gridley Howe condemned those who, like Charles Sumner, had paused to count the cost of a war against Russia. "I am not at all moved by what

7. Ibid., 26 February 1852.
8. Ibid., 15 January 1852.
9. Ibid., 22 January 1852; *The Liberator*, 16 January 1852.
10. *Resolves Passed by the Legislature of Massachusetts*, 1852, chapter one; *National Era*, 15, 22 January 1852.
11. *The New York Tribune*, quoted in *The Liberator*, 23 January 1852.

you . . . say about a war costing us five hundred millions," he wrote Sumner, "of course we must settle if it be *right*, and then meet the cost as we best may." Howe, though not a Garrisonian, was opposed to slavery and was convinced that a war should be waged in Europe to defend the rights of man.[12]

In Springfield, Illinois, Abraham Lincoln actually sanctioned the principles of secession and civil war to justify Kossuth's cause. With eight other prominent citizens of that city, Lincoln called a "Kossuth meeting" at the city's courthouse on 8 January. At that meeting he introduced nine resolutions, the first of which declared:

> Resolved, 1. That it is the right of any people, sufficiently numerous for national independence to throw off, to revolutionize, their existing form of government, and to establish such other in its stead as they may choose.

In the proposals that followed, Lincoln recommended that the United States keep its hands off such movements but insisted that "we should at once announce to the world our determination to insist upon this mutuality of non-intervention as a sacred principle of the international law." Then, after condemning Russia's involvement in Hungary as a violation of that principle, he declared, "To have resisted Russia in that case, or to resist any power in a like case, would be no violation of our own cherished principles of non-intervention, but, on the contrary, would be ever meritorious, in us, or any independent nation." Whether or not the United States chose to use force in such situations, he concluded, would depend on the particular circumstances of the case. Lincoln's resolutions won approval by the citizens present, who added more of their own, including one decision to send their minutes to Kossuth and to the entire Illinois congressional delegation.[13]

Even some who logically should have rejected Kossuth's appeal were now championing his cause. Kossuth was, above all else, a nationalist, and his demands for help from the United States were anchored

12. Samuel Gridley Howe, *Letters and Journals of Samuel Gridley Howe,* ed., Laura E. Richards, 2:354; Laura E. Richards, *Samuel Gridley Howe,* pp. 203–7.

13. Roy P. Basler, ed., *The Collected Works of Abraham Lincoln,* 2:115–16.

to that fact. Indeed, the quality of nationality constituted in his thinking the highest imaginable evolution of human society. When he described that emotion-laden abstraction *nationality*, he conjured images few men could resist:

> Community of interests, of rights, of duties, of history, but chiefly community of institutions; by which a population, varying perhaps in tongue and race, is bound together through daily intercourse in the towns, which are the centres and home of commerce and industry;—besides these, the very mountain-ranges, the system of rivers and streams,—the soil, the dust of which is mingled with the mortal remains of those ancestors who bled on the same field, for the same interests, the common inheritance of glory and of woe, the community of laws and institutions, common freedom or common oppression;—all this enters into the complex idea of Nationality.[14]

"To fight for liberty," he had told one audience in New York, "is to fight for nationality."[15]

But Charles Goepp, the German-born internationalist, chose to ignore Kossuth's rhetoric and instead redefined the Hungarian cause in entirely different terms. Goepp, although he had been in the United States since the 1830s, had become a leader of the most radical element of German "Forty-Eighters," the political exiles of the 1848 revolution. In a short book with the revealing title *E Pluribus Unum*, Goepp declared that "all nationality is a fiction." It was because of this judgment, and not in spite of it, that Goepp urged his government to help to revive the Hungarian revolution. That struggle, and others like it, provided the United States with an opportunity to kill once and for all the antique ideas that had hindered human progress for too many centuries. To realize that goal, Goepp contended, the United States needed only to adopt a simple, three-step foreign policy. First, the administration should suspend diplomatic relations with those governments that did not profess to derive their powers from the consent of the governed. Second, it should create a series of offensive and defensive alliances, all aimed

14. Louis Kossuth, *Select Speeches of Kossuth. Condensed and Abridged, with Kossuth's Express Sanction*, p. 80.
15. Ibid., p. 84.

toward the elimination of despotic regimes. And third, the United States should take the lead in building a universal republic that would represent all peoples who had won or were fighting for their freedom. The purposes of this new international sovereign would be, as Goepp's title suggested, "forming a more perfect union, establishing justice, ensuring domestic tranquility," and the other stated goals of the Constitution of the United States.[16]

As public support for the interventionist movement continued to mount, one alarmed editor feared that the conservative administration and the opposition of the South would prove "an insufficient barricade against the rush of popular feeling towards intervention in European broils."[17] Intervention-minded Democrats were convinced they could make that happen.

II.

In Washington, the most prominent Young Americans in the Democratic party were moving to seize exclusive ownership of the cause. As early as 16 December, Sen. Isaac P. Walker of Wisconsin had condemned the nation's traditional posture toward the Old World as "a policy so criminally neutral," and had declared that "what was our policy in our infancy and weakness has ceased to be our true policy now that we have reached manhood and strength." Walker did not advocate wars of conquest or aggression, but he insisted that struggles of national liberation were of a different, less selfish nature. They would be fought in defense of "morals," "the laws of nations," "self-emancipation, self government and freedom." "Sir, peace is beautiful," he avowed at one point; "but war, with all its tragedy and blood, is less to be dreaded than dishonorable or 'ignoble peace;'—peace at the expense of peace, justice, liberty and the rights of man." America's new mission in the council of nations, Walker was contending, was to inject the dictates of morality

16. Charles Goepp, *E Pluribus Unum: A Political Tract on Kossuth and America*; the quotations are from pp. 26 and 32.

17. *Charleston* (South Carolina) *Courier*, 13 January 1852.

into the corrupted diplomatic structure of the Western world.[18] Walker's was an extreme statement of the principles of Young America. But, as events would indicate, he was not alone in that opinion.

On 8 January, the Jackson Democratic Association welcomed Kossuth to its annual banquet, celebrated each year on the anniversary of the battle of New Orleans. Nearly five hundred party luminaries crowded into Jackson Hall that night, and nearly all of them were sympathetic toward Kossuth's program for their nation. Those who were not stayed home—a group which included most of the Southern membership. Among those who did attend were two of the party's leading presidential contenders: Lewis Cass, the standard-bearer in 1848, who would descend on the Baltimore convention in June with strong support for another run at the elusive prize; and Stephen Douglas, "the Little Giant" from Illinois, who at forty-nine years of age was the youngest serious candidate. Douglas's lieutenants expected to capitalize on his youth with a semantic play on the Young America slogan. Present also were a host of potential darkhorses—in their number Joe Lane and Jesse D. Bright, both of Indiana, and Sam Houston, the towering and magnetic Texan. Among those who could not attend were James Buchanan, the third important candidate for the presidency, who was operating quietly from his Wheatland estate near Lancaster, Pennsylvania; Martin Van Buren in New York, who despite his recent flirtation with the Free-Soilers still hoped that with some luck he might return to the White House after a twelve-year absence; and Franklin Pierce of New Hampshire, himself the center of a subtle, patient, and eventually successful presidential strategy.[19]

Kossuth's presence at this political function indicated that the Young Americans were determined to identify their presidential campaign with his cause. Standing beneath the American, Hungarian, and Turkish flags that hung intertwined throughout the banquet room, one

---

18. *Congressional Globe*, 32d Cong., 1st sess., pp. 104–6.

19. *Proceedings at the Banquet of the Jackson Democratic Association, Washington, Eighth of January, 1852* (Washington, D.C., 1852); *Daily Union*, 31 December 1851; *The New York Tribune*, 31 December 1851.

speaker after another endorsed Kossuth's principles in a political game that Francis P. Blair later described as "leap frog": each man tried to express his commitment in terms more sweeping than those of his rivals. Blair himself, though not a candidate for any office, set the tone for this rhetorical competition by proposing as his toast: "Our countrymen will not assent to the one-sided doctrine [of neutrality]. They will intervene to lift up those stricken down by intervention. The Exiles from Europe—Liberty and Louis Kossuth."

Later toasts echoed Blair's sentiments. "Non-Intervention: A wrong principle in our political system when despots are waging unholy war against Liberty!" declared one Democrat; "The people of the United States: Their freedom was established by foreign intervention; can they, then, look coldly on and see the struggle of any people for the same freedom they possess, overcome by despotic might? No, never!" pronounced another.[20] As one speaker after another proposed spirited toasts identifying themselves with the Hungarian revolution, Blair regretted that Martin Van Buren's letter to the association had not yet arrived, for as he wrote the former president later, "I intended to prepare a toast following it to identify you with the Hero of the Day."[21] Blair soon concluded that Van Buren's political enemies had interfered with its progress. "I am a little suspicious that it might have been taken out at the Post Office," he advised Van Buren.[22]

Late in the evening, one Major Stephens of the Army Corps of Engineers was called to address the association. In his remarks he assured the Democrats that intervention was militarily feasible, should a Young American win the coming election. "Gentlemen, this much vaunted Russian Power has received some attention at the hands of our own able military men," he declared. "In any contest with the United States, Russia could not float an inch board anywhere below the low-

20. *Proceedings of the Jackson Association*, pp. 12, 13, 15.
21. Blair to Van Buren, 9 January 1852, Van Buren papers, Library of Congress.
22. Blair to Van Buren, 11 January 1852, ibid.

water mark, except by sufference." Major Stephens seemed as eager for
war as his civilian friends.

> Let . . . the necessity of interposition arise, and with the immense means
> of transportation, we could knock at the gates of St. Petersburgh, and before
> the Autocrat could call to the defence of his capital, his armies striking down
> liberty in Hungary and the Caucasus, that magnificent monument of the
> genius of Peter would be a monument of the prowess and heroism of the
> sons of the New World.[23]

Throughout this orgy of rhetoric, both Lewis Cass and Stephen
Douglas remained aloof from Kossuth's principles. Cass had been identified throughout his career with the idea of a moralistic foreign policy,
but he had relied upon that principle as a *means* of diplomacy, a tool by
which goals could be achieved through the agency of condemnation and
censure. In 1848 that had been a radical position. But by January 1852,
it lagged far behind those interventionist spokesmen who saw a moral
world order as an *end* of diplomacy and who were prepared to use
military force to achieve that end. Cass found it impossible to span that
intellectual gulf; in his address to the assembled Democrats he could
manage little more than a bland proposal that the United States should
"insist" on Russian non-intervention in Hungary. The nature of that
insistence he left undefined.[24]

Stephen Douglas's reticence was more politically calculated. He had
built his presidential campaign upon a coalition with conservative Southerners. He had, in fact, broken all precedent by selecting in advance his
choice for his vice-presidency: R. M. T. Hunter, a Virginian who had
opposed the Compromise of 1850 and who had solid support among
many politicians in the deeper South.[25] Although he was already associated in the popular mind with Kossuth's principles and had con-

23. *Proceedings of the Jackson Association*, pp. 16–17.
24. Ibid., p. 7.
25. Robert W. Johannsen, *Stephen A. Douglas*, p. 347; Gerald A. Capers,
Stephen A. Douglas, Defender of the Union, p. 82; George Fort Milton, *The Eve
of Conflict: Stephen A. Douglas and the Needless War*, p. 83.

ferred privately with the Magyar at least once since his arrival in the capital,[26] he could find no reason this night to risk his Southern constituency with a strong endorsement of interventionism in Europe. He did, however, employ a clever alternative. After congratulating Kossuth for his brief speech (which had ended with the toast "Intervention for Non-Intervention"), Douglas condemned the Fillmore administration for interfering with the aborted López filibustering expedition against Cuba. Southerners generally were sympathetic to López and had provided much of his manpower. It was within this context of a slave-state issue that Douglas attacked the principle of neutrality and called for "a foreign policy in accordance with the spirit of the age."[27]

Politically safe as it might have been for his own presidential ambitions, Douglas's speech was a bitter disappointment to Kossuth, who walked out of the banquet immediately after the Little Giant sat down.[28] Neither man knew that within a month Douglas would be identified irrevocably with the Hungarian cause, for neither man would make that decision. It would be made instead by George Nicholas Sanders, the new owner and editor of *The Democratic Review*.

III.

George Nicholas Sanders bore all the earmarks of a fanatic. A scion of the once-prestigious Nicholas dynasty in Virginia, he had had the bad luck to be born into the family just as its fortunes—both economic and political—were declining and as its members were drifting into the North and West to seek new prominence and prosperity.[29] Sanders had matured in Kentucky but had departed that border state with its rural complexion for the business and political opportunities of New York,

26. *Daily Union*, 1 January 1852.
27. *Proceedings of the Jackson Association*, pp. 10–11.
28. Ibid., p. 11.
29. The decline of the Nicholas family is detailed in V. Dennis Golladay, "The Nicholas Family of Virginia, 1722–1820."

Washington, and the capitals of the Old World. In all these arenas he had demonstrated an almost compulsive preoccupation with revolutionizing Europe. In that crisis year of 1848 he had crisscrossed the Continent fomenting rebellion, peddling firearms to the republicans, and, during Paris's bloody June Days, actually manning the barricades himself.[30] Throughout these years, Sanders had developed an ego as massive as his great frame, brushing aside the advice and criticism of others with all the confidence of a genius and all the obstinacy of a madman.

Some time in 1851 Sanders identified Stephen Douglas as his candidate for the presidency, and within weeks the Illinois senator had allowed Sanders to attach himself to the fledgling campaign organization. That was a colossal blunder. Sanders was no man to be invited to participate in any political campaign; to Douglas's he could bring only disaster. The balance between the Little Giant's distinct appeals to the Northwest and to the South was too delicate for Sanders's undisciplined mind to appreciate and too restrictive for his most unique talent, writing invective. But Douglas seems not to have recognized that fact until it was too late to act. When in December 1851, Sanders bought the expansionist monthly *The Democratic Review* and converted it into a national organ for the Douglas campaign, the candidate was pleased and actually promised to try to raise money if it was necessary for the project.[31]

Sanders's first issue shattered Douglas's assumption that the journal would benefit his campaign. In an article entitled "Eighteen Fifty Two and the Presidency," Sanders identified Douglas with the interventionist movement in implied but unmistakable terms. After ridiculing the foreign policies of the Taylor and Fillmore administrations as "our Quaker policy," Sanders declared, "We must transfer the field of war to the soil of Europe, and change the issue from a contest, whether monarchs shall beard us here [through continued intervention in the Western hemi-

30. Merle Eugene Curti, "George N. Sanders—American Patriot of the Fifties," is still the only study of Sanders's career.
31. Douglas to Sanders, 28 December 1851, in Robert W. Johannsen, ed., *The Letters of Stephen A. Douglas*, pp. 233–34.

sphere], to a contest whether they and their impious practices shall for an hour longer be tolerated there." Two hundred and fifty million people in Europe would be the armies in such a war, he continued; "250 millions of suffering humanity, to whose ideas the United States is a heaven beyond the setting sun—who dream in gladsome ecstasy of the day when our flag shall be unfurled, or even our nod . . . for the liberation of nations." In such a contest, Sanders assured the American people, "We can conquer, and not fight."[32]

Sanders pledged that only Stephen Douglas, referred to simply as "a second Hercules," would transform the nature of the country's foreign policy, for he alone represented the "new generation of American statesmen." The other hopefuls were a collection of "old fogies," and the Kentuckian described each in turn. Of Lewis Cass he wrote disdainfully, "Age is to be honored, but senility is pitiable." Martin Van Buren was the champion of "humanitarian bigots," and "a beaten horse, whether he ran for a previous presidential cup as first or second"; James Buchanan was a "mere lawyer, trained in the quiddities of the court, but without a political idea beyond a local election"; and William O. Butler, whom Sanders despised for personal reasons,[33] was a "mere wire puller and 'judicious bottle holder.'" Only Douglas, "a statesman of sound democratic pluck," "a bold man, who can stand the brunt of foreign war," and "a man astute and wise as Cato, who can . . . crush the despots of the world in their very dens" could satisfy Young America's demands for "young blood" and "young ideas."[34]

The fierceness of Sanders's manifesto shocked Douglas, and he immediately wrote the editor. "The friends of other candidates will hold me responsible for the assaults made by you upon their favorites," he feared. "It is no answer to say that I am not responsible. You know and I know that my voice in this respect has been disregarded, and yet they will not believe it." He further warned that "the man whose active

32. "Eighteen Fifty Two and the Presidency," *The Democratic Review* 30 (January 1852):1–12; the quotations are from pp. 4, 5, 6.

33. Siert Riepma, "Young America," p. 99n, analyzes this feud.

34. "Eighteen Fifty Two"; the quotations are from pp. 3, 9, 10, 12.

friends will try to advance his interests by assaulting others is sure to be defeated."[35] Sanders was unimpressed. To Caleb Cushing he promised, "The more fire the better as we intend to make the times hot."[36] And in his February issue, after denying half-heartedly that Douglas was responsible for anything the *Review* said, he published a vicious diatribe against Kentucky's favorite-son candidate, Butler, and stormed into an open controversy with James Buchanan's official organ, *The Pennsylvanian*. That newspaper, Sanders fumed, was a mere "mouthpiece," and it resembled a "dexterous thief in an orchard."[37]

Douglas's campaign was obviously collapsing under the burden of such help. Frantically the candidate begged Sanders to call a halt to his assaults. "If you cease now and make no more attacks upon anybody, and especially none on Gen'l Cass, possibly I can yet regain my lost position. If these attacks are repeated, my chances are utterly hopeless."[38] But the irrepressible Sanders was now in the driver's seat, and he was oblivious to danger. "Dont [*sic*] be scared," he assured Douglas at one point. "I hope to turn the tables on all our enemies."[39]

Douglas's friends denied on the floor of Congress that he was connected with the *Review*'s tactics and even circulated rumors that the proofsheets of the journal had been seen in the hands of his political enemies.[40] Finally, in April, the Little Giant tried to dissociate himself completely from the uncontrollable Sanders, begging him to "assail me with them, and at the same time select somebody else as your candidate."[41] Sanders responded with the most vitriolic issue yet, in which

35. Douglas to Sanders, 10 February 1852, in Douglas, *Letters of Douglas*, p. 239.

36. Quoted in Johannsen, *Douglas*, p. 361.

37. "The Presidency and the Review," *The Democratic Review* 30 (February 1852):183–85; "Miscellany," ibid., pp. 187–88.

38. Douglas to Sanders, 15 April 1852, in Douglas, *Letters of Douglas*, p. 246.

39. Quoted in Johannsen, *Douglas*, p. 362.

40. *Congressional Globe*, 32d Cong., 1st sess., *Appendix*, p. 302; James S. Pike, *First Blows of the Civil War: The Ten Years of Preliminary Conflict in the United States. From 1850 to 1860. A Contemporaneous Exposition . . .*, p. 115.

41. Douglas to Sanders, 15 April 1852, in Douglas, *Letters of Douglas*, pp. 246–47; Milton, *Eve of Conflict*, p. 88.

he described the other candidates as "imbeciles," "nincompoops," "parasites," "hucksters," "harmless fools," and even "vile toads."[42]

This chain of events, begun in December and January 1852, had two effects. First, it identified Douglas as the candidate of Young America and of interventionism—at least in the public mind. Second, it insured that he would not win the party's nomination.[43] If Kossuth could have anticipated these events as he listened to Douglas's evasive speech to the Jackson Association, he might have been less disturbed by what he heard, but his actions would not have been different. Already he was convinced that he could not win his demands for American intervention by remaining in the capital. On 12 January, therefore, he departed Washington for a series of speeches and rallies throughout the West and South.

42. "The Nomination—The 'Old Fogies' and Fogy Conspiracies," *The Democratic Review* 30 (April 1852): 367, 370, 377; Curti, "Patriot of the Fifties," p. 80.
43. Milton, *Eve of Conflict*, p. 88, describes the decline in Douglas's campaign fortunes; see also *The New York Herald*, 25 May, 5, 8 June 1852; Campbell to William L. Marcy, 12 March 1852, Marcy papers, Library of Congress.

IX.

THE WESTERN TOUR

"The question of our intervention in behalf of the oppressed in foreign countries is rapidly becoming the great question," reported the Baltimore *Sun* on 15 January 1852.[1] Despite his failure to win pledges of diplomatic or military assistance from the federal government, Kossuth continued to attract the support of thousands of private citizens outside the capital. And these Young Americans were eager to demonstrate their commitment to the cause of Hungarian liberty.

It was this reservoir of sympathy that the Magyar hoped to exploit as he journeyed into the West during the early months of the new year. Eighteen fifty-two was a presidential election year, and Kossuth believed that if he could mobilize the Young Americans into effective local organizations, he could bring enormous pressure to bear on both major political parties. He told an audience in Salem, Ohio:

> The cheers of the people are not recorded in Washington city, but when I can show the records of these ["Friends of Hungary"] associations; when they have joined together and act in unison; when they consist of hundreds of thousands, perhaps millions of people; when out of the small drops of individual sympathy a vast ocean has been formed, then, indeed, though their cheers may not be weighed, their names and influence will be.[2]

As Kossuth barnstormed through the western states, therefore, the meaning of his crusade changed subtly. He had looked to the federal government as a potential ally when he arrived in the United States more than a month earlier. But by January the current leadership in

1. *The Baltimore Sun*, 15 January 1852.
2. Quoted in H. A. Boardman, *The New Doctrine of Intervention, Tried by the Teachings of Washington*, p. 37.

Washington had become his rival for the allegiance of the people. In the western states, at least, there was a good chance that he could overwhelm his competition in the coming elections.

I.

That the "Magyar mania epidemic" had not abated seemed clear when Kossuth visited Harrisburg, Pennsylvania, en route to the West.[3] Hours before he was scheduled to address the state legislature there on 14 January, hundreds of women forced themselves into the state house and occupied the House chamber where Kossuth was to speak. "The Rotunda and entrance to the Hall presented a scene of dire confusion— an immense crowd struggling and swaying to and fro," reported *The Liberator's* correspondent in the building. Those women who could squeeze into the room stationed themselves at the legislators' desk or sat down in the aisles; those who could not shouted curses and threats at the sergeant at arms, demanding that he find them places inside. Speaker Rhey, huddled with his colleagues in the front of the room, called for order, and asked the women to leave. "His entreaty was turned to ridicule by the mob, who shouted and hooted all the more," reported Garrison's agent. One legislator moved to adjourn until the following day in order to clear the building: the proposal lost a voice vote in which the women participated loudly. Even the National Guard, summoned hastily by the Speaker of the House, could not restore order. When the captain in charge announced that he would arrest those who refused to leave, they only laughed. The guardsmen managed to occupy all doors into and out of the hall, but they could not close them because the corridors were filled with Kossuth's pushing admirers. Throughout the confusion of shouts and threats, Kossuth sat calmly behind the Speaker's platform, "not a feature of his face disturbed." Finally, when

3. The term was George Templeton Strong's, George Templeton Strong, *The Diary of George Templeton Strong: The Turbulent Fifties, 1850–1859*, ed., Allan Nevins and Milton Halsey Thomas, p. 76.

all other alternatives had failed, the legislators sacrificed their dignity and stood wherever they could find a place as Kossuth addressed the entire crowd. The next day he returned to speak to the legislature in closed session.[4]

More profitable demonstrations of Kossuth's popularity occurred throughout the state. In Philadelphia, Young Americans donated nearly five hundred dollars in one day; in Hollidaysburg, two hundred dollars; and in Pittsburgh, factory workers donated a week's wages in a "Kossuth festival" where a total of thirty-five hundred dollars was raised.[5] In the wake of such public support, it was not surprising that Pennsylvania's governor, in a speech on 16 January, declared himself and his administration in favor of military intervention against Russia.[6]

The drama of the Harrisburg demonstration notwithstanding, it was in Ohio that Kossuth received his most unqualified welcome. Support for Kossuth was strong throughout the West,[7] but two special circumstances made Ohioans even more intensely Young American than the citizens of other Northwestern states. First, it was a strongly antislavery state, especially within the northern tier of counties that constituted Connecticut's old Western Reserve; except for the Garrisonians, most antislavery spokesmen continued to identify Kossuth's appeals for human rights with their individual conceptions of morality.[8] Second, Ohio contained a huge German population, including thousands of "Forty Eighters" who had fled the Continent after the aborted revolutions of that year. They had strongly interventionist sympathies, of course, as did many of the Germans who had preceded them.[9]

4. *The Liberator*, 23 January 1852; *National Era*, 22 January 1852.
5. See, for example, *The Liberator*, 27 February 1852; *National Era*, 29 January 1852; Fredrick Trautmann, "Kossuth in Indiana," p. 300.
6. *The New York Tribune*, 17 January 1852; *The Liberator*, 23 January 1852.
7. See John W. Oliver, "Louis Kossuth's Appeal to the Middle West—1852."
8. See Chapter 11.
9. Eitel W. Dobert, "The Radicals," in A. E. Zucker, ed., *The Forty-Eighters: Political Refugees of the German Revolution of 1848*, pp. 157–81, describes the sentiments of one militant wing of these immigrants.

Even before Kossuth arrived in the state, therefore, it was clear that he would find strong support for his principle of "Intervention for Non-Intervention." Already the Ohio legislature had adopted the most bellicose series of resolutions to emerge from any state in the Union. After declaring that the Hungarians had fought for "the great principles that underlie the structure of our Government," the Ohioans pledged that "an attack in any form upon them is impliedly [or "implicitly"] an attack upon us; that any narrowing of the sway of these principles is a most dangerous weakening of our own influence and power; and that all such combinations of kings against people should be regarded by us now as they were in 1776, and so far as circumstances will admit the parallel, should and will be so treated."[10] The state's Democratic convention echoed these sentiments and added its conviction that the United States would "encounter the shock of arms in the field of battle" before it would tolerate the extinction of republican institutions in Europe.[11]

As Kossuth swept through Ohio during early February, he met unqualified support. In Cleveland thousands attended his speeches, and the *True Democrat* in that city pronounced him worthy of America's greatest weapons in the struggle for liberty: "Money, muskets and men! Powder, pistols and prayer!"[12] The citizens of Hamilton County donated to the Hungarian five hundred muskets belonging to the county's militia arsenal.[13] And at least one editor related with obvious approval the behavior of a fanatic in Newburgh:

A young man was seen pushing through the crowd, shouting "Eljen Kossuth! Eljen Kossuth!" said he, "God bless you, you are a political Christ." "Say not that," said the Magyar, putting both his hands on his head and blessing him. "He is the holy one; but for freedom I am willing now, in

10. *Daily Enquirer* (Cincinnati), 11 February 1852; *Daily Union*, 14 January 1852; *The Liberator*, 6 February 1852; *National Era*, 29 January 1852.

11. *Cleveland True Democrat*, 12 January 1852; Eugene H. Roseboom, *The Civil War Era*, vol. 4 in *The History of the State of Ohio*, ed., Carl Wittke, p. 265.

12. *Cleveland True Democrat*, 31 January 1852.

13. John Bach McMaster, *A History of the People of the United States, from the Revolution to the Civil War*, 8:153; *Daily Enquirer*, 10 February 1852, said the number was 200.

humble imitation of Him, to bear the cross and die on it for Freedom."
The young man wept.[14]

This account of almost religious reverence for Kossuth and his
mission was no isolated incident, for as one member of the entourage
noted in his diary, "Many religious fanatics listen to Kossuth with holy
ecstacy and confess him to be a prophet of God."[15] Even presumably
rational men sometimes expressed their support in biblical similes. Almost simultaneous with the incident in Newburgh, the editor of the
Cincinnati *Enquirer* proclaimed, "Kossuth's mission, we think, is like
that of JOHN'S—it is to prepare the way for the coming of a brighter
day to the nations."[16] The pastors of that city, emphasizing their welcome to Kossuth "as *protestant* clergymen," invoked the blessings of
morality and the will of God in predicting that Kossuth would overcome Russian and Austrian tyranny.[17]

Kossuth did not hesitate to exploit these Christian sentiments. In his
address to the state General Assembly he reverted to King James English to advance his cause. "Thou wast, oh! my nation, often the martyr
who by thy blood, didst redeem the Christian nations on earth," he
declaimed theatrically, referring to Hungary's successful defense against
Moslem invaders some four centuries earlier. "Even thy present nameless
woes are Providential. They are necessary that the Star Spangled Banner
of America should wave over a new Sinai—the mountain of law for all
nations." And then, like a new Moses, he pronounced a series of international commandments. "Hear, ye despots of the world, henceforward
this shall be law in the name of the Lord your God and Our God.

"Ye shall not kill nations.

"Ye shall not steal their freedom.

"And ye shall not covet what is your neighbor's."[18]

14. *Cleveland True Democrat*, 2 February 1852, quoted in Leffler, "Kossuth
in Cleveland," p. 252.
15. Quoted in Andor M. Leffler, "The Kossuth Episode in America," p. 110.
16. *Daily Enquirer*, quoted in Trautmann, "Kossuth in Indiana," p. 301.
17. *Daily Enquirer*, 15 February 1852.
18. Ibid., 11 February 1852.

II.

Only one incident marred Kossuth's visit to Ohio, a vicious verbal attack by Orestes Brownson. Brownson, a former Unitarian preacher and once a member of the free-thinking transcendentalist movement in New England, had converted to Roman Catholicism in 1844; in the intervening eight years he had won a national reputation as an uncompromising champion of the Roman church and had founded a quarterly magazine to propagate the political as well as the theological principles of the Church's most conservative wing.[19]

Kossuth never had been popular with the Catholic hierarchy in the United States. A Lutheran, he had played a leading role in agitating for religious reforms in the Hapsburg empire before 1848, and despite his protests to the contrary, many Americans had identified him and his war for independence in essentially theological terms, as a struggle against domination by the established church.[20] But by identifying Kossuth with Protestantism as well as republicanism, these Americans were implicitly identifying the Hapsburgs with Catholicism as well as with tyranny. One Prostestant publication wrote of Kossuth's position, "On this basis the Pilgrims stood and the English Puritans . . . on this stood Knox, Calvin and Luther, and all the mighty wrestlers against that which is the centre and life of all European despotism, the Papacy. . . . The plea of Kossuth is, that despots are combining to crush liberty out of existence."[21]

19. For surveys of Brownson's career, see Hugh Marshall, *Orestes Brownson and the American Republic: An Historical Perspective*; Henry F. Brownson, *Life of Orestes Brownson*.

20. It was not; in fact, Kossuth could claim the support of most of the bishops of Hungary during his stormy tenure in power; for a detailed narrative of Kossuth's religious agitation in Hungary and the attitude of the Church there, see Leffler, "Kossuth Episode," pp. 86–94; *National Era*, 8 January 1852; Kossuth made his strongest appeal for Roman Catholic support in his speech at St. Louis, copied in *The New York Tribune*, 24 March 1852.

21. Carroll John Noonan, *Nativism in Connecticut, 1829–1860*, p. 170.

It was by this process of association that Kossuth became identified by many as an anti-Catholic crusader.[22] "The enthusiasm of some of the Protestant sects—and particularly the clergymen and ladies—amounts almost to a religious mania," remarked the London *Times*. "They regard him as a sort of second Luther, who is destined to shake the Papal system to pieces with his preaching."[23] The Washington *Union*'s correspondent in New York agreed that the clergy seemed to see the Magyar as "a special agent sent by God to overthrow Romanism and establish true Christianity, as they understand it, throughout the world. It is a little strange that those who have heretofore interpreted the Gospel as able to make its way to the hearts of men by peace should now be willing to cooperate in spreading it by the sword."[24]

American Catholic leaders tended to see Kossuth's revolution in the same light and condemned him as a "humbug," "a demagogue," and "a tyrant and an enemy of Christianity." The *Catholic Freeman's Journal* called Millard Fillmore "an imbecile" for allowing him even to enter the United States and dismissed those Young Americans who sympathized with his cause as "vipers too pestiferous and disgusting to be longer endured in society."[25] From Boston, Orestes Brownson launched

22. Democrats, eager to endorse the liberal movements in Europe while maintaining their traditional appeal to Roman Catholic voters, had been seeking to identify the Church with the republican cause; see, for example, W. L. G. Smith, *The Life and Times of Lewis Cass*, pp. 638–39; "Gossip of the Month," *The Democratic Review* 22 (January 1848):86; "The Present Reforms of Pope Pious IX," *The Democratic Review* 22 (April 1848):301–8.

23. *Daily Union*, 24 December 1851; *The* (London) *Times*, 2 January 1852; Strong, *Diary*, p. 76; *National Era*, 20 November 1851.

24. *Daily Union*, 24 December 1851.

25. Dobert, "The Radicals," p. 169, in Zucker, ed., *The Forty-Eighters*; *National Era*, 20 November 1851; Ray Allen Billington, *The Protestant Crusade, 1800–1860: A Study of the Origins of American Nativism*, p. 331; Archbishop John Hughes, Report to the Vatican, 23 March 1858, in John Tracy Ellis, ed., *Documents in American Catholic History*, pp. 341–43. See also, Archbishop Hughes to Horace Greeley, 21 November 1851, *The Morning Courier and New York Enquirer*, 22 November 1851; Bishop O'Conner of Pittsburgh to ———, in Jánossy Dénes, ed., *A Kossuth-Emigráció Angliában és Amerikában, 1851–1852*,

a lecturing tour to counter the enthusiasm evoked by the Hungarian cause. He caught up with Kossuth in Cincinnati.

Brownson's decision to confront Kossuth anywhere was unwise; the Magyar's eloquence and his magnetic personality were too overpowering to challenge directly. In Cincinnati, with its German population and connections with the West, the confrontation was utterly foolish. But the quixotic Brownson had, after all, courted controversy throughout his career, and on 17 February he stormed into the Queen City to address the Young Men's Mercantile Library Association in the city's new concert hall. Without mentioning the Magyar's name, Brownson ridiculed the idea of intervention in European affairs and assailed those who could find any merit in the "Red Republicanism" that had appeared in the Old World during recent years. The audience was already uneasy when Brownson suddenly shouted, "We have no traitors in this country —but we import traitors from Europe and make heroes of them!" After a moment of shocked silence, the audience broke into a rage, hurling insults and hisses toward the platform. Immediately Brownson's friends began cheering the speaker, finally silencing his critics. Only within an atmosphere of bitter and uneasy coexistence could he complete his speech. He finished by denying that peoples had the right to rebel against tyrannical governments and by declaring the Hungarian revolution to be without legal or moral foundation.[26]

Brownson's effort did his cause little good; three days later one of Cincinnati's most respected jurists told a cheering crowd that Brownson's speech had been an outrage. And a week later the president of the group that had sponsored the anti-interventionist address apologized publicly for the embarrassing incident, professed not to have known what Brownson was going to talk about, and condemned the Catholic's

---

1:437–43. Similar attacks had prompted the *National Era* to gloat as early as 20 November 1851, "We are glad these slaves of a foreign potentate are beginning to unmask themselves."

26. I have drawn heavily from David Mead's account of this incident, "Brownson and Kossuth in Cincinnati," Historical and Philosophical Society of Ohio *Bulletin* (April 1949):90–94.

"wanton personal attack" against the Magyar. Even Kossuth could express satisfaction that Brownson had been answered so vigorously that he needed to make no personal reply.[27]

Weeks later, however, he did make a weak and half-hearted appeal for Catholic support. He had never been anti-Catholic, he told a gathering in St. Louis; but after making that statement, he proceeded to advise his hosts that the Society of Jesus—the Jesuits—coveted "the historical ambition . . . to rule the world" and revealed that eight priests in Missouri were Austrian natives.[28] If Kossuth wished to attract Roman Catholic support, his statements in making the attempt were not well chosen.

It is impossible to determine the degree to which Catholics outside the Church's power structure opposed Kossuth's mission. At least one politician reported that "the Catholics are all, to a man, against the doctrine of Kossuth,"[29] but it is clear that sentiment among them was never so unanimously hostile. The only two Catholic congressmen, Senators Shields of Indiana and Mallory of Florida, voted in favor of Kossuth's reception at the capitol.[30] And years later even the conservative archbishop of New York, John Hughes, admitted that a large number of priests had sympathized with the Magyar and had endorsed his program.[31] The religious dimension so many Americans saw in the Kossuth hysteria did exist, but its scope and significance may have been more apparent than real.

III.

"Treaties or no Treaties, it is vain to talk of compromise with tyranny," editorialized the Detroit *Free Press* on 11 December 1851. "There

27. Ibid.
28. *The New York Tribune*, 24 March 1852.
29. Thomas to William L. Marcy, 22 December 1851, Marcy papers, Library of Congress.
30. *Congressional Globe*, 32d Cong., 1st sess., p. 90; *National Era*, 1 January 1852.
31. Hughes, Report to the Vatican, in Ellis, *Documents in Catholic History*, p. 343.

is and can be no such compromise." Evangelical and ideological in their own approach to foreign policy, many western Young Americans could not understand why other nations were not similarly motivated. In their minds, the confrontation between liberty and despotism was not confined to the plains of Hungary; it was global in scope and absolute in nature. Either the United States would prevail in its struggle to bring republican institutions to the Old World, or it would itself become a victim of Russian tyranny; the two systems could never coexist.[32]

As he traveled toward the Mississippi River, Kossuth subtly adjusted his rhetoric in order to exploit this sense of an approaching Armageddon. In previous speeches he had emphasized the idea of nationality and had begged the American people to assume the responsibility for defending that abstraction. But now he was defining his cause in wholly different terms. "The fate of mankind is sealed for centuries," he told one Indianapolis audience—unless the United States joined the European revolutionaries in an ideological war against all totalitarian governments. If America chose to ignore its own interests, it would not survive the nineteenth century.[33] Kossuth told his audiences that Czar Nicholas, aware that his iron rule at home would not be secure as long as one free government existed anywhere in the world, would focus the power of a conquered Europe against the United States. He would exploit the nation's sectional tensions to disrupt the Union; and with that accomplished, Kossuth predicted, it would be a simple matter to invade the United States and reduce the entire North American continent to colonial status.[34] The time when the American people could hide behind the Atlantic Ocean had passed forever. "That country is most vulnerable which can be approached at thousands and thousands of points from the seas," he reminded his hosts at St. Louis; "since the steam engine works, the ocean is not a barrier—it is a high way—it is a door."[35]

32. Detroit *Free Press*, 11 December 1851; see also, ibid., 10 October 1851.
33. Madison, Indiana, *Daily Banner*, 5 March 1852, quoted in Trautmann, "Kossuth in Indiana," p. 307; Kossuth's address in Indianapolis cited, ibid., p. 305.
34. Ibid., see also *The New York Tribune*, 24 March 1852.
35. Ibid.

Louis Napoleon's coup d'état in France in the last weeks of 1851 reduced the prospects of a new revolution on the Continent. Kossuth's "asking money *since* the establishment of a military despotism in France, is entirely a different thing from his asking it *before* that event," remarked one Cincinnatian.[36] And in Pennsylvania, James Buchanan agreed. After expressing alarm and disappointment over the progress of events in Paris, he confided to one correspondent, "There is not a spot on the continent of Europe where Kossuth can land in safety; and how he is to commence a revolution in Hungary is beyond human conception." The presidential hopeful professed confidentially that with the support of a republican France and the backing of the British fleet he would have considered intervention against Russia. But without a French alliance the United States would be militarily inert. A war between America and Russia would be "the most harmless war ever waged between two powerful nations. Russia would not be mad enough to send troops here and we could not, if we would, send any considerable number of troops to Russia."[37]

But to those Young Americans who accepted Kossuth's warnings, Napoleon's coup provided visible evidence of the immediacy and terrible efficiency of a universal conspiracy. The nature of that conspiracy was defined by Henry Winter Davis in his widely read and terrifying book, *The War of Ormuzd and Ahriman in the Nineteenth Century*.[38] Taking

---

36. Daniel Drake manuscripts, 29 February 1852, from the Collections of the Cincinnati Historical Society.

37. James Buchanan to Ellen Ward, 6 February 1852, quoted in Leffler, "Kossuth Episode," p. 195.

38. Henry Winter Davis, *The War of Ormuzd and Ahriman in the Nineteenth Century*. Davis invoked the original, nonpartisan meaning of Young America throughout his work. "The American People have passed the season of youth when withdrawn from the eye of the world their pleasures might blamelessly be their pursuits," he wrote in his foreword. "In the maturity of years and strength they are amenable to mankind for the conformity of their conduct to the higher motives of policy and duty." And in another passage he spoke of the republic as having "passed in seventy years from the gristle of unformed youth to the bone and sinew, the developed form and well-knit limbs of perfect manhood" (pp. iii–iv, 347).

his title from the Zoroastrian religion's account of a cosmic battle between the spirits of Good and Evil, Davis drew an analogy between that conflict and the current one between America and Russia. His grim exploration of the czarist threat to American values reinforced Kossuth's rhetoric in absolute terms. "For the first time in the history of the world has freedom been thus attacked, by a universal conspiracy," he told his readers. "The only issue in Europe now is freedom or slavery. On that question all the princes of Europe are of one mind and of one heart. They make common cause, have a common purse, swear by and invoke the same devil, and ply with rival skill his borrowed flames."[39]

Davis asserted that it was absurd to pretend that the United States could escape Russian domination simply by ignoring the danger, for the process of encirclement already had begun. On the Continent, Russian institutions and power were supreme; in Asia, the Czar was moving steadily to consolidate his holdings and to monopolize the strategic wealth of China. And even on the western coast of North America he had planted military outposts, "nearer to our possessions

In his book, Henry Winter Davis drew an analogy between the Zoroastrian religion's account of a cosmic battle between Good and Evil and the threat of Russian "Cossackism" to American republicanism.

39. Ibid., pp. 324, 281.

than ourselves—and capable of attacking them with superior naval force ere we can even hear of the contemplated hostilities."[40]

With the exception of the British, America's only allies in the confrontation would be Kossuth and his fellow revolutionaries. If they were crushed in their next war for liberal institutions, America's destruction would be inevitable. "The only alternatives are war, in Europe, now with allies—and war hereafter, on our own soil, without allies." Within the context of Davis's premises and his logic of an existing conspiracy, the United States had no choice. She must "fling her sword into the trembling scale which weighs the destiny of the world."[41]

IV.

Kossuth continued to win converts during his trip through the West. Perhaps the most famous was Thomas Hart Benton, once the very symbol of Jacksonian thought and now forced into political retirement by enemies within Missouri. In January, Benton had written Martin Van Buren, "Have left [sic] all my friends know that I cannot go with them in this new crusade"; he also promised to return to St. Louis and "act a man's part in opposing intervention to prevent intervention."[42] And even in late February, Francis P. Blair wrote that Benton recently had denounced the Magyar for "swindling" the public with his worthless Hungary bonds.[43] But by March, after Van Buren had written the Missourian in Kossuth's behalf and after he had seen Kossuth's progress through the West, Benton changed his mind, and endorsed the nation's guest and his program.[44]

Ironically, however, Kossuth's successes throughout the West had been in the long view superficial, temporary and actually counterproductive. He had raised money, captured headlines, and enrolled

40. Ibid., pp. 302, 344, 361, 358.
41. Ibid., pp. 277, 428.
42. Benton to Van Buren, 11 January 1852, Van Buren papers, Library of Congress.
43. Blair to Van Buren, 22 February 1852, ibid.
44. Blair to Van Buren, 3 April 1852, ibid.

thousands of Americans in his Associations of the Friends of Hungary. But at the same time he had drawn to a climax that section's agitation for intervention. For more than two years western Young Americans had focused their attention on the Hungarian cause and had supported it unequivocally. But these same people were incapable of sustaining the emotional frenzy they had reached upon his arrival in their city or town and lost interest soon after he moved on. Wild jubilation and total commitment lapsed into apathy, sometimes into actual hostility. In Pittsburgh, for example, his most active supporters abandoned him after a dispute over who would pay the costs of the Hungarian festival there.[45] In the Pennsylvania legislature, the scene of his recent triumph, the members voted to pay the costs of his visit only after stormy debate.[46] And even in Ohio, one of the Magyar's sympathizers noted that by 21 March, "the Kossuth fever is entirely allayed here."[47]

45. *The Liberator*, 27 February 1852.
46. *Charleston Courier*, 16 April 1852.
47. William Fairchild to Isaac Strohm, 21 March 1852, Federal Writers Project Transcript, from the Collections of the Cincinnati Historical Society.

X

THE COLLAPSE OF INTERVENTIONISM

Few congressional debates in American history have been marked by genuine profundity. During February and March 1852, the Senate reached that plateau intermittently during the debates on foreign policy that followed Kossuth's departure from the capital. While the Magyar marched triumphantly through the western states, one senator after another took the floor to explain his understanding of the issues raised by Kossuth and his lost revolution. The conflicts that appeared in these debates were not new; they had vibrated through the Senate chambers even before 1848. But never had they been presented so cogently, and never so often in terms of the general principles of statecraft.

It now seemed clear that the intervention issue had degenerated into a matter of party and sectional interests. Western and most northeastern Democrats were allied with antislavery Whigs in favor of the evangelical and idealistic principles of Young America; opposing them were the administration Whigs and Southerners of both parties. Even two months earlier these groups had not coalesced firmly, for a majority of each had joined to welcome Kossuth to the capital. But as the Magyar came to symbolize military intervention in Europe, rather than the abstractions *progress* and *justice* or the equally intangible power of moral force, the positions of most political figures hardened. No longer could Young Americans rationally endorse the Hungarian cause by invoking sympathy and hope, for Kossuth already had pronounced both emotions to be worthless.[1] The issue had become what John C. Calhoun had predicted, in a different context, some six years earlier. "Will mere bravado have any practical effect?" he had asked his colleagues in debates over the Monroe Doctrine. "No." "You must arm, equip, fit out your navies,

---

1. Quoted by Senator Barrien, *Congressional Globe*, 32d Cong., 1st sess., p. 44.

raise a powerful revenue," and wage a war to enforce the moral sense of the American people; to do less would make statements of sentiment utterly meaningless. "The affairs of nations are not determined by mere declarations," he had warned.[2]

I.

On 19 January, just six days after Kossuth left Washington, John H. Clarke, the Rhode Island Whig, introduced a set of resolutions designed to answer Kossuth's demands for American aid. After reaffirming the United States' commitment to human rights, the resolutions declared that those principles could never be allowed to interfere with the nation's fundamental interests overseas. Clarke rejected the Magyar's appeal for diplomatic recognition of his imaginary government-in-exile and stated that the United States would continue to deal with "governments *de facto*, without inquiring by what means they have been established, or in what manner they exercise their powers." Only when the United States was threatened directly would it fight a despotic government, the Rhode Island senator concluded; until that danger appeared the nation would recognize its true policy "in the great fundamental principles given to us by Jefferson: 'Equal and exact justice to all men, of whatever State or persuasion—religious or political—peace, commerce, and honest friendship with all nations, entangling alliances with none.' "[3]

The perimeters of debate were set a day later when two Young Americans offered substitute resolutions. Lewis Cass, soon to be labeled an "old fogy" by the *Democratic Review*, wished to warn European powers that the United States Senate would not watch "without deep concern" a renewed violation of Hungary's nationality; and William Seward employed even stronger language:

The United States, in defence of their own interests and the common interests of mankind, do solemnly protest against the conduct of Russia . . .

2. *Congressional Globe*, 29th Cong., 1st sess., p. 245.
3. Ibid., 32d Cong., 1st sess., p. 298.

as a wanton and tyrannical infraction of the laws of nations. And the United States do further declare, that they will not hereafter be indifferent to similar acts of national injustice, oppression, and usurpation, whenever or wherever they may occur.[4]

These two substitutes, taken separately or together, marked the most advanced position to which Young Americans were willing to push the country. Taken at face value they pledged a military alliance with any future republic—or any professedly republican revolution—in Europe.

Ironically, it was neither Cass nor Seward who delivered the most effective speech in favor of the principles they had announced. Instead, Pierre Soulé, the flamboyant expansionist from Louisiana, carried the primary burden. Soulé was himself an exiled European republican. Thirty years earlier, in 1822, he had been forced to flee France to escape imprisonment for publishing attacks against the court of Charles X. Eventually landing in New Orleans, the excitable Soulé had risen to prominence within the city's political establishment and had won appointment to the Senate twice, in 1847 and in 1849. By 1852 the former Frenchman had developed a mammoth ego toward himself and his adopted country. He dreamed of the expansion of American power and influence throughout the world. His eccentricity allowed him to reconcile his Young American principles with the fire-eating states' rights philosophy he had learned from John C. Calhoun. Both positions, he believed, were bulwarks against tyranny.[5]

"I am decidedly against this country being pent up within the narrow circle drawn around it by the advocates of the policy of impassiveness," he announced on 17 March, in speaking for the Cass resolution. The United States, like any developing youth, had progressed beyond its former helplessness, he continued. "The lusty appetite of its manhood

4. Ibid., 310; for Seward's resolution and his speech in its behalf, see also William H. Seward, *The Works of William H. Seward*, ed. George E. Baker, 1:196–221.

5. There is still no published biography on Soulé. The closest to a full-length study in Amos Aschbach Ettinger's *The Mission to Spain of Pierre Soulé, 1853–1855: A Study in the Cuban Diplomacy of the United States*, which discusses Soulé's earlier career passim.

Pierre Soulé, an exiled European republican and Louisiana senator, dreamed of the expansion of American influence throughout the world.

[fares ill] with what might satisfy the soberer demands of a younger age." He compared America's isolation behind two oceans during its infancy with the sheltered existence of the Christian church during the Dark Ages:

> We boast exultingly of our wisdom. Do we mean to hide it under a bushel, from fear that its light might set the world in flames? As well might Christianity have been confined to the walls of a church, or the enclosures of a cloister.What had it effected for mankind, what had it effected for itself, without the spirit that promulgated it to the world?[6]

Like the Church in the post-medieval age, the United States must eventually recognize its destiny to revolutionize and reform the world by spreading abroad the principles of free and enlightened self-government. That mission, Soulé proclaimed, was nothing less than a divine mandate: "Onward! onward! is the injunction of God's will as much as *Ahead*! ahead! is the aspiration of every American heart." And that combination of destiny with the popular will made it futile for conservatives to attempt to prevent intervention in European affairs. "At-

6. *Congressional Globe*, 32d Cong., 1st sess., *Appendix*, pp. 349–54.

tempt not, therefore, to stop it in its forward career," he concluded, "for as well might you command the sun not to break through the fleecy clouds that herald its advent in the horizon."[7]

Soulé's appeals to the nation's sense of destiny won strong support from Robert Field Stockton, the freshman Democratic senator from New Jersey. Unlike many of his colleagues, Stockton had devoted little of his career to the conduct of foreign policy. Before reaching his teens he had run away to join the navy. He had risen through the ranks, eventually being appointed commodore. Slim and dashing in personal appearance, the youthful Stockton had won a hero's reputation during the Mexican War as "the conquerer of the whole of California."[8] Stockton's reasons for supporting the interventionist movement clearly manifested his military bent.

Stockton believed that a total war between liberty and despotism was inevitable, and during the Senate debates on 2 February he explained why. "Sir, when we cast our eyes over the world—everywhere—with the exception of America—we see the surface of the whole earth appropriated by absolute monarchs." All the republics of the past had vanished, the victims of aggressive tyrants; in 1852 the United States stood alone as a nation of free men. "We are, in truth, the residuary legatees of all that the blood and treasure of mankind expended for four thousand years have accomplished in the cause of human freedom," he continued. "In our hands alone is the precious deposit. Before God and the world we are responsible for this legacy."[9]

America's duty, Stockton argued, was to promote the cause of liberty overseas, in whatever manner circumstances might require. Although he refused to counsel an immediate declaration of war against "our old, and true, and faithful friend" Russia, he did demand that the United States announce its commitment to the principle of interventionism in the

7. Ibid.
8. For a brief and not entirely accurate sketch of Stockton's life, see *The New York Times*, 9 October 1866; see also Glenn W. Price, *Origins of the War with Mexico: The Polk-Stockton Intrigue*; the standard short study is contained in *The Dictionary of American Biography*.
9. *Congressional Globe*, 32d Cong., 1st sess., pp. 438–39.

cause of liberty. The United States should stand prepared to implement that principle whenever it would benefit the peoples of the Old World; "and when the great contest begins, as before 1900 it must, between free principles and despotic power, then let it be inscribed upon all our banners—everywhere—wherever they float, on every sea, on land, and ocean and continent, where the warfare rages, let it herald the advent of freedom and national independence, and the discomforture of tyranny and oppression."[10]

Such pleas for a selfless, altruistic foreign policy evoked scorn from Jeremiah Clemens. In a brilliant address on 12 February, the Alabama Democrat explained again the principles of realpolitik that had governed the nation's diplomacy since its earliest years. Leaders functioned in a capacity of attorneyship, Clemens contended; they were selected under the social contract to defend the interests of their constituents, and to further those interests when a careful weighing of means and ends indicated that that was prudent. To sacrifice the interests of one's constituents in order to advance those of a third party was the worst form of tyranny, he continued, for it violated the only rational relationship between a republic's governors and its governed—the principle of attorneyship. "The heart is a bad counsellor at best," he remarked in prelude to a splendidly simple statement of political philosophy: "An individual may be pardoned for yielding to its promptings when the risk is all his own; but no code of morals, no precept of religion can excuse or extenuate the guilt of him who idly perils a nation's welfare, a people's happiness."[11]

Within the context of this ethical system, a national crusade to extend democracy to Europe would be profoundly immoral. "Russia has done us no injury," he reminded his listeners, "we have, therefore, no wrongs to avenge. Russia has no territory of which we wish to deprive her, and from her there is no danger against which it is necessary to guard. Enlightened self-interest does not offer a single argument in favor of embroiling ourselves in a quarrel with her." And without a firm

10. Ibid.
11. Ibid., *Appendix*, pp. 179–81.

justification in self-interest, intervention would be a crime against the rights of the American people.[12]

Young Americans had never denied the altruistic nature of their program, Clemens recalled. Instead, they had defined it in terms of a mandate from God to "strike the manacles from the hands of all mankind." The only evidence that the United States had been chosen for that mission, he reminded his listeners, was the rhetoric of Pierre Soulé and his like-minded colleagues. "And, for one, I prefer waiting for some clearer manifestation of the Divine Will," he declared.[13]

If Clemens challenged the contentions of the interventionists with appeals to logic and realpolitik, it was Jacob Miller of New Jersey who attacked them with arguments they could understand and appreciate. Miller, a Whig, was of German extraction and was violently opposed to slavery. He had, in fact, voted against the compromise measures of 1850, and in 1855 he would join the new Republican party in reaction against the Kansas-Nebraska Act. The ideals that animated Miller were the ones that excited many Young Americans, for throughout the North, Germans and Free-Soilers were among Kossuth's most devoted sympathizers. The New Jersey senator understood the mystique of Young America, and when he announced his opposition to the interventionist cause, he explained his position in the rhetoric of idealism.

Miller made clear immediately that he had no wish to criticize the acts of the American people in welcoming Kossuth. On the contrary, he said, "my remarks are intended to apply solely to the Government." The senator congratulated private citizens for their "noble and liberal sympathy ... toward the oppressed of other lands" and was gratified that "liberty and humanity are not merely embodied in the forms of our Government, but that they have also a deep and warm place in the hearts of the American people." "Nevertheless," he cautioned, "the feelings of individuals may lead one way, while the duty of the government points to the opposite direction."[14]

12. Ibid.
13. Ibid.
14. Ibid., pp. 212–15.

In advancing his plea for that "opposite direction," Miller appealed to the very idealism and sense of national destiny that motivated Young Americans. "We have enough to do at home," he challenged the ambitious interventionists, and he listed schools, churches, roads, and harbors that needed improvement. Furthermore, he scolded his antislavery brethren for having confused their priorities. "While the masses in Europe are the objects of their most ardent sympathy, the masses at home are abandoned with cold indifference."[15]

Americans could afford to devote their energies to improving their own country, he assured his colleagues, for the United States' power already had been established within the council of nations. "She has proven her existence, not by arrogant proclamations, by Congressional paper resolutions, or bombastic dinner speeches, but by high and noble deeds, telling upon the world's history and affecting the world's destiny." Senate resolutions threatening intervention in Europe were unnecessary, for "all Europe at this moment feels our power at work at the foundations of her despotisms, not by intervention, armed or unarmed, but by the wisdom and justice of our national policy."[16] For sheer emotional impact, Miller's speech could hardly have been better conceived, for it accepted the premises upon which many Young Americans acted and drew a straight line from them to the traditional principles of American diplomacy.

Perhaps the most pathetic figure in these debates was Lewis Cass. Although in 1849 he had been Kossuth's first and most eloquent spokesman and it had been he who had moved to suspend diplomatic relations with the Hapsburgs in the wake of Hungary's collapse, after Kossuth had stormed into the United States demanding military intervention against Russia, the intellectual position of the two men had grown progressively different. Cass had clung tenaciously to his theory that diplomacy could be conducted by mobilizing the force of international public opinion. In the debates of 1852, Cass was continuing to champion a cause that had deserted him; he was claiming the leadership of a move-

15. Ibid.
16. Ibid.

ment in which he was advocating precisely what its beneficiary did not want. Kossuth insisted that military aid alone could win the freedom of Europe, but Cass, totally committed to the effectiveness of moral principles, pronounced him wrong.

Instead he argued on 10 February that the United States must lead the liberal forces of the world in an assault upon the old tools of diplomacy. The balance of power—"that fertile source of war and oppression"—must be abandoned as both a weapon and a goal of statecraft, he insisted. In its place, the United States must proclaim the binding quality of international law and demand that other nations obey its dictates. "The elementary commentaries of wise and learned men, the decisions of enlightened jurists, and the discussions of able statesmen, have built up the system, and it is a beautiful monument of the progress and improved condition of society," declared the Michigan senator at one point. "I assume at once the duty of all Christian people to recognize its binding force, and to aid its operations, so far as they properly can do it." But how he would enforce that duty Cass would still not make clear. Already he had advised Kossuth that under no circumstances would the United States defend Hungary by war. And in this speech he assured his fellow senators that his proposed resolution was intended only to "exert our moral influence in support of the existing principles of public law."[17]

Cass's theory of peaceful change through the popular will of the world had grown totally irrelevant to the Kossuth episode. "The Senator from Michigan says we cannot stand still," remarked Jacob Miller with ill-disguised contempt, "but he neglects to tell us whither we shall go."[18] James C. Jones, the Tennessee Whig, agreed. In a long analysis of Cass's speech, Jones heaped scorn upon the middle ground to which the Michigan senator continued to subscribe. He could understand the position of the radical interventionists, Jones admitted.

If it is the policy of this Government to interfere in the affairs of foreign countries, though I shall oppose it at every step, I want to see gentlemen come up and speak boldly, fearlessly, frankly, independently, and authori-

17. Ibid., pp. 158–65.
18. Ibid., p. 212.

tatively, and when we have spoken, then, to borrow the language of a distinguished gentleman of your party, let us maintain it, "at all hazards, and to the last extremity."

But Cass's middle road made no sense whatever to the Tennessean. "Do you remember . . . the speech of that learned gentleman, in which he inveighed with such touching and powerful eloquence against the cruelties, the enormities, and the outrages of the Czar of Russia?" he asked rhetorically. "Why, sir, the veriest monster that ever disgraced the image of God is an angel transformed into the brightness of light, compared with that miserable wretch, and yet the Senator from Michigan thinks there is virtue enough in this protest to rouse the moral sensibilities of such a devil." "I would not give a straw for all the moral influences of your declarations," he told Cass pointedly, "unless there be a power behind the throne greater than the throne. There must be physical power, and force, and will, to execute and require obedience to the protest."[19]

Even before these debates ended, it had become clear that Kossuth's cause was thoroughly discredited among half the Senate. Two months earlier that body had voted 33 to 6 to welcome the Magyar hero in open session; but on 18 February, a resolution to print Kossuth's letter of thanks for that honor passed by only one vote. Of the twenty-one votes in favor of the resolution, twelve were cast by Democrats from the Northeast and Northwest, five were antislavery Whigs, and one, Salmon Chase, was a Free-Soiler; all of the latter six would eventually join the Republican party, and one of the Democrats—Hannibal Hamlin of Maine—would be Abraham Lincoln's first vice-president. Of the twenty votes opposed, all were Southerners or Whigs, and only one, Jacob Miller, would eventually join the Republican party.[20]

Neither the Clarke resolution nor the Seward and Cass amendents to that resolution ever appeared for a vote. Debate continued only intermittently throughout the spring, and consideration of the proposals was

19. Jones's speech is printed, ibid., pp. 303–8.
20. *Congressional Globe*, 32d Cong., 1st sess., p. 590.

maintained only through weekly delays of continued debate. After 6 May, all three motions were forgotten, the victims of declining interest in interventionism.[21]

II.

Opposition to Kossuth continued to mount during the months of debate, as the anti-interventionist forces began to focus upon Washington's Farewell Address as their line of defense against the Young American crusade. On 21 February, the capital's Whigs held a public dinner for the announced purpose of "evincing a becoming respect to [the first President's] high character and illustrious services, and for the purpose of affirming and reasserting the principles set forth by him in his Farewell Address to the American people."[22] The dinner turned out to be nothing less than an anti-Kossuth rally.

It was John J. Crittenden of Kentucky who led the attacks upon the visiting rebel. In mid-1849 Crittenden had boasted that the example of the United States had inspired the people of Europe to fight for republican governments. "The great conflict is now going on between popular rights & Monarchical or despotic power," he had added. "That is the issue before mankind."[23] It had been within that context of total support for Kossuth and the other European republicans that the Kentuckian had urged the Taylor administration to speak out in favor of the republican movement. "Must our voice be unheard?" he had asked Secretary of State John M. Clayton. "God forbid! Such a course would not be *neutrality*, it would be the *abandonment* & *betrayal* of our own principles & of every just and general and noble sympathy."[24]

But never had Crittenden considered armed intervention in behalf of the rebels.[25] By February 1852, Kossuth's persistent demands for that

21. Ibid., p. 1259.
22. Printed invitation, dated 29 January 1852, in John M. Clayton papers, Library of Congress.
23. Crittenden to Clayton, 20 July 1849, ibid.
24. Ibid.
25. Ibid.

type of aid had led the Kentucky Whig to retreat from his earlier sympathy for the Hungarian cause. "We are Americans," he told the Washington's Birthday audience.

> "The father of our Country" has taught us, and we have learned, to govern ourselves. If the rest of the world have not learned that lesson, how shall they teach us? Shall they undertake to expound to *us* the Farewell Address of our Washington, or to influence us to depart from the wise policy recommended by him? *We* are the teachers, and they have not or will not learn, and yet they come to teach us![26]

Kossuth's decision to make an issue of the Farewell Address had provided a convenient weapon for those who sought to discredit the interventionist movement. Its advice was quoted repeatedly during the Senate debates of February and March.[27] Newspapers critical of Kossuth sometimes published the Farewell verbatim.[28] And Reverend H. A. Boardman of Philadelphia wrote a short book, *The New Doctrine of Intervention, Tried by the Teachings of Washington*, in which he described Kossuth's challenge to the first president's valedictory as insolent, disrespectful, and selfish. "Almost before the spray of the ocean was dry upon his clothes," Boardman complained bitterly, the Magyar had dared to attack America's most illustrious hero.[29]

New, less expected support for the anti-interventionist forces was appearing as well, for Kossuth's Hungarian enemies were beginning to speak up. The foreign minister of the short-lived Hungarian republic, Casimir Batthianyi, had published a vicious assault on his former chief in the London *Times* on 30 December 1851, and by the early months of the new year it was being reprinted in American newspapers and maga-

26. Quoted in Nathan Sargent, *Public Men and Events from the Commencement of Mr. Monroe's Administration, in 1817, to the Close of Mr. Fillmore's Administration, in 1853*, 2:384. For an account of this meeting, see *The National Intelligencer* (Washington, D.C.), 26 February 1852.

27. *Congressional Globe*, 32d Cong., 1st sess., *Appendix*, pp. 137, 139, 181, 213, 245, 305, 307, 350.

28. See, for example, *Southern Advocate*, 18 February 1852.

29. H. A. Boardman, *The New Doctrine of Intervention, Tried by the Teachings of Washington*; the quotation is from p. 22.

zines. "Kossuth's impetuous and restless temper, and the inherent weakness of his character and laxity of principle, predominated over his better feelings," inveighed the bitter Batthianyi.

> Ambition, and a hankering after notoriety, and the suppleness with which he always yielded to the most pressing and least scrupulous, placed him first in contradiction with himself, and then involved him—and it may be said, also, the other ministers—in an inconsistent policy, and finally led him to self-willed and arbitrary measures, which accelerated the fall of the Batthyany [Batthianyi] ministry. It is unnecessary to charge a man with more failings and follies than he has been guilty of.[30]

Bartholomaeus Szcmere, the former president of the Hungarian Ministerial Council, added from Paris a week later that Kossuth was also a coward, who had fled his homeland prematurely, "giving himself no thought for the fate of his party, his friends, his army, the fortunes of the nation," and who had avoided his friends to make good his escape.[31] That these accusations came from men who had good reason to hate Kossuth did not destroy their credibility; as fellow exiles, their sentiments carried weight among some Americans.

III.

In the face of this mushrooming opposition, Kossuth ventured into the South to confront his most vocal critics in their home territory. In contrast with the North, where Kossuth had received invitations to visit nearly every state, the South managed to extend only two offers of hospitality. One came from the city of New Orleans, and already its invitation had been virtually repudiated by the Louisiana legislature.[32]

30. *The* (London) *Times,* 30 December 1851; *The North American Review* 75 (September 1852):458n; *Vicksburg Weekly Whig,* 25 February 1852.
31. *Morning Courier and New York Enquirer,* 9 February 1852; *The New York Times,* 2 February 1852.
32. An apparent draft of a telegraphic message, in Kossuth's hand, 22 March 1852, from the Collections of the Ohio State Archeological and Historical Society; Louisiana's legislature refused to invite Kossuth as a guest of the state. One resolution introduced there, but not adopted, had declared expressly that he would not

The second was a personal gesture by Henry Foote, by then governor of Mississippi, obliging the Hungarian's request to visit at his home in Vicksburg.[33]

Kossuth first touched the slave states at Louisville on 7 March. "Kentucky did not bleed freely on the application of the Great Hungarian Leech," reported the Natchez *Mississippi Free Trader*.[34] Local officials had not bothered to invite him to the state, and his only public speech there was an impromptu affair, scantily attended and greeted with only lukewarm applause.[35] "The anti-Kossuth feeling is almost universal in Kentucky," Richard Hawes had reported from Lexington a week earlier. In that state the abolitionists and Free-Soilers seemed to be the most dedicated Young Americans. "Cassius Clay sought the opportunity to make a Kossuth speech on the night of the 24 [of February], with a view of catching the Whigs, but although he had a large hearing, principally of democrats, he only raised $15 after a speech of three hours," Hawes continued. "He enquired of me if I thought he could raise some money in Boston, and I told him that I did not know anyone who would give him a dime."[36]

The deep South was even less kind. The Magyar traveled from Louisville to St. Louis, then steamed down the Mississippi to Jackson and New Orleans. From there he moved by rail to Mobile, Alabama, and Charleston, South Carolina. Nearly everywhere he met audiences sullenly contemptuous of his mission.

Kossuth did everything he could reasonably have done to win sup-

---

be treated as a guest, and that unless he repudiated an earlier criticism of Henry Clay he would not be welcome in the state; quoted in William Warren Rogers, "The 'Nation's Guest' in Louisiana: Kossuth Visits New Orleans," p. 359.

33. An apparent draft of a telegraphic message, in Kossuth's hand, 22 March 1852, from the Collections of the Ohio State Archeological and Historical Society.

34. Natchez *Mississippi Free Trader*, 24 March 1852.

35. Rogers, "Nation's Guest," p. 358.

36. Hawes to John J. Crittenden, 28 February 1852, Crittenden papers, Library of Congress. Kossuth was similarly identified with the antislavery cause in St. Louis: see Edward Younger, *John A. Kasson: Politics and Diplomacy from Lincoln to McKinley*, p. 64.

port in the South. He warned at one point that Southerners might well lose their cotton markets in Europe, reasoning that if the Continent passed under Russian domination, the despots would declare economic war against the world's remaining republics.[37] At another place he disclaimed even a remote interest in either slavery or abolitionism. "What have I to do with abolitionism or anti-abolitionism?" he asked the citizens of New Orleans. "Nothing in the world. That is not my matter; I am no citizen of the United States; I have neither the right nor the will to interfere with your domestic concerns; I claim for my nation the right to regulate its own institutions; I therefore must respect, and indeed I do respect, the same right in others."[38]

And in some speeches he even made a plausible argument that he was fighting the South's own battle—that Hungarian rights and Southern rights were synonymous. At Mobile, for example, he declared that centralization and foreign interference were the two great enemies of self-government.

> I frankly confess I should feel highly astonished if the Southern States prove not amongst the first, and amongst the most unanimous to join in such a declaration [in favor of "intervention for non-intervention"]. Because, of all the great principles guaranteed by your constitution, there is none which they more cherish,—than the principle of self-government; the principle that their own affairs are to be managed by themselves, without any interference from whatever quarter, neither from another state, though they are all estates of the same galaxy, nor from the central government, though it is an emanation of all the states.[39]

It is impossible to determine if Kossuth was also identifying himself with the Southern construction of the Constitution when he spoke of the federal government as "emanating" from the states; if he was, no one seemed to notice.

37. Louis Kossuth, *Select Speeches of Kossuth. Condensed and Abridged, with Kossuth's Express Sanction,* pp. 303–5; for a less pointed declaration, see Rogers, "Nation's Guest," p. 363.

38. Quoted ibid., p. 362; *The New York Tribune,* 12 April 1852; *Daily Union,* 17 March 1852.

39. Kossuth, *Select Speeches,* pp. 296–97.

It was in this address, too, that Kossuth made a subtle but unmistakable appeal for votes in the coming election. After complaining that Alabama Sen. Jeremiah Clemens was as critical of the interventionist movement as the czar himself, the exile reminded his listeners that congressmen presently sitting "have not been elected upon the question of foreign policy, that question being then not discussed. I therefore humbly entreat the sovereign people of the United States to consider the matter and to pronounce its opinion, in such a way as is consistent with law, and with their constitutional duties and rights."[40] But for the reference to "constitutional duties," Kossuth could have meant messages to Congress.

These appeals fell on deaf ears. Like their national representatives, Southerners were deeply suspicious of the Young Americans and their crusading spirit. Some, like the editor of the *Vicksburg Weekly Whig*, identified him with the Free-Soil movement and advised Southerners that "there is no surer test of the correctness of the course of Southern politicians and papers, than to find them in opposition to the views of the abolitionists and free soilers."[41] Others, like Gen. John E. Wool, feared that his passionate and persuasive speeches would lure the United States into an unprofitable and unnecessary war. "There appears to be no limit to his influence over the humn mind," the alarmed general and possible candidate for the presidency wrote in late December.

> In the seeming honesty of his purpose, and by his zeal and eloquence, he carries all with him; even he who, in his moments of reflection, would shudder at the thought of war and bloodshed, enters fully into all his plans, and declares himself ready to shoulder the musket, and commence a crusade against all crowned heads or oppressors of the human family.

At least one Southern newspaper reprinted the general's letter to warn its readers to beware of the Magyar's rhetoric.[42]

40. Ibid., pp. 394–95.
41. *Vicksburg Weekly Whig*, 25 February 1852.
42. John E. Wool to ———, 31 December 1851, published ibid., 10 March 1852; for Wool's presidential hopes, see Henry Bull to William L. Marcy, 23 December 1851, William L. Marcy papers, Library of Congress.

For these and other reasons, Kossuth's tour through the South was an almost unbroken series of humiliations. At Montgomery a crowd of a few hundred listened in "cold, unsympathetic and even hostile" silence;[43] at Jackson, one irate citizen swore out a warrant for the exile's arrest, claiming that he had willfully violated the federal neutrality law of 1818.[44] And in South Carolina, that haughtiest and most contrary of states, Kossuth had arrived, stayed two days and left before the *Charleston Courier* announced his visit; understandably, perhaps, no one there asked him to speak.[45]

IV.

Kossuth was virtually ignored when he returned to Washington in mid-April. Senators Cass, Shields, and Seward, his official hosts, called on him briefly the evening he arrived. Otherwise, reported one newspaper, "he was left to himself."[46] Only the Sewards and Mrs. Horace Mann bothered to see him off when he departed the capital for New England. Seward himself recalled with little exaggeration, "Hungary and Kossuth have passed from the memory of all men here but myself."[47]

43. Francis Pulszky and Theresa Pulszky, *White, Red, Black: Sketches of American Society in the United States During the Visit of Their Guests*, 2:221.
44. *Charleston Courier*, 12 April 1952.
45. Ibid.; Pulszky and Pulszky, *White, Red, Black*, 2:222.
46. *Charleston Courier*, 19 April 1852.
47. Frederic Bancroft, *The Life of William H. Seward*, 1:322; Andor M. Leffler, "The Kossuth Episode in America," p. 84; Frederick W. Seward, *Reminiscences of a War-Time Statesman and Diplomat, 1830–1915*, pp. 102–5.

XI.

THE FINAL WEEKS

As Kossuth reentered the North it was clear that the mystique which had earlier surrounded him and his crusade had vanished from the national mood. Westerners had lost interest in the Young American movement as it pertained to Europe. "I must say it is strange for me to see the friends of General Cass in Michigan . . . not only not supporting my cause, but openly attacking & undoing what I had done there," Kossuth remarked bitterly.[1] And Southern journals—now confident that the interventionist forces could not succeed—were not bothering even to discuss their opposition to the Magyar. By late April, when the Hungarian arrived in Jersey City, New Jersey, he was confronting enemies who no longer debated the issues he had raised; instead they made cruel jokes about his future. "I had millions at my disposal, yet I went into exile penniless," he lashed out at one group of detractors in that city. "Who now are *ye* . . . to insult my honour and call me a sturdy beggar, and ask in what brewery I will invest the money I get from Americans?"[2]

Still, the interventionist movement was not yet dead. New Englanders awaited Kossuth's arrival with promises of strong sectional support, and the national political party conventions, scheduled for June, conceivably could yet nominate candidates sympathetic to his cause. During these last weeks of his tour, Kossuth tried desperately to mold his remaining friends into a coalition capable of determining the course of American foreign policy. Yet even as he acted, the exile admitted that he could not succeed. "The spirit of liberty takes itself wings,—you are

1. Kossuth to Edmund Burke, 24 May 1852, Burke papers, Library of Congress.
2. Louis Kossuth, *Select Speeches of Kossuth. Condensed and Abridged, with Kossuth's Express Sanction*, pp. 307–8.

happy to be the first-born of that spirit," he told one audience; "but we accept our condition just to be one of its martyrs."[3]

I.

On 24 April, aboard a special train sent from Boston, Kossuth entered New England for the first time. Immediately, the promise of a vigorous welcome in that section, tendered months earlier, was confirmed.[4] At New Haven, Connecticut, church bells tolled that city's commitment to the principle of European liberty, and cannon salutes symbolized the attitude of its citizens toward military intervention in the Old World. At Springfield, Massachusetts, five thousand people crowded around the nation's guest to hear him plead his country's cause. And at Boston the city fathers prepared the most elaborate greeting he had seen since his first day in the United States. Thirty-four militia companies formed a procession to lead him through the city; public and private buildings were dotted with signs expressing welcome and support, which were flanked by Hungarian and American flags. At Boston Commons an estimated fifty thousand citizens gathered to watch him review the local troops and perform other ceremonial duties. At the statehouse, workmen had constructed a giant arch painted with the slogan that would become Kossuth's motto in New England: "There is a Community in the Destinies of Humanity."[5]

Equally gratifying were the persistent offers of financial aid. Germans at nearly every stop gave the exiles money in amounts varying from a few dollars to more than one hundred; the Congregational church at Brookfield, Massachusetts, sent one hundred dollars via its preacher, the Reverend William B. Greene; the George Mirriam family

3. Quoted in George S. Boutwell, *Reminiscences of Sixty Years in Public Affairs*, p. 187.

4. *Kossuth in New England: A Full Account of the Hungarian Governor's Visit to Massachusetts; with His Speeches, and the Addresses That Were Made to Him, carefully revised and corrected*, pp. 2–4.

5. Ibid., pp. 11, 25, 68–73, and passim, details the public response to his visit there; see also Louis Kossuth, *Memories of My Exile*, pp. xvii, xviii.

of Springfield gave one hundred and fifty dollars. Citizens donated to civic "Kossuth funds," which were presented to the Magyar when he visited in or near their towns. And more than once, Kossuth's scheduled lectures were closed to all who could not show a Hungary bond at the door.[6] Occasionally, Kossuth's refusal to detail how he was spending these contributions evoked some criticism; but his standard explanation, "I cannot tell the public (which is to tell my country's enemy), how I dispose of the sums which I receive," seemed to satisfy his supporters, for there was no apparent decline in their generosity.[7]

Kossuth had warned on his arrival in the Northeast that his visit there would necessarily be short. But the public response to his presence was so gratifying and profitable that he delayed his departure for nearly a month. In that time he crisscrossed the state, making more than twenty stops and delivering at least thirty prepared speeches, as well as many more impromptu talks.[8] At times his barnstorming tour had the appearance of a formal diplomatic visit, as the citizens of Massachusetts escorted him from one tourist attraction or historical landmark to another. In New Haven, Eli Whitney, the son of the inventor of the cotton gin, conducted him through his arsenal and gave him twenty rifles for use in the coming revolution.[9] On 27 April he visited the national armory at Springfield; on 3 May he traveled to the Bunker Hill monument, and a week later to Lexington and Concord.[10] Everywhere New Englanders. gathered to greet him and to cheer his calls for intervention.

Those with whom Kossuth spoke included the nation's most prestigious minds. At Faneuil Hall he met Josiah Quincy, the state's most venerable link with its revolutionary past. At Concord he was greeted by Ralph Waldo Emerson; at Samuel Gridley Howe's home he spoke with

6. *Kossuth in New England*, pp. 20, 21, 26, 41.
7. Kossuth, *Select Speeches*, p. 308.
8. *Kossuth in New England*, passim; Boutwell, *Reminiscences*, pp. 306, 308.
9. *Kossuth in New England*, p. 18. Samuel Colt had set a precedent in this regard; Jack Rohan, *Yankee Arms Maker*, pp. 224–25.
10. Joseph Szeplaki, " 'The Nation's Guest': Bibliography on Louis Kossuth, Governor of Hungary with Special Reference to His Trip in the United States, December 4, 1851–July 14, 1852," p. 3; Kossuth, *Selected Speeches*, p. 348.

William Francis Channing, Theodore Parker, Charles Sumner, and Henry Wadsworth Longfellow. Without exception, these thinkers were impressed by the exile and most were sympathetic to his cause.[11] At Howe's home he also met Laura Dewey Bridgman, the first blind and deaf mute ever to receive a systematic education; upon meeting Kossuth, Ms. Bridgman said in finger-writing, "I am glad he is out of Turkey. Kings are cruel."[12]

Kossuth's ideas had grown familiar through months of constant repetition, and there was little he could say he had not said before. Yet as he traveled through the cities and towns of Massachusetts, the exile continued to find new ways of expressing his central message—that the United States must intervene in European politics. In Washington he had spoken of America's interest in protecting the principles of international law; in the expansive and nationalistic West he had raised the specter of foreign invasion of the United States and had reminded his listeners of Russia's foothold in the hemisphere; and in the South he had pled for protection of local government and states' rights.

In New England, that cradle of ideology during the American Revolution, he stressed the blessings of liberty and proclaimed the need for Americans to extend those rights to the people of other nations. With telling effect upon these sons of Puritanism, he put his case in religious terms. He told a mammoth rally in Boston's historic Faneuil Hall:

> You have grown prodigiously by your freedom of seventy-five years, but what is seventy-five years as a charter of immortality? No, no, my humble tongue tells the records of eternal truth. A *privilege* never can be lasting. Liberty restricted to one nation never can be sure. You may say, "We are the prophets of God;" but you shall not say, "God is only our God." The Jews said so, and their pride, old Jerusalem, lies in the dust. Our Saviour

11. Richard Henry Dana, Jr., *The Journal of Richard Henry Dana, Jr.*, ed. Robert F. Lucid, 2:489; Kossuth, *Select Speeches*, pp. 348, 349; *Kossuth in New England*, p. 224ff; Russell M. Jones, ed., "A Letter from Dr. William Francis Channing to Louis Kossuth," *The New England Quarterly* 39 (March 1966):88–93; Sumner, *Complete Works*, 3:172.

12. Dana, *Journal*, 2:489.

taught all humanity to say, "Our Father in heaven," and his Jerusalem is lasting to the end of days.[13]

Kossuth's meaning was clear: Americans must make liberty universal, or watch it perish from their own land.

Kossuth's appeals proved irresistible to most political figures within the state. Gov. James Boutwell, speaking for the Democratic party in Massachusetts, wholeheartedly endorsed military intervention in Europe.[14] And Anson Burlingame, designated by the antislavery Conscience Whigs in the legislature as the Magyar's official host in the state, adopted the rhetoric of Young America in referring to the continuing national debate over the relevance of the Farewell Address for the 1850s. Washington's valedictory had been designed to meet the "exigency of those early times," Burlingame told one audience at Worcester.

> Why a nation can have no such thing as a fixed policy. It must have fixed *principles*. The eloquent speaker [Kossuth] has told us that policy is one thing, and principle quite another thing. One takes its hues and form from the passing hour; the other is eternal, and may not be departed from in safety. . . . Let us not wrong our fathers by believing they intended to chain this nation to the cradle of its infancy.[15]

With the dominant figures of both parties in the Young America camp, there were few New Englanders who dared to criticize the Magyar. Besides Boston's Irish immigrants, who were alarmed by the anti-Catholic implications of Kossuth's cause,[16] his only critics seemed to be those who endorsed his ideals but pronounced them impossible to attain. Such critics aroused a special ire in the exile and evoked from him the most petulant statement of his American tour:

> Some take me here as a visionary. Curious, indeed, if that man who, a poor son of the people, has abolished an aristocracy of a thousand years old,

13. Kossuth, *Select Speeches*, p. 323.

14. Ibid., p. 328, relates Boutwell's interventionist remarks at Faneuil Hall on 30 April 1852.

15. *Kossuth in New England*, p. 63.

16. Oscar Handlin, *Boston's Immigrants: A Study in Acculturation*, pp. 141, 336n.

created a treasury of millions out of nothing, an army out of nothing, and directed a revolution so as to fix the attention of the whole world upon Hungary, and has beated the old, well-provided power of Austria, and crushed its future by his very fall, and forsaken, abandoned, alone, sustained a struggle against two empires, and made himself by his very exile feared by Czars and emperors, and trusted by foreign nations as well as his own,—if that man be a visionary therefore, so much pride I may be excused, that I would like to look face to face into the eyes of a practical man on earth.[17]

II.

Kossuth's visit to New England enriched his war chest by thousands of dollars. Despite their near unanimity in favor of his cause, however, New Englanders were of little import in Kossuth's dwindling crusade for a new, evangelistic foreign policy for the American people. Instead, the only remaining hope for his success was the Democratic national convention, then summoning delegates to Baltimore. On 21 May, therefore, Kossuth and his entourage departed New England en route back to the Empire City. There, Kossuth believed, he could bring political pressure to bear upon the party's eventual nominee and force him to endorse interventionist policies in exchange for the votes of the Magyar's remaining friends.

Even before he arrived in New York City, Kossuth moved to win new allies within the Democratic hierarchy. From Niagara Falls he wrote to Edmund Burke, formerly Thomas Ritchie's coeditor at the Washington *Union*, and currently, although ostensibly devoted to his private law practice, still an influential member of the party's inner circle at the capital. On 24 May, in a letter shadowed with hints of bribery and pleas for secrecy, Kossuth asked Burke to accept a position as his confidential agent. If the Democrats won the presidential election, Kossuth explained, it would be Burke's responsibility to supply him "from time to time a confidential statement of the course of affairs" and to act

17. Quoted in Boutwell, *Reminiscences*, p. 190.

as a go-between in Kossuth's negotiations with the administration. "It is quite natural that such a position is connected with expenses etc., which I most gladly will bear," Kossuth advised the former editor. What expenses Burke might encounter, aside from postage, Kossuth left diplomatically vague.[18]

Furthermore, Kossuth advised the Democrat that his party would be wise to nominate a candidate sympathetic to the cause of the European republicans. Germans were prepared to vote "without party respect" for the candidate who espoused their interests most openly, he warned. In the absence of a genuine interventionist among the prominent candidates, the Magyar implied that Lewis Cass was his personal choice. Whether or not Burke's influence in the Michigan senator's behalf was included under "expenses etc." depended on how Burke interpreted Kossuth's remarkably subtle and suggestive letter.[19]

III.

Kossuth's efforts to influence the course of the Democratic convention proved futile. The pathetic eloquence of his New England tour could not rekindle the national hysteria that had existed when he had arrived six months earlier. By 1 June, when the delegates assembled in Baltimore's American House hotel to choose a presidential ticket, the Hungarian cause had become irrelevant to the national political scene. If there was a sense of mission among those party regulars, it was focused upon exclusively domestic issues—the maintenance of the Union and victory in the November elections. To achieve either would require a platform and a candidate acceptable to Northerners and Southerners alike.

The nominating process was tortuous. Saddled with a two-thirds rule for nomination and three strong front-runners, the party staggered through thirty-nine ballots, as the lieutenants of Cass, Douglas, and Buchanan maneuvered for advantage. None ever came within seventy

18. Kossuth to Burke, 24 May 1852, Burke papers, Library of Congress.
19. Ibid.

votes of the necessary 188. Then, on the fortieth poll, Virginia turned to Franklin Pierce of New Hampshire as a part of a pre-arranged plan. The move, as anticipated, broke the deadlock, and nine ballots later Pierce won the nomination almost unanimously.[20]

That Pierce was the party's new standard-bearer could not have disturbed Kossuth greatly, for the New Hampshire politician was an unknown quality. His national reputation was barely mediocre—that of a hard-drinking local operator who disliked Catholics and who had served passably as a general during the Mexican War. His stance on issues of foreign policy was also unknown, probably even to himself. His victory in the convention testified to his safeness on the slavery issue, and to nothing else.[21]

What must have disturbed Kossuth, however, was the text of the platform adopted at Baltimore. "In view of the condition of popular institutions in the Old World," declared the Democrats in the last plank of that document, the United States must recognize its "high and sacred duty" to protect the principles of liberty and states' rights—at home.[22] This statement, coupled with the platform's utter silence regarding Kossuth and interventionism, constituted a virtual repudiation of the evangelical Americanism that the Magyar had hoped would characterize the party's official position on foreign policy.

The Whigs were more direct. On 19 June, after nominating Winfield Scott for the presidency, they adopted a platform that condemned the Young America movement categorically. In the third article they declared:

> While struggling freedom everywhere enlists the warmest sympathy of the Whig party, we still adhere to the doctrines of the Father of his Country, as announced in his Farewell Address, of keeping ourselves free from all

20. Roy F. Nichols, *Franklin Pierce: Young Hickory of the Granite Hills*, pp. 202–4; Allan Nevins, *Ordeal of the Union*, 2:18–20.

21. The standard biography is Nichols, *Franklin Pierce*; for a critical analysis of Pierce's potential and reputation, see Nevins, *Ordeal of the Union*, 2: chapter 1.

22. Kirk H. Porter and Donald B. Johnson, eds., *National Party Platforms, 1840–1956*, p. 18.

entangling alliances with foreign countries, and of never quitting our own to stand on foreign grounds; that our mission as a republic is not to propagate our opinions, or impose upon other countries our forms of government by artifice or force, but to teach by example, and show by our success, moderation and justice, the blessings of self-government and the advantages of free institutions.[23]

The absolute refutation of interventionism, and its location near the beginning of the platform, made it clear that the Whigs had identified foreign policy as a popular issue in this election year.

IV.

By late June, Kossuth's fortunes had grown desperate. Instead of forcing the contending parties to vie for his good will, the presidential campaign had fragmented the interventionist forces beyond any political effectiveness. The continuing friendship of William Seward and other politicians of his persuasion was now worthless; the Whigs had repudiated the Young America movement in absolute terms, and in this election year the Sewardites could not abandon their party, their candidate, and their platform for a hopeless cause.[24] Similarly, the Democratic party had resolved to avoid any issues that might divide the South against the North; and within that context, Young America could serve better as an empty platitude than as a statement on foreign policy.

In the West and in New England the Free-Soilers were seeking to capture leadership of the interventionist movement. Indeed, in their August convention the members of that party would incorporate the principles of Young America into their national platform:

Every nation has a clear right to alter or change its own government, and to administer its own concerns in such a manner as may best secure the

23. Ibid., p. 20; Thomas Hudson McKee, *The National Conventions and Platforms of all Political Parties, 1789 to 1900: Convention, Popular and Electoral Vote* (Baltimore, 1900), pp. 78–79.
24. They could, however, continue to speak out; see *The New York Tribune*, 5 June 1852.

rights and promote the happiness of the people; and foreign interference with that right is a dangerous violation of the law of nations, against which all independent governments should protest, and endeavor by all proper means to prevent; and especially it is the duty of the American government, representing the chief republic in the world, to protest against, and by all proper means to prevent, the intervention of kings and emperors against nations seeking to establish for themselves republican or constitutional governments.[25]

But this support—foreshadowed in the attitude of politicians such as Joshua Giddings and Gamaliel Bailey[26]—was of no inherent value, for no one gave the Free-Soilers even a remote chance of capturing the White House.

Even among the Democrats, Kossuth's support was vanishing. Southern opposition, the general decline of interest throughout the country, and the imperative of party unity during a national campaign had silenced many of Kossuth's sympathizers. Lewis Cass was at least temporarily quiet about foreign policy; Stephen Douglas had said nothing on the subject since he had repudiated George Sanders's endorsement. Even Edmund Burke, to whom Kossuth had offered either a retainer or a bribe, was counseling Pierce to deceive the Magyar with friendship only long enough to obtain his political blessing. "Kossuth should be invited to New Hampshire, but should receive nothing from you but courtesy and civilities," he advised the nominee in early June. The Democrats could anticipate the Magyar's support *"without any assurance* that a Northern administration will sympathize more with the popular movements in Europe than a Southern or Whig administration."[27]

Kossuth could now count on the fingers of one hand his most prominent supporters within the Democratic party: George Sanders, who was,

25. Porter, *National Party Platforms*, p. 19; McKee, *National Conventions*, p. 83.

26. For Giddings's attitude, see *Congressional Globe*, 32d Cong., 1st sess., *Appendix*, pp. 143–45.

27. Burke to Pierce, 6 June 1852, Franklin Pierce papers, Library of Congress.

as the result of his vituperative essays in the *Democratic Review,* thoroughly disliked by nearly every element of the party; Isaac O. Barnes, a second-rate Democratic New York politician who could win the ears of party dignitaries, but who had no influence over policymaking; Dr. G. C. Hebbe, a Swedish scholar and party functionary who was little more than a liaison with the nation's German community; and Pierre Soulé and John L. O'Sullivan, who were the only two among the five who could boast respectable credentials within the national party structure. Aside from these men, Kossuth could count upon the support of a few Democrats like Thomas Baermann—men whose influence was strictly local and based solely on their German extraction. Throughout the rest of the party, Kossuth had so little prestige that when he let it be known that he wished to meet the party's nominee, Pierce responded with stony silence.[28]

The remaining interventionists then resorted to the mails and to the printed word. Barnes advised Pierce that the Whigs "will resort to anything & everything in their power" to capture control of the "Kossuth mania," a patently absurd threat that was, nevertheless, repeated by Soulé.[29] And O'Sullivan, anticipating the Free-Soilers' convention two months in the future, expressed alarm that the antislavery party might attract the German vote on the issue of Young America.[30]

Kossuth did what he could to reinforce this pressure. On 23 June, the Magyar addressed New York City's Germans at the Broadway Tabernacle. In his speech, he predicted that the Whigs might be persuaded to reverse the foreign policy plank of their platform. Even if they did not, he declared, the Democrats could not consider the German vote as safe, *"for there is a third course yet open,* viz: that the German citizens . . . *may unite with a third independent party, or refrain from voting* . . . and throw the election into Congress."[31] This threat earned

28. Ibid. Jacob Thompson to Pierce, June —, 1852, ibid.; Roy F. Nichols, *The Democratic Machine, 1850–1854,* p. 149; and notes following.

29. Soulé to Pierce, 30 June 1852, Pierce papers.

30. O'Sullivan to Pierce, 26 June 1852, ibid.

31. *The New York Tribune,* 26, 28 June 1852.

some teeth when the assembled Germans adopted resolutions warning, "We expect that the candidate of the Democratic party will adopt the principles of this policy," meaning interventionism.[32]

The only practical course for Pierce to follow, the interventionists contended, was to announce his commitment to the principles of Young America; if he would make such a declaration, Kossuth would endorse the Democratic ticket. "Kossuth is, I am sure, heart and soul with us," Soulé confided to Pierce on 30 June, after meeting with the Magyar, "but he is still more so with the cause which he so devotedly defends and apostolizes. He expresses a wish that something were done by us that might afford him an excuse for pressing more strenuously than he has heretofore done, upon those who seem disposed to be guided by his judgments, the claims of the Democratic party to their undivided and unreserved support." Soulé explained that he believed Kossuth's endorsement could determine the outcome in the critical states of Ohio, New York, Pennsylvania, and Louisiana. He concluded by asking Pierce to state his attitude on the neutrality laws, promising "immense advantage" if the response would satisfy the Hungarian.[33]

George Sanders chose to apply his own peculiar brand of pressure. In the June issue of his *Democratic Review*, he pretended perfect satisfaction with Pierce's nomination. The candidate was, Sanders declared, "the type of candidate we have indicated" in six months of agitation for Young America. "Our contest was worth forty-eight [*sic*] ballots at all events—it was the contest of two generations, of great and living principles against the dead and unworthy, of the young green tree against the old and wrinkled trunk—and with us it has been victorious." Twice Sanders edited the party's platform, twisting it into an interventionist manifesto.[34] At another point he admitted that the foreign policy plank had been weak but explained:

32. Ibid.
33. Soulé to Pierce, 30 June 1852, Pierce papers.
34. Article 20 of the platform read: "*Resolved*, That in view of the condition of popular institutions in the Old World, a high and sacred duty is devolved, with increased responsibility, upon the Democracy of this country, as the party of the people, to uphold and maintain the rights of every state, and thereby the union of

Our young men desired neither to humiliate the beaten, cramp themselves, nor dictate to their selected executive. It was sufficient for them to assert practically the principles they advocated, to install a new man as representative of those principles, to make a platform large enough, and tolerant enough to include all opinions and all sections.[35]

Sanders's attempts to identify Pierce publicly with the interventionist movement dominated the entire issue.[36]

Pierce resisted these desperate maneuvers. Simultaneous with them, letters were arriving at his home in Concord, reminding him that the entire South was now opposed to the Magyar. Furthermore, the traditionally Democratic Germans probably would not abandon the party. Besides, wrote Jacob Thompson, "Kossuth is not the man to give any assurances in your behalf on any subject, least of all, of your views of Foreign policy."[37]

V.

Kossuth's personal integrity reached its nadir during these weeks. Upon his arrival in the United States he had assured the public, "I would

states, and to sustain and advance among them constitutional liberty by continuing to resist all monopolies and exclusive legislation for the benefit of the few at the expense of the many, and by a vigilant and constant adherence to those principles and compromises of the Constitution which are broad enough to embrace and uphold the Union as it is, and the Union as it should be, in the full expansion of the energies and capacity of this great and progressive people." McKee, *National Conventions*, p. 76; Porter, *National Platforms*, p. 18. Sanders edited that article to read, "That in view of the condition of popular institutions in the old world, a high and sacred duty is devolved with increased responsibility upon the Democracy of this country, as the party of the people." "Eighteen Fifty-Two and the 'Coming Man,'" *The Democratic Review* 30 (June 1852):486.

35. Ibid.

36. See "The Neutrality Law: What Does It Mean, What Prohibit and What Permit," ibid., pp. 497–512; "The Crisis in Europe. Number Two. Intervention of the United States," ibid., pp. 554–69.

37. Thompson to Pierce, June 1852, Pierce papers; I. W. Bradbury to Pierce, 30 June 1852, ibid. George Templeton Strong, *The Diary of George Templeton Strong: The Turbulent Fifties, 1850–1859*, ed., Allan Nevins and Milton Halsey Thomas, p. 98.

rather starve than rely for myself and family on foreign aid."[38] But as the interventionist movement collapsed the Magyar sought new claims on his hosts' pocketbooks. On 21 June, in his last public speech in America, he pleaded for money to bring his mother to the New World so that she might open a school in the West.[39] He was presumably referring to the same woman he had reported dead of anguish some five months earlier.[40] His mother was indeed still alive, but her health was so delicate that she could not withstand an ocean voyage; she would die in January 1853, without trying to reach America.

Such pleas were made necessary by the hopelessly tangled and insolvent financial structure Kossuth had built over the preceding months—a structure so confused and so informal that it is impossible to determine how much money he received or where it went.[41] During Kossuth's last days in the United States, the full burden of his fiscal incompetence became apparent: the Philadelphia printer who had supplied the entire stock of "Kossuth Bonds" had not yet been paid; weapons bought on credit for two dollars apiece were pawned for half that amount; two munitions factories opened by Kossuth, using exile labor, produced hundreds of thousands of bullets, among other supplies—all of which were left behind because Kossuth had not set aside money to transport them across the Atlantic.[42] Kossuth appointed C. F. Henningsen, a scoundrel whom he had been specifically advised to ignore, as agent for these supplies; later, Henningsen sold them and apparently

38. *National Era*, 18 December 1851.

39. Louis Kossuth, *The Future of Nations: In What Consists Its Security*, pp. iii–v, 44; *The New York Tribune*, 9 June 1852.

40. *Daily Union*, 9 January 1852.

41. Kossuth's tally, dated 10 June 1852, was $84,096.34 in contributions, with only $1,132.34 remaining after expenses; see Jánossy Dénes, ed., *A Kossuth-Emigráció Angliában és Amerikában, 1851–1852*, 2:867–68. In one request for a loan, Kossuth instructed his patron that after he (Kossuth) had left for Europe, the patron was to give $600.00 to an unnamed agent who would present the matching half of a torn piece of paper; ibid., 2:935. Such practices, along with the discrepancies between newspaper reports of donations and Kossuth's announced receipts, cast doubt on the accuracy of the Hungarian's official figures.

42. Ibid., 2:930, 935, 949, 990.

kept the money.[43] And still Kossuth contracted for more munitions, simultaneously addressing frantic appeals for loans to George Sanders, Samuel Gridley Howe, even Franklin Pierce.[44]

It was at this point and probably because of these desperate circumstances that Kossuth became involved in a madcap and utterly despicable scheme to invade and conquer the black-ruled "empire" of Haiti. Months earlier, in New Orleans, Kossuth had received overtures from Col. John C. Pickett, a would-be filibusterer, regarding a possible expedition against that nation. The details, such as they were, remain sketchy. Apparently, Kossuth was to furnish ammunition, money, men, and his goodwill in the American press; Pickett was to provide additional men and military leadership. Then, operating either as allies with or as mercenaries for the white-ruled Dominican Republic, the invading forces would occupy Haiti, extort an indemnity (Kossuth's share would be one million dollars), and the battle-seasoned invaders would then presumably move to Central Europe to liberate Hungary.[45]

Kossuth's correspondence with Pickett indicates that he took the offer seriously, and by June he was telling the American people, ridiculously, that Haitian "Emperor" Faustin Elié Soulouque was a czarist agent. On his last full day in the United States, Kossuth executed a brief but sweeping authorization for Henningsen to represent him in future negotiations that would lead to the planned invasion.[46] Fortunately for Kossuth's later reputation, the scheme failed to materialize;[47] even in its preliminary form, however, it indicates the degree to which the idealism

43. Toulmin Smith to Kossuth, 2 December 1851; Kossuth to Smith, 15 January 1852; both, ibid., 1:95–98, 369–74. John H. Louis Komlos, *Kossuth in America, 1851–1852*, p. 161.

44. Jánossy, *Kossuth-Emigráció*, 2:921, 936, 987, 988–90.

45. Pickett to Kossuth, 3 May 1852, in ibid., 2:814–15; Henningsen memorandum, ibid., 2:1002–5.

46. *Kossuth in New England*, p. 105; Kossuth [to Pickett?], 13 July 1852, in Jánossy, *Kossuth-Emigráció*, 2:934.

47. Pickett traveled to Santo Domingo but apparently met new and unexpected resistance from authorities there; see Basil Rauch, *American Interest in Cuba, 1848–1855*, pp. 217–18.

of Young America might have been channeled, unknowingly, into the service of a Southern filibusterer.

And then, on 14 July, Kossuth and his wife slipped aboard the Cunard Liner *Africa* under the aliases "Mr. and Mrs. Alexander Smith."[48]

More than a month earlier, Kossuth had written his own denouement for his American mission. He told the citizens of Albany:

> More than five months have passed since my landing in New York. The novelty has long since subsided, and emotion has died away. The spell is broken which distance and misfortune cast around my name. The freshness of my very ideas is worn out. Incessant toils spread a languor upon me, unpleasant to look upon. The skill of intrigues, aspersing me with calumny; willful misrepresentations, pouring cold water upon generous sympathy. . . . And in addition to all this, the Presidential election, absorbing public attention and lowering every high aspiration into the narrow scope of party spirit, busy for party triumph; all these circumstances, and many besides too numerous to record, joined to make it probable that the last days of my wanderings on American soil would be different from those in which the hundred thousands of the 'Empire City' thundered up to the high heaven the cheers of their hurrahs, till they sounded like a defiance of a free people to the proud despots of the world.[49]

48. *The New York Tribune*, 15 July 1852.
49. Kossuth, *Select Speeches*, p. 373.

XII.

"THE SOBER SECOND THOUGHT"

Kossuth could not complain that he had not been heard. Through more than seven months he had traveled across the United States, exhorting his sympathizers to take up the burden of international morality. He had delivered more than four hundred prepared addresses, each one a variation of his central theme.[1] Newspapers had followed his progress with exhaustive and highly detailed stories, often reprinting the entire text of even his longest speeches. He had conferred with governors, congressmen, senators, and members of the cabinet, as well as with the president. As Ralph Waldo Emerson reminded him on 11 May, "You have got your story told in every palace, and log hut, and prairie camp throughout the continent."[2]

Despite that fact, the evangelical Americanism that had characterized the national mood in December 1851 had vanished. Neither Kossuth nor his American allies had succeeded in translating the emotions of Young America into a coherent, practicable foreign policy for the United States, nor had they discredited the conservative wisdom of the past. Instead, they had precipitated the collapse of the very attitude they had hoped to exploit. As Kossuth sailed out of New York harbor, new evidence of Young America's decline continued to appear.

Kossuth's war chest, built from the idealism and good faith of the

1. Andor M. Leffler, "The Kossuth Episode in America," p. 31; this number is, of course, an estimate. Kossuth addressed Americans more than a thousand times, but many of these statements were little more than impromptu remarks. Fifty speeches were significant enough to reprint in Louis Kossuth, *Select Speeches of Kossuth. Condensed and Abridged, with Kossuth's Express Sanction.*

2. Quoted in *Kossuth in New England: A Full Account of the Hungarian Governor's Visit to Massachusetts; with His Speeches, and the Addresses That Were Made to Him, carefully revised and corrected,* p. 224; George S. Boutwell, *Reminiscences of Sixty Years in Public Affairs,* p. 184.

American people, would eventually become a sizable retirement fund. Not once in his remaining three decades of life would the exile make a genuine effort to revive his revolutionary movement. Instead, he would devote his attention to an endless series of letters, begging other nations to win his battles for him and to return him to the governorship of an independent Hungary.

I.

"He entered the city with all the pomp, and ceremony, and enthusiasm, which of old attended the victorious general in a Roman triumph, and has left it secretly and in disguise, without a solitary huzza to bid him God-speed," gloated the *New York Herald* a week after Kossuth's departure. "This is, indeed, a profound depth to which Kossuth has fallen." Like many other Americans, in December, James Gordon Bennett, the editor of the *Herald*, had welcomed Kossuth as the future savior of the Old World. But by 22 July, he was ridiculing the exile's monarchical habits and "flunky character" and intimating that he had departed the country secretly to escape lawsuits being contemplated by his creditors in New York.[3]

Orestes Brownson was positively ecstatic about the Hungarian's fortunes. "Greeley's *Tribune* and Raymond's *Times* are the only journals of any note that still make a show of adhering to him," Brownson reported with little exaggeration. "The Kossuth plume has drooped, the Kossuth hat will soon go, if it has not already gone, out of fashion, and there will be few willing to remember that they ever shouted a welcome to the Magyarized Sclave."[4]

Everywhere the mood of expansiveness had disappeared. Even Kossuth's last stronghold, the German Forty-Eighters, had lost interest in Young America. In September 1852, their most radical spokesmen or-

3. *The New York Herald*, 22 July 1852.
4. "Literary Notices and Criticism," *Brownson's Quarterly Review* 6 (October 1852):552.

ganized a convention at Wheeling, Virginia, to build strategy toward American intervention in the Old World. Charles Goepp, whose latest book, *The New Rome: The United States of the World*, was then being published in New York, provided the intellectual leadership of the Wheeling conference, and the gathering adopted a series of resolutions taken from that book. Comparing the United States to the ancient Roman Empire, Goepp contemplated American expansion into Latin America, the British Empire, and finally into Europe. The result of this messianic vision was a dream of a universal republic created by the force of American arms. Neither the enthusiasm of Goepp nor the wild rhetoric of the adopted resolutions could disguise the fact that only sixteen delegates attended, from a possible 1,112. Like the rest of the nation, these German firebrands had begun to focus their attention on the domestic institutions of the United States and to make a serious effort to reform their adopted homeland.[5]

"The sober second thought has come apace. The danger is over," declared Robert Winthrop on 22 July. After recounting in frightening detail Kossuth's disruption of the nation's conservative traditions, the Massachusetts Whig pronounced Young America dead.

> The case does not now exist, nor is it within the prospect of belief that any such case will soon exist, which can tempt us to peril our own peace, to disregard our own Constitution, to trample under foot the precepts and principles of the Father of his Country, and to involve and implicate the New World, in the more than doubtful experiment of setting up republics in Europe for emperors and would-be emperors to overthrow.

Having sustained the eloquent tongue and pen of Kossuth for half a year without intervening in Europe, Winthrop concluded, "the American masses are not [now] capable of being fanaticized into such madness as this." The only lesson Kossuth could now teach the American people,

5. Dobert, "The Radicals," pp. 162–69, in A. E. Zucker, ed., *The Forty-Eighters: Political Refugees of the German Revolution of 1848*, discusses the course and aftermath of the Wheeling convention.

Winthrop said, was the dangerous power of "one earnest and heroic man . . . to agitate the mighty heart of a vast continent, and even to affect and modify the public opinion and the public affairs of the world." In Winthrop's judgment, it was not a power that Americans should encourage in the future.[6]

Others recognized different benefits from the interventionist movement. Some believed its collapse encouraged a new appreciation of Washington's Farewell Address as the touchstone of the nation's foreign policy. As the *North American Review* remarked concerning Kossuth's assault on that document:

> The result has been, not to weaken the influence of Washington's great name and divine wisdom, but to freshen, in the minds of the people, a knowledge of his doctrines. . . . American intervention in European affairs is less likely to occur since Kossuth's visit than it was before; because the people are better informed on all the bearings of the question, by the questions to which his presence and his appeals have given rise.[7]

Francis Parkman, the Unitarian preacher at Boston's New North Church and father of the historian, revealed the new fervor with which some men would now defend the Farewell. He told friends in November 1852:

> No one respects the talents of Louis Kossuth more than I do. But if the Archangel Gabriel and his brother Michael were to quit their celestial homes and come to Boston, clothed in white robes and bearing palms in their hands and should undertake to teach us the doctrines of Washington's Farewell Address—so help me heaven, not meaning to be profane, I should pluck them by their robes and say to them, go back where you came from, praise God, and mind your own business.[8]

6. Robert Winthrop, "The Obligations and Responsibilities of Educated Men in the Use of the Tongue and Pen," in *Addresses and Speeches on Various Occasions*, 2:29–30.

7. "Review, Stiles's *Austria in 1848*," p. 465.

8. Quoted in Richard Henry Dana, Jr., *The Journal of Richard Henry Dana*, 2:520.

II.

From New York, Kossuth sailed to Britain, where he lingered for years, surrounded by Giuseppe Garibaldi, Giuseppe Mazzini, and the other defeated rebels of 1848. He maintained a close relationship with George Sanders, who in 1853 wheedled a consulship from the new administration of Franklin Pierce. With all these men he plotted new revolutions on the Continent. Occasionally he smuggled documents across the channel in Sanders's diplomatic pouch.[9] He also continued a correspondence with those Americans who still sympathized with his movement; constantly he urged them to continue agitation in behalf of the interventionist cause.[10]

War in the Crimea in 1854 offered Kossuth his last real opportunity to return to Hungary as a hero. In that conflict Russia stood alone against Britain, France, and Turkey. The Hapsburg empire would collapse, Kossuth believed, if czarist power in Eastern Europe failed to survive the war. But while Sanders implored the Turkish sultan to allow Kossuth to lead an invading army up the Danube, the Magyar seemed satisfied to discharge his responsibilities to his homeland by writing long letters to the *New York Times*. In those letters, Kossuth censured the United States for refusing to declare war against Russia and contended that President Pierce was personally to blame. With bile-soaked humor, the exile proposed an essay contest and offered a prize to that American who could answer the question, "'What is the difference, for the better, between the America of President Franklin Pierce and the America of President Millard Fillmore, either in principles, diplomacy, activity, or policy?' The slightest indication of the slightest difference for the better, shall be considered a satisfactory reply," he continued. "The Democratic majority in both Houses of Congress [are] requested to act as prize judges."[11]

9. See Merle Eugene Curti, "George N. Sanders—American Patriot of the Fifties," passim.
10. See, for example, the long series of letters in the Coggeshall papers, in the collections of the Ohio State Archeological and Historical Society.
11. *The New York Times*, 23 February 1855.

Kossuth believed the entire responsibility for the future of republicanism in Europe had become the burden of the American people. Sitting in his London apartments, thousands of miles from the scene of battle, Kossuth declared, "If this war is not made a war of freedom, if the providential opportunity is spoilt, the fault . . . of it rests with America." "No man ever had a similar opportunity to become a great man, at so small a price, than President Pierce had," the exile continued bitterly. "What did he do all this while? Why! he was creating clerks and postmasters." But Kossuth was not prepared to absolve the American people from ultimate responsibility. "His was the guilt; but whose was the fault?" he demanded. "I cry out to heaven and to earth; it is yours! people of America; who accepted the shame of that nothingness from your servant, whom you could command."[12]

Kossuth's invective was ignored. Most Americans had lost interest in the prospect of extending liberty and republican institutions throughout the world. Instead, their attitude toward the Crimean War emerged from other, more traditional considerations: the hope that war would prevent Britain from interfering with America's territorial ambitions in the New World; their longstanding concern for the rights of neutral powers; and—incredibly—the heritage of friendship that many Americans now assumed to exist between their country and Russia. Ironically, it was the "Young America" administration of President Pierce that led the nation in unofficial and semiofficial support of the czar. The leading champions of the Allied cause were Whig organs and *Brownson's Quarterly Review*. Horace Greeley's *Tribune*, which had outlasted almost every other journal in support of both Kossuth and interventionism, did not bother even to choose a favorite. This war between Britain and the late villain, Russia, evoked no ideological response whatever from the American people.[13]

12. Ibid., 11 August 1855; see also, Kossuth's letter, ibid., 19 March 1855.
13. Alan Dowty, *The Limits of American Isolation: The United States and the Crimean War*, is a good interpretive study of the subject; see particularly chapter 3. See also, John G. Gazley, *American Opinion of German Unification, 1848–1871 (Studies in History, Economic and Public Law*, 191 New York, 1926): 88–89; L. Jay Oliva, "America Meets Russia, 1854."

III.

Young America did not disappear in 1852. But the movement that survived Kossuth's visit embodied a mellower, more domesticated attitude toward the world than it had possessed in December 1851. The unbridled sense of destiny that had characterized the national mood for a decade before 1852 had collapsed, the victim both of disillusionment with Kossuth and of a seven-month orgy of self-indulgence. Evangelical Americanism could not survive the experience. By 1853, Andrew Johnson's election to the Senate on a platform of free homesteads seemed to the Cleveland *True Democrat* the epitome of "expansive Young America."[14] When the movement focused on foreign policy at all, it seemed best embodied in William Marcy's famous Dress Circular, or in his insistence that only "the American language" appear in diplomatic correspondence. Both directives were pious reaffirmations of republican simplicity and, perhaps, genuine efforts to reform the world by example, rather than by active interference in the affairs of other states. Marcy's gestures, regardless of the motives behind them, contained a mere shadow of the urgency and moral fervor that once had typified the movement. They represented not Young America, but its decline.

14. Cleveland *True Democrat*, 11 August 1853, quoted in Siert Riepma, "Young America," p. 208n.

XIII.

YOUNG AMERICA AND THE DIPLOMACY OF SYMBOLISM

Diplomacy, like war, reveals the fundamental values of any society. The process by which a nation identifies its interests, the nature of those interests, and the tactics employed to pursue them all emerge from the social and intellectual patterns that define that state and that society.

For those who subscribed to its principles, Young America captured the internal strength, vigor, and vision of a people purposefully at war with tradition and its presumed handmaiden, tyranny. To those critics who rejected its appeal, that crusade seemed a misshapen and awkward caricature of the American dream, a movement at best quixotic and at worst malign. But from either perspective, Young America was a function of its particular time and place—a welding of two explosive forces, nationalism and altruism, which often are found in conflict.

I.

Louis Kossuth did not invent Young America. On the contrary, that movement evolved from four separate impulses, three of which were anchored firmly within the domestic history of the United States. Most general of these ingredients was the centuries-old awareness among the American people that they possessed a special mission among the nations of the world. "Mission" is one of those abstractions for which it is impossible to find a precise definition. At various times in their history Americans have translated the word into political, religious, philosophical, and even economic terms; but always it has implied a liberal dose of altruism—a seeming eagerness to bear any burden in furthering the redemption of a less than worthy world. By the 1840s, at least on the level of rhetoric, this peculiarly American calling was firmly entrenched in the nation's mythology.

If mission was the collective conscience of the American people, nationalism was their collective ego. Americans of the 1840s rode the crest of a strident nationalism perhaps unequaled at any other point of the nineteenth century. Whether rallying to the banner of Manifest Destiny or contemplating, with Edwin De Leon and Ralph Waldo Emerson, the mediocrity of the outside world, that decade Americans discovered within themselves those selfish aspirations for the future which distinguish true nationalism from mere cultural pride. And with that discovery came—as indicated during the Mexican War—the martial spirit required to satisfy their ambitions.

A third component in Young America was the nation's perception of progress. As Lewis Cass, Daniel Webster, and even John C. Calhoun agreed, progress was an inevitable attribute of the modern world. Yet the inescapability of that process did not necessarily imply that the United States should passively await its arrival. Between 1848 and 1852, Young Americans believed that they were the most advanced exponents of progress and felt a special obligation to hurry it along its way. Despite its inherent irony, this was not the first time a dynamic and activist ideology had fomented change in the name of historical inevitability, nor would it be the last.

And fourth among the impulses toward Young America was the revolutionary fervor of 1848 in Europe. Those midcentury revolutions provided most obviously the spark that ignited the evangelical phase of the movement. But they also offered confirmation, to those who wished to find it, that their nation's mission was a righteous one—that America's special values, hacked from a wilderness on the edge of Western civilization, were those for which other men would also fight and die. Thus by 1848 the United States had discovered in its traditional Mission, its newly perceived power, and the revolutions of 1848 the motive, means, and opportunity to adopt a crusading spirit toward the Old World.

II.

And yet from any reasonable perspective, a military or even a diplomatic crusade for the independence of an ethnic minority half a world away seems alien to the intellectual milieu of the midnineteenth century; that earnest public officials seriously debated the wisdom of such a course seems equally unexplainable. There were, after all, other questions of infinitely greater urgency, many of them embodying nothing less than the survival of the Union. Indeed, measured against such crucial choices, the fate of Louis Kossuth's already shattered revolution shrinks into profound insignificance. That this is so suggests that the Kossuth episode possessed symbolic as well as inherent importance for the American people and that Kossuth's appeal transcended the question of Hungary or even of Europe.

Most obviously, Young America symbolized those ideas that had given it birth—mission, nationalism, progress. At this level Young America was the celebration of an idealized expression of the nation's self-perception—of exaggerated virtues and a unique capacity to sway the world. And it was also at this level that Louis Kossuth most fully appreciated—and exploited—his hosts. In almost all of his important speeches Kossuth repeated a single theme: that the United States was no longer simply the mecca of republicanism but had become its arsenal as well. Even when he bullied his hosts, as he did regularly, he reinforced this theme by challenging them to accept their destined role as a world power.

This level of symbolism is revealed also in the Young Americans' image of Russia as the stereotypical negation of everything for which their movement stood. Despite generally favorable relations between the Russian and United States governments throughout the nineteenth century, and despite the obvious fact that it was Austria and not Russia that had owned and presumably tyrannized the Hungarian people for centuries, it was nevertheless Russia that bore the brunt of Young America rhetoric throughout the period 1848–1852. In the eyes of Young Americans, that nation's' despotic government contradicted every political and social value to which the American people subscribed; the czar's self-proclaimed role as the guardian of stability in Eastern Europe seemed a reactionary force, poised at any moment to destroy those who wished to follow the United States' revolutionary example; and his ambition to play a larger role in the European balance of power positively marked him as a menace to the future of Western civilization. For all these reasons Russia's graphic representation as a bear held more than passing significance: like its symbol that nation seemed huge, aggressive, greedy, and completely amoral.

It may be an exaggeration to assert that this perceived conflict between Russia and the United States reflected the dualism inherent in Western ethical schemes. Nevertheless the suggestion holds thematic appeal. Two huge nations, each expansive and expanding, and each destined, as Tocqueville had predicted nearly two decades earlier, to sway the future of half the globe—the theme recurs again and again in the rhetoric of Young America. It is worth repeating here that this vision won its fullest expression in Henry Winter Davis's apocalyptic and avowedly dualistic volume, *The War of Ormuzd and Ahriman in the Nineteenth Century*, in which Davis adopted the ancient Zoroastrian images of light and darkness, good and evil, as symbols for the United States and Russia. Such symbolism held special relevance for Americans in 1848, for that generation was torn internally by a variety of domestic issues, at least two of which—slavery and the Mexican War—had sparked intense debate about the nation's moral sense.

But it was the relationship between Young America and slavery that evoked the most intriguing and greatest variety of symbolic responses. The association between Hungarian freedom and domestic slavery was inescapably clear—as clear as the rhetoric employed toward both subjects. No American could praise "freedom" and "independence" and "liberty" in Hungary without noticing the simultaneous absence of those rights among the black slaves at home. And if someone could have somehow temporarily compartmentalized the contemporary perception of these issues, the compartmentalization would have collapsed under the weight of abolitionist reminders. Within the rhetorical framework of Young America, freedom was good and slavery was bad and there were few nuances that could be drawn to qualify either judgment. Thus abolitionists endorsed Kossuth as long as he was a symbol for abstract freedom and abandoned him when he refused to cooperate with them, while more moderate opponents of slavery clung to Kossuth throughout his American tour.

And for Southerners too Young America (and Kossuth) possessed significance on more than one level. To many Yankee contemporaries, Southern opposition was easily explained: Kossuth's dilemma was identical to that of the slaves, and Southerners chose to reject Kossuth's pleas because they consciously recognized that fact. Such an explanation contained more than a grain of truth, for there were important voices in the South who perceived the analogy and responded to it, labeling Kossuth a Trojan horse who could, without ever mentioning slavery, undermine its philosophical and political defense.

But such an explanation is ultimately flawed, for it assumes that the South's was a one-dimensional civilization—a society identical to the North's except for the presence of slaves. It was not. Slavery, and the need for Southern thinkers to rationalize its existence, had created a society holding values remarkably different from those in the Northern states. For decades influential Southerners had denied the universality of human freedom; indeed, they had predicated their civilization on such a rejection. And from that judgment had flowed a variety of other conclusions—conclusions questioning the merits of capitalism, women's rights, unbridled democracy, and a host of other current "reforms." Southerners rejected Young America not only because it smacked of abolitionism; they rejected it because Young America and abolitionism (and a host of other "isms") violated the zeitgeist of that slaveholding region.

It was therefore unnecessary for Southerners to associate Young America with antislavery in order to reject it. They held already a logically consistent and theoretically sound approach to foreign policy, which excluded movements such as Young America regardless of their connection with other issues. Their approach was, in fact, intellectually superior to that of the Young Americans: its premises were more carefully drawn, its logic was more rigorously applied, its conclusions were more reflective of reality and more accurately analogous to the nation's (and the world's) diplomatic history. To such men mission was a romantic fiction, progress was a dangerous and degenerative force, and altruism was at best a diplomatic absurdity. To argue, as did Horace Mann and others, that Southerners constructed these elaborate theories merely to disguise their presumed sensitivity about slavery is to ignore the intellectual divorce that separated Northern Americans from Southern Americans during the decades before the Civil War. And if that divorce had its roots in the slavery question, by 1848 it had become more pervasive and much more fundamental.

Young America did possess symbolic significance in the South, therefore. It represented the strange eccentricities and enthusiasms that defined the Northern mind in the Southern press; it shared the rhetoric of Garrison and Douglass; and its interventionist catchwords struck Southerners as dangerous precedents at home as well as abroad. But while Young America's symbolic content was central to its appeal among many Northerners, that same symbolism was but a nuance in the South. Far more revealing was the literalness of that section's spokesmen and the skewed lines on which they and the Young Americans interacted.

III.

If Louis Kossuth did not invent Young America, he did exploit it deftly. In the minds of his supporters he was a republican and a revolutionary, a hero cut from the same cloth as Washington. And with a thoroughly disarming mixture of humility, conceit, idealism, grasping practicality, eloquent flattery, and biting contempt, he maintained that image through months of constant public exposure.

And yet it was also Kossuth who ultimately weakened that movement. By December 1851, the principles of Young America as they pertained to Europe were nearly four years old; in less precise form they were much older still. Kossuth's arrival in the New World did not raise his supporters to a new and higher plateau of sustained commitment to its principles. On the contrary, it sparked the emotional climax of that movement and its principles—a climax that followed Kossuth from New York to Washington, through the West and into New England. Kossuth drained the fervor that his adherents had expressed before his arrival. Rather than function as the spark needed to inaugurate an interventionist foreign policy, Kossuth served as a lightning rod, attracting the energy of the Young Americans to his own presence, energy that spent itself impotently in demonstrations and resolutions.

More subtly, perhaps, Kossuth also weakened Young America by wrenching it from its symbolic context and by intruding it into the arena of rational debate. Whatever the extent of his personal commitment to the abstractions he represented, Kossuth's primary loyalty was to Hungarian independence. He repeated that fact endlessly, in nearly every speech, in nearly every town. When Young Americans praised him with generalizations he responded with concrete demands; when they offered him the endorsement of enlightened opinion he pronounced such support worthless; when they sought to lump him by analogy with issues unrelated to Hungary he scorned such identification and reminded his hosts of why he had crossed the Atlantic.

It was by this process that Kossuth forced the Young Americans to recognize the reality of his appeal, and its literal meaning; and confronted by that reality the entire crusade collapsed, the victim, as Henry Clay had earlier predicted, of its "want of sympathy between the premises and conclusion." Among the Garrisonians that revelation carried with it a wildly emotional condemnation of Kossuth; for other men, as for Lewis Cass and Daniel Webster, the process was less sensational but no less dramatic. As the Senate debates of February 1852 proved clearly, Young America could not stand the test of literal and rational examination.

BIBLIOGRAPHY

MANUSCRIPT COLLECTIONS

Edmund Burke papers. Manuscript Division, Library of Congress, Washington, D.C.

John M. Clayton papers. Manuscript Division, Library of Congress, Washington, D.C.

John Hartwell Cocke papers. Manuscript Division, Alderman Library, University of Virginia, Charlottesville.

John J. Crittenden papers. Manuscript Division, Library of Congress, Washington, D.C.

Andrew Jackson Donelson papers. Manuscript Division, Library of Congress, Washington, D.C.

Daniel Drake papers. Collections of the Cincinnati Historical Society, Cincinnati, Ohio.

Louis Kossuth papers. Manuscript Division, Library of Congress, Washington, D.C., and in Collections of the Ohio State Archeological and Historical Society, Columbus, Ohio.

William L. Marcy papers. Manuscript Division, Library of Congress, Washington, D.C.

Franklin Pierce papers. Manuscript Division, Library of Congress, Washington, D.C.

Isaac Strohm papers. From the Collections of the Cincinnati Historical Society, Cincinnati, Ohio.

Martin Van Buren papers. Manuscript Division, Library of Congress, Washington, D.C.

PUBLISHED PAPERS

Calhoun, John Caldwell. *Correspondence of John C. Calhoun, Annual Report of the American Historical Association for the Year 1899*, vol. 2. Edited by James Franklin Jameson. Washington, D.C., 1900.

Channing, William Francis. "A Letter from Dr. William Francis Channing to Louis Kossuth." Edited by Russell M. Jones. *The New England Quarterly*, 39 (March 1966) :88–93.

Dana, Richard Henry, Jr. *The Journal of Richard Henry Dana*. Edited by Robert F. Lucid. 3 vols. Cambridge, 1968.

Dickinson, Daniel S. *Speeches, Correspondence, etc., of the Late Daniel S. Dickinson, of New York. . . .* Edited by John R. Dickinson. 2 vols. New York, 1867.

Douglas, Stephen A. *The Letters of Stephen A. Douglas*. Edited by Robert W. Johannsen. Urbana, 1961.

Emerson, Ralph Waldo. *The Complete Works of Ralph Waldo Emerson in Six Volumes*. Edited by Edward W. Emerson. 6 vols. New York, 1923.

Fillmore, Millard. *Publications of the Buffalo Historical Society: Millard Fillmore Papers*. Edited by Frank H. Severance. 10 vols. Buffalo, New York, 1907.

Howe, Samuel Gridley. *Letters and Journals of Samuel Gridley Howe*. Edited by Laura E. Richards. 2 vols. Boston, 1909,

Kossuth, Louis. *The Future of Nations: In What Consists Its Security*. New York, 1852.

————. "A Letter of Louis Kossuth." Edited by Heinrich H. Maurer. *Journal of Modern History*, 2 (1930) :66–67.

————. *Select Speeches of Kossuth. Condensed and Abridged, with Kossuth's Express Sanction*. Edited by Francis W. Newman. New York, 1854.

Lincoln, Abraham. *The Collected Works of Abraham Lincoln*. Edited by Roy P. Basler. 9 vols. New Brunswick, New Jersey, 1953.

Marsh, George Perkins. *Life and Letters of George Perkins Marsh*. Edited by Caroline Crane Marsh. 2 vols. New York, 1888.

Phillips, Wendell. *Speeches, Lectures and Letters by Wendell Phillips*. Edited by Theodore Calvin Pease. Boston, 1891.

Seward, William H. *The Works of William H. Seward*. Edited by George E. Baker. 5 vols. Boston, 1887.

Strong, George Templeton. *The Diary of George Templeton Strong: The Turbulent Fifties, 1850–1859*. Edited by Allan Nevins and Milton Halsey Thomas. New York, 1952.

Sumner, Charles. *Charles Sumner: His Complete Works*. 20 vols. New York, 1969.

Sumner, William Graham. *Essays of William Graham Sumner*. Edited by

Albert Galloway Keller and Maurice R. Davies. 2 vols. New York, 1934.

Washington, George. *The Writings of George Washington, from the Original Manuscript Sources, 1745–1799*. Edited by John C. Fitzpatrick. 39 vols. Washington, D.C., 1931.

Webster, Daniel. *The Letters of Daniel Webster*. Edited by C. H. Van Tyne. New York, 1902.

———. *Works of Daniel Webster*. Boston, 1877.

———. *Writings and Speeches of Daniel Webster*. 18 vols. Boston, 1903.

Winthrop, Robert. *Addresses and Speeches on Various Occasions*. 2 vols. Boston, 1867.

CONTEMPORARY SOURCES AND PERIODICALS

The Advocate of Peace. 1848–1852.

Abel, Annie Heloise, and Frank J. Klingberg, eds. *A Sidelight on Anglo-American Relations, 1839–1858*. Lancaster, Pennsylvania, 1910.

Appleton's Cyclopaedia of American Biography.

Boardman, H. A. *The New Doctrine of Intervention, Tried by the Teachings of Washington*. Philadelphia, 1852.

Boutwell, George S. *Reminiscences of Sixty Years in Public Affairs*. 2 vols. New York, 1902.

Brace, Charles L. *Hungary in 1851, with an Experience of the Austrian Police*. New York, 1852.

Brownson's Quarterly Review.

Cass, Lewis. *Address . . . Before the Association of the Alumni of Hamilton College*. Utica, N.Y., 1830.

Conway, Moncure Daniel. *Autobiography, Memories and Experiences*. 2 vols. Boston, 1904.

Davis, Henry Winter. *The War of Ormuzd and Ahriman in the Nineteenth Century*. Baltimore, 1852.

De Leon, Edwin. *The Positions and Duties of Young America*. Charleston, 1845.

Dénes, Jánossy, ed. *A Kossuth-Emigráció Angliában és Amerikában, 1851–1852*. 2 vols. Budapest, 1844.

Dewey, Orville. *Autobiography and Letters of Orville Dewey, D.D.* Edited by Mary E. Dewey. Boston, 1884.

DePuy, Henry W. *Kossuth and His Generals*. Buffalo, N.Y., 1858.

Ellis, John Tracy, ed. *Documents in American Catholic History*. Milwaukee, 1956.

Fitzhugh, George. *Cannibals All! or Slaves Without Masters*. Edited by C. Vann Woodward. Cambridge, 1960.

Garrison, William Lloyd. *Letter to Louis Kossuth Concerning Freedom and Slavery in the U.S*. Boston, 1852.

Giddings, Joshua. *History of the Rebellion: Its Authors and Causes*. New York, 1864.

[Goepp, Charles]. *E Pluribus Unum: A Political Tract on Kossuth and America*. Philadelphia, 1852.

Green, Duff. *Facts and Suggestions: Biographical, Historical, Financial and Political, Addressed to the People of the United States*. New York, 1866.

Headley, Phineas Camp. *The Life of Louis Kossuth . . . Including . . . His Principal Speeches*. Auburn, N.Y., 1852.

Helper, Hinton Rowan. *The Impending Crisis of the South: How to Meet It*. New York, 1857.

Jay, William. *The Kossuth Excitement*. Boston, 1852.

Kossuth, Louis. *Memories of My Exile*. Translated by Ferencz Jausz. New York, 1880.

Kossuth in New England: A Full Account of the Hungarian Governor's Visit to Massachusetts; with His Speeches, and the Addresses That Were Made to Him, carefully revised and corrected. Boston, 1852.

The Liberty Bell. 1852.

Living Age. 1851–1852.

McClure, Alexander K. *Colonel Alexander K. McClure's Recollections of Half a Century*. Salem, Mass., 1902.

McKee, Thomas Hudson, ed. *The National Conventions and Platforms of All Political Parties, 1789 to 1900: Convention, Popular and Electoral Vote*. Baltimore, 1900.

National Cyclopaedia of American Biography.

The North American Review. 1848–1852.

Pike, James S. *First Blows of the Civil War: The Ten Years of Preliminary Conflict in the United States. From 1850 to 1860. A Contemporaneous Exposition. . . .* New York, 1879.

Porter, Kirk H., and Donald Bruce Johnson, eds. *National Party Platforms, 1840–1956.* Urbana, Ill., 1956.

Proceedings at the Banquet of the Jackson Democratic Association, Washington, Eighth of January, 1852. Washington, D.C., 1852.

Pulszky, Francis, and Theresa Pulszky. *White, Red, Black: Sketches of American Society in the United States During the Visit of Their Guests.* 2 vols. New York, 1853.

Sargent, Nathan. *Public Men and Events from the Commencement of Mr. Monroe's Administration, in 1817, to the Close of Mr. Fillmore's Administration, in 1853.* 2 vols. Philadelphia, 1875.

Seward, Frederick W. *Reminiscences of a War-Time Statesman and Diplomat, 1830–1915.* New York, 1916.

Skinner, P. H. *The Welcome of Louis Kossuth to Philadelphia, by the Youth.* Philadelphia, 1852.

Tefft, Benjamin. *Hungary and Kossuth.* Philadelphia, 1852.

United States Democratic Review. 1848–1852.

GOVERNMENT DOCUMENTS CITED

American State Papers, Foreign Relations. 6 vols. Washington, D.C., 1833–1859.

Congressional Globe. 29th Cong., 1st sess.; 30th Cong., 1st sess.; 31st Cong., 1st sess.; 31st Cong., 2d sess.; 32d Cong., 1st sess.

Records of the Department of State, National Archives, Record Group 59: Microfilm Publications M46, Role 14; M77, Role 162; M99, Role 27; T220, Role 5

Special Missions, Volume 1

Messages and Papers of the Presidents, ed. James D. Richardson. 11 vols. Washington, D.C., 1896.

U.S. Congress, House of Representatives. *Documents.*

———. *Journal of the House of Representatives,* 32d Cong., 1st sess.

U.S. Congress, Senate. *Executive Documents,* 32d Cong., 1st sess., 8, no. 78.

———. *Journal of the Senate,* 31st Cong., 1st sess.

———. *Senate Documents,* 31st Cong., 1st sess., 10, no. 43; 32d Cong., 1st sess., 8, no. 78; 61st Cong., 2d sess., 58, no. 279.

Resolves Passed by the Legislature of Massachusetts. 1852.

NEWSPAPERS, 1848–1852

Albany (New York) *Argus.*
Baltimore, Maryland, *American and Commercial Daily Advertiser.*
The Baltimore Clipper.
The Baltimore Sun.
Brownlow's Knoxville (Tennessee) *Whig, and Independent Journal.*
Charleston (South Carolina) *Courier.*
Cincinnati, Ohio, *Daily Enquirer.*
Detroit, Michigan, *Free Press.*
Huntsville, Alabama, *Southern Advocate.*
The Liberator.
The (London) *Times.*
Macon *Georgia Telegraph*
Natchez *Mississippi Free Trader.*
The National Anti-Slavery Standard.
New Orleans, Louisiana, *Daily Picayune.*
The New York Herald.
The New York Independent.
New York, *Morning Courier and New York Enquirer.*
The New York Times.
The New York Tribune.
New York *Young America!*
The Oquawka (Illinois) *Spectator.*
The Daily Scioto (Ohio) *Gazette.*
Rochester, New York, *Frederick Douglass's Paper.*
Vicksburg (Mississippi) *Weekly Whig.*
Washington, D.C., *Daily Union.*
Washington, D.C., *The National Era.*
Washington, D.C., *National Intelligencer.*
Washington, D.C., *Republic.*
Worchester, Massachusetts, *Burritt's Christian Citizen.*

UNPUBLISHED STUDIES

Campbell, Randolph Bluford. "Henry Clay and the Emerging Nations of

Latin America, 1815–1829." Ph. D. dissertation, University of Virginia, 1966.

Golladay, V. Dennis. "The Nicholas Family of Virginia, 1722–1820." Ph. D. dissertation, University of Virginia, 1973.

Leffler, Andor M. "The Kossuth Episode in America." Ph. D. dissertation, Western Reserve University, 1949.

Riepma, Siert. "Young America." Ph. D. dissertation, Western Reserve University, 1939.

Szeplaki, Joseph. "'The Nation's Guest': Bibliography on Louis Kossuth, Governor of Hungary with Special Reference to His Trip in the United States, December 4, 1851–July 14, 1852." Mimeograph study available from Ohio University Library, Athens, Ohio, 1972.

BOOKS

Bancroft, Frederic. *The Life of William H. Seward.* 2 vols. New York, 1900.

Bartlett, Irving H. *Wendell Phillips, Brahmin Radical.* Boston, 1961.

Beecher, William C., and Samuel Scoville. *A Biography of Rev. Henry Ward Beecher.* New York, 1888.

Benson, Lee. *The Concept of Jacksonian Democracy: New York as a Test Case.* Princeton, 1961.

Billington, Ray Allen. *The Protestant Crusade, 1800–1860: A Study of the Origins of American Nativism.* New York, 1938.

Blumenthal, Henry. *A Reappraisal of Franco-American Relations, 1830–1871.* Chapel Hill, N. C., 1959.

Brown, Samuel Gilman. *The Life of Rufus Choate.* Boston, 1870.

Brownson, Henry B. *Life of Orestes Brownson.* 3 vols. Detroit, 1898–1901.

Capers, Gerald A. *Stephen A. Douglas, Defender of the Union.* Boston, 1959.

Commager, Henry Steele, *The Search for a Usable Past.* New York, 1967.

Crouthamen, James R. *James Watson Webb: A Biography.* Middleton, Conn., 1969.

Curti, Merle Eugene. *Austria and the United States, 1848–1852: A Study in Diplomatic History.* Smith College Studies in History 11 (April 1926).

Dalzell, Robert F., Jr. *Daniel Webster and the Trial of American Nationalism, 1843–1852.* Boston, 1973.

Dowty, Alan. *The Limits of American Isolation: The United States and the Crimean War.* New York, 1971.

Dunbar, Willis Frederick. *Lewis Cass.* Grand Rapids, Mich., 1970.

Eaton, Clement. *Freedom of Thought in the Old South.* Durham, N. C., 1940.

Einstein, Lewis. "Lewis Cass," *The American Secretaries of State and Their Diplomacy,* vol. 6. Edited by Samuel Flagg Bemis. New York, 1958.

Ekirch, Arthur A., Jr. *The Idea of Progress in America, 1815–1860.* New York, 1944.

————. *Ideas, Ideals and American Diplomacy: A History of Their Growth and Interaction.* New York, 1966.

Elkins, Stanley. *Slavery: A Problem in American Institutional and Intellectual Life.* New York, 1959.

Ettinger, Amos Aschbach. *The Mission to Spain of Pierre Soulé, 1853–1855: A Study in the Cuban Diplomacy of the United States.* New Haven, 1932.

Fellman, Michael. *The Unbounded Frame: Freedom and Community in Nineteenth Century American Utopianism.* Westport, Conn., 1973.

Filler, Louis. *The Crusade Against Slavery, 1830–1860.* New York, 1960.

Fogel, Robert W., and Stanley E. Engerman. *Time on the Cross: The Economics of American Negro Slavery.* 2 vols. Boston, 1974.

Foner, Eric. *Free Soil, Free Labor, Free Men: The Ideology of the Republican Party Before the Civil War.* Oxford, 1970.

Formisano, Ronald P. *The Birth of Mass Political Parties: Michigan, 1827–1861.* Princeton, 1971.

Fredrickson, George M. *The Inner Civil War: Northern Intellectuals and the Crisis of the Union.* New York, 1965.

Fuller, J. D. F. *The Movement for the Acquisition of All Mexico, 1846–1848.* Baltimore, 1936.

Garrett, William. *Reminiscences of Public Men in Alabama, for Thirty Years.* Atlanta, 1872.

Garrison, Wendell Phillips. *William Lloyd Garrison, 1805–1879.* 4 vols. Boston, 1889.

Gazley, John G. *American Opinion of German Unification, 1848–1871,* in *Studies in History, Economics and Public Law,* 191, 1926.

Genovese, Eugene. *The Political Economy of Slavery.* New York, 1965.

Graebner, Norman A. *Ideas and Diplomacy.* New York, 1964.

Griffis, William Eliot. *Millard Fillmore: Constructive Statesman*. Ithaca, N.Y., 1915.

Hamilton, Holmon. *Zachary Taylor: Soldier in the White House*. Indianapolis, 1951.

Handlin, Oscar. *Boston's Immigrants: A Study in Acculturation*. New York, 1968.

Higham, John. *From Boundlessness to Consolidation: The Transformation of American Culture, 1848–1860*. Ann Arbor, 1969.

Hofstadter, Richard. *The American Political Tradition and the Men Who Made It*. New York, 1948.

Holcombe, John W., and Hobert M. Skinner. *Life and Public Services of Thomas A. Hendricks, with Selected Speeches and Writings*. Indianapolis, 1886.

Johannsen, Robert W. *Stephen A. Douglas*. New York, 1973.

King, Alvy L. *Louis T. Wigfall: Southern Fire-eater*. Baton Rouge, 1970.

Komlos, John H. *Lewis Kossuth in America, 1851–1852*. Buffalo, 1973.

Lasserman, Max M. *The American Impact on Russia: Diplomatic and Ideological, 1784–1917*. New York, 1950.

Louis Kossuth, as He Was Known to His Contemporaries. Pittsburgh, 1902.

Lowenthal, David. *George Perkins Marsh, Versatile Vermonter*. New York, 1958.

McMaster, John Bach. *A History of the People of the United States, from the Revolution to the Civil War*. 8 vols. New York, 1883–1913.

McWhiney, Grady. *Southerners and Other Americans*. New York, 1973.

Mann, Mary Peabody. *Life of Horace Mann*. Washington, D.C., 1937.

Marshall, Hugh. *Orestes Brownson and the American Republic: An Historical Perspective*. Washington, D.C., 1971.

May, Arthur M. *Contemporary American Opinion of the Mid-Century Revolutions in Central Europe*. Philadelphia, 1927.

May, Robert E. *The Southern Dream of a Caribbean Empire, 1854–1861*. Baton Rouge, 1973.

Merk, Frederick. *Manifest Destiny and Mission in American History: A Reinterpretation*. New York, 1963.

Milton, George Fort. *The Eve of Conflict: Stephen A. Douglas and the Needless War*. Boston, 1934.

Neilson, Joseph. *Memories of Rufus Choate, with Some Considerations of*

His Studies, Methods, and Opinions, and of His Style as a Speaker and Writer. Boston, 1884.

Nevins, Allan. *Ordeal of the Union.* 2 vols. New York, 1947.

Nichols, Roy F. *Franklin Pierce: Young Hickory of the Granite Hills.* Philadelphia, 1931.

————. *The Democratic Machine, 1850–1854.* New York, 1923.

Noonan, Carroll John. *Nativism in Connecticut, 1829–1860.* Washington, D.C., 1938.

Parker, Edward Griffin. *Reminiscences of Rufus Choate, the Great American Advocate.* New York, 1860.

Parrington, Vernon Louis, *Main Currents in American Thought: From the Beginnings to 1920.* 3 vols. New York, 1930.

Peterson, Merrill D. *The Jefferson Image in the American Mind.* New York, 1960.

Pivany, Eugene. *Webster and Kossuth: A Discourse on the Relations of Daniel Webster and Louis Kossuth.* Philadelphia, 1909.

Price, Glenn W. *Origins of the War with Mexico: The Polk-Stockton Intrigue.* Austin, Tex., 1967.

Rauch, Basil. *American Interest in Cuba, 1848–1855.* New York, 1948.

Rayback, Robert J. *Millard Fillmore: Biography of a President.* Buffalo, N.Y., 1959.

Richards, Laura E. *Samuel Gridley Howe.* New York, 1935.

Rohan, Jack. *Yankee Arms Maker.* New York, 1935.

Roseboom, Eugene H. *The Civil War Era,* vol. 4 in *The History of the State of Ohio.* Edited by Carl Wittke. Columbus, Ohio, 1944.

Sewell, Robert H. *John P. Hale and the Politics of Abolition.* Cambridge, 1965.

Sherwin, Oscar. *Prophet of Liberty: The Life and Times of Wendell Phillips.* New York, 1958.

Smith, W. L. G. *The Life and Times of Lewis Cass.* New York, 1856.

Spengler, Oswald. *The Decline of the West.* Translated by Charles Francis Atkinson. London, 1926.

————. *Man and Technics: A Contribution to a Philosophy of Life.* Translated by Charles Francis Atkinson. London, 1932.

Stewart, James Brewer. *Joshua R. Giddings and the Tactics of Radical Politics.* Cleveland, 1970.

Széplaki, Joseph. *Louis Kossuth: "The Nation's Guest," A Bibliography on His Trip in the United States, December 4, 1851–July 14, 1852.* Ligonier, Penn., 1976.

Thomas, Benjamin Platt. *Russo-American Relations, 1815–1867.* Baltimore, 1930.

Thompson, William Y. *Robert Toombs of Georgia.* Baton Rouge, 1966.

Tolis, Peter. *Elihu Burritt: Crusader for Brotherhood.* Hamden, Conn., 1968.

Tyler, Alice Felt. *Freedom's Ferment: Phases of American Social History from the Colonial Period to the Outbreak of the Civil War.* Rochester, Minn., 1944.

Tyler, Lyon G. *The Letters and Times of the Tylers.* 2 vols. Richmond, Va., 1885.

Van Deusen, Glyndon G. *The Life of Henry Clay.* Boston, 1937.

————. *William Henry Seward.* New York, 1967.

Wish, Harvey. *George Fitzhugh: Propagandist of the Old South.* Baton Rouge, 1943.

Wittke, Carl. *Refugees of Revolution.* Philadelphia, 1952.

Woodford, Frank B. *Lewis Cass: The Last Jeffersonian.* New Brunswick, N. J., 1950.

Younger, Edward. *John A. Kasson: Politics and Diplomacy from Lincoln to McKinley.* Iowa City, 1955.

Zucker, A. E., ed. *The Forty-Eighters: Political Refugees of the German Revolution of 1848.* New York, 1950.

ARTICLES

Curti, Merle Eugene. "George N. Sanders—American Patriot of the Fifties." *South Atlantic Quarterly* 27 (January 1928) :79–87.

————. "Young America." *American Historical Review* 32 (October 1926) : 34–49.

Leffler, Andor M. "Kossuth Comes to Cleveland." *Ohio State Archeological and Historical Society Quarterly* 56 (April 1947) :242–57.

Luthin, Reinhard. "A Visitor from Hungary." *South Atlantic Quarterly* 47 (January 1948) :29–34.

Mead, David. "Brownson and Kossuth in Cincinnati." Historical and Philosophical Society of Ohio *Bulletin* (April 1949) :90–94.

Moore, John Bassett. "Kossuth: A Sketch of a Revolutionist." *Political Science Quarterly* 10 (March 1895) :95–131; (June 1895) :257–91.

Oliva, L. Jay. "America Meets Russia, 1854." *Journalism Quarterly* 40 (Winter 1968) :65–69.

Oliver, John W. "Louis Kossuth's Appeal to the Middle West." *Mississippi Valley Historical Review* 14 (March 1928) :481–95.

Pratt, Julius. "The Origins of 'Manifest Destiny.' " *American Historical Review* 32 (July 1927) :795–800.

Rogers, William Warren. "The 'Nation's Guest' in Louisiana: Kossuth Visits New Orleans." *Louisiana History* 9 (Fall 1968) :355–64.

Shewmaker, Kenneth E. "Daniel Webster and the Politics of Foreign Policy, 1850–1852." *Journal of American History* 63 (September 1976) :303–15.

Spencer, Donald S. "Lewis Cass and 'Symbolic Intervention':1848–1852." *Michigan History* 53 (Spring 1969) :1–17.

Trautmann, Fredrick. "Kossuth in Indiana." *Indiana Magazine of History* 43 (December 1967) :299–314.

Urban, C. Stanley. "The Ideology of Southern Imperialism: New Orleans and the Caribbean, 1845–1860." *Louisiana Historical Quarterly* 39 (January 1956) :48–73.

INDEX

Abolitionists: described, 65–66; and Kossuth, 66–81; mentioned, 12, 22, 64, 76, 80, 109, 148, 181–83
Adams, John Quincy: mentioned, 32
Africa: Kossuth departs on, 168
Allen, William: on French Revolution (1848), 15–16; mentioned, 21
Allen, William G.: quoted condemning Kossuth, 79
American (Baltimore), 29
American Bible Society: elects Kossuth vice president, 62
Atlantic and Pacific Telegraph Company, 57
Austria: seeks Kossuth's extradition from Turkey, 2, 36; move to suspend relations with, 31–35, 74, 142; and Mann mission, 38–39; mentioned, 1, 2, 14, 22, 24, 27, 30, 31–32, 36, 37, 40, 44, 54, 55, 68–69, 90–91, 104, 126, 129, 173

Baermann, Thomas: supports Kossuth, 163
Bailey, Gamaliel: as interventionist, 108–9; mentioned 24, 69, 162
Baltimore *American. See American* (Baltimore)
Baltimore Clipper: quoted opposing interventionism, 103
Baltimore Sun: quoted, 121
Bar Association (New York): donates to Kossuth, 57; banquet of, 63
Barnes, Isaac O.: supports Kossuth, 163
Batthianyi, Casimir: criticizes Kossuth, 146–47
Beecher, Henry Ward: raises funds for Kossuth, 57; compares U.S. and Austria, 69
Bennett, James Gordon: quoted on manifest destiny, 13; condemns Kossuth, 170; mentioned, 14, 15
Benson, Lee, 21

Benton, Thomas Hart: adopts Young American principles, 133
Blair, Francis: reprimanded by Clay, 94; at Democratic banquet, 114; mentioned, 133
Bloomer, Amelia, 59
"Bloomerism," 98
Boardman, H. A.: defends Farewell Address, 146
Boutwell, James: as interventionist, 109, 157
Bowen, Francis: attacks Kossuth, 43; denied Harvard chair, 43, 44
Brace, Charles Loring, 69
Breese, Sidney, 21
Brick, Josef, 49
Bridgman, Laura Dewey: meets Kossuth, 156
Bright, Jesse D.: as presidential darkhorse, 113; mentioned, 21
Brownson, Orestes: attacks Kossuth, 126, 127–28, 170
Brownson's Quarterly Review, 174
Bryant, William Cullen, 34
Buchanan, James: as presidential hopeful, 113, 159; attacked by *Democratic Review*, 118, 119; quoted on impossibility of intervention, 131
Buel, Alexander: quoted, 13, 36
"Bunker Hill Casket": given to Kossuth, 58
Burke, Edmund: approached by Kossuth, 158–59; mentioned, 162
Burlingame, Anson: quoted, 157
Burritt, Elihu: compares U.S. and Austria, 69
Butler, C. M.: quoted, 90
Butler, William O.: feud with George Sanders, 118; attacked by *Democratic Review*, 119

Calhoun, John C.: lacks hope for French Revolution, 16–18; as "realist," 100; condemns rhetorical diplomacy, 135–36; mentioned, 93, 99, 137, 178

Calvin, John, 126

Capitalism, 95–96, 95n–96n

Caruthers, William Alexander, 97

Cass, Lewis: welcomes French Revolution, 16–17, 73; described, 18–21; quoted on public opinion, 19–20, 22; theory of diplomacy, 19–20; on suspending Austrian relations, 31–35, 74; on moral authority, 32; attacked by Clay, 33–34; Hülsemann's opinion of, 37; corresponds with Kossuth, 43; condemns Hale, 75; hosts Kossuth, 88; rebuked in Southern press, 101; attacked by Democratic Review, 118; as presidential contender, 113, 159; left behind by Young America, 115, 142–43; supported, 137–39; mentioned, 136, 144, 151, 153, 159, 162, 178, 183

Catholic Church. See Roman Catholic Church

Catholic Freeman's Journal: attacks Kossuth, 127

Central Hungarian Committee, 58

Central Southern Association to Promote the Cause of Liberty in Europe, 23

Channing, William Ellery, 71, 79

Channing, William Francis, 156

Charles X (France), 137

Charleston Courier: ignores Kossuth, 151

Chartists, 15

Chase, Salmon P., 34, 144

Cincinnati Enquirer. See Enquirer (Cincinnati)

Clark, William, 18

Clarke, John H.: rejects Young America, 136; mentioned, 144

Clay, Cassius M.: supports interventionism, 109; seeks funds for Kossuth, 148

Clay, Henry: early idealistic diplomacy of, 32; attacks Young America, 33–34; opposes Hülsemann letter, 42; prestige of, 92–93; meeting with Kossuth, 93–94; mentioned, 65, 74, 108, 148n, 183

Clayton, John M.: instructions to A. Dudley Mann, 25–26; seeks Kossuth's release, 36; receives Hülsemann's protest, 38; on Hülsemann letter, 42; mentioned, 27, 145

Clemens, Jeremiah: quoted condemning Kossuth, 100–102, 105; diplomatic theory of, 140–41; attacked by Kossuth, 150; mentioned, 100

Cleveland True Democrat. See True Democrat (Cleveland)

Compromise of 1850, 40, 65, 67, 85–86, 115

Conway, Moncure Daniel: quoted, 98

Corcoran, W. W.: philanthropy of, 49

Correy, William: role in inviting Kossuth, 44n; as interventionist, 45

Courier and Enquirer (New York), 24, 35, 63

Crafts, William, 97

Crimean War: predicted by Kossuth, 94; American response to, 173–74

Crittenden, John J.: abandons Young America, 145–46

Crozier, H. P.: condemns Kossuth, 79

Cushing, Caleb, 119

Daily Picayune (New Orleans): quoted on intervention, 101; mentioned, 55, 105

Daily Union (Washington): quoted on Whig "monarchists," 36; supports intervention, 45–46; on Kossuth's popularity, 64; abandons Kossuth, 104; on Kossuth and protestantism, 127; mentioned, 58, 64, 158

Dallas, George M., 24

Davis, Henry Winter: apocalyptic warnings of, 131–33, 180

DeBow, J. D. B., 96

De Leon, Edwin: on Young America, 11, 178

Democratic party: convention of 1852, 159–60; platform, 164n

Democratic Review: on French Revolution, 17–18; on 1852 campaign, 117–20, 164–65; mentioned, 116, 136, 163

Detroit Free Press. See Free Press (Detroit)

Dewey, Orville: quoted, 50

Dickinson, Daniel S., 34

Dominican Republic, 167

Donelson, Andrew Jackson: gift to Kossuth, 58

Douglas, Stephen A.: supports Hülsemann letter, 42; as presidential contender, 113, 159; avoids endorsing Kossuth, 115–16; political strategy of, 115–16; endorses filibustering, 116; *Democratic Review* on, 118; rebukes George Sanders, 118–19; mentioned, 21, 86, 162

Douglass, Frederick: contrasts Kossuth's speeches and slavery, 68; quoted, 70; mentioned, 79, 182

Downing, George, 76–77

Draper, Simeon, 35, 58

Dress Circular, 175

Duer, William, 63

E. Anthony, 61

Eaton, Peggy, 19

Emerson, Ralph Waldo: quoted, 169; mentioned, 97, 155, 178

Enquirer (Cincinnati), 125

E Pluribus Unum: quoted, 111–12

Evans, George Henry, 14

Ewing, Presley: quoted, 101; mentioned, 93

Farewell Address. *See* Washington's Farewell Address

Fillmore, Millard: criticizes Young America, 84, 86–87; as realist, 84–86; foreign policy of, 86; meets Kossuth, 88–89; criticized, 116, 127; mentioned, 41, 53, 92, 107, 117, 173

Fillmore, Millard, Jr., 56

Fitzhugh, George: quoted, 98; mentioned, 99

Foote, Henry S.: supports Kossuth, 44, 74, 105, 148; offers to lynch John P. Hale, 73

"Forty-Eighters." *See* Germans in the United States

Foster, Stephen, 97n

France: attitude toward Kossuth, 4; Revolution of 1848, 14–18, 24, 30, 73

"Francis Joseph," 104

Free Press (Detroit): quoted, 15, 44–45, 129–30

Free-Soilers: and Kossuth, 71; platform of

1852, 161–62; mentioned, 22, 66, 73, 148, 163

"Friends of Hungary," 121, 134

Fugitive Slave Law, 68, 71, 85–86

Furness, William H.: quoted, 78

Garibaldi, Giuseppe: in London, 173

Garrison, William Lloyd: quoted, 71; attacks Kossuth, 78–79; mentioned, 67, 122, 182

Garrisonians. *See* Abolitionists

Genin, John Nicholas, 59–61

Germans in the United States, 63, 123, 128, 154, 159, 163–64, 170–71

Germany, 14, 15

Giddings, Joshua: quoted on Free-Soilers and Kossuth, 71; sees Kossuth's opponents as proslavery, 104; mentioned, 103, 162

Goepp, Charles: supports Kossuth, 111–12; at Wheeling Conference, 171

Gould, Walter, 62

Greece: war of independence in, 32

Greeley, Horace, 15, 84, 91, 108, 170, 174

Greene, William B., 154

Gregg, William, 96

Haiti: Kossuth's designs on, 167

Hale, John Parker: quoted, 16, 105; described, 72–73; on foreign policy, 73–75; mentioned, 103

Hamlin, Hannibal, 144

Hannegan, Edward, 21

Hapsburg Empire. *See* Austria

Hartford Republican: quoted, 79

Harvard University: Bowen dismissed at, 43–44

Hawes, Richard: quoted, 148

Hawley, Charles: quoted on progress, 12

Hawthorne, Nathaniel, 97

Hebbe, G. C., 163

Helper, Hinton Rowan: mentioned, 96, 99

Hendricks, Thomas A.: identifies Kossuth's opponents as proslavery, 104

Henningsen, C. F., 166–67

Herald, New York. *See New York Herald*

Holy Alliance: mentioned, 32

Hornblower, Chief Justice, 24
Houston, Sam: as presidential darkhorse, 113
Howe, Samuel Gridley: supports interventionism, 109–10; hosts Kossuth, 155–56; Kossuth asks loan from, 167
Hughes, John, Archbishop: quoted, 129
Hülsemann, G. J.: quoted on American attitudes toward Austria, 30; opinions on American politics, 37–38; protests Mann's mission, 38–40; departs Washington, 91–92; mentioned, 75, 108
Humboldt: mentioned, 1, 5, 60, 71
Hungarian Liberty Fund, 59
Hungary: revolution in, 1–2, 22–23, 26–27, 29–30, 38, 43; mentioned, 9, 26, 31, 36, 39, 43, 44, 53, 58, 59, 68, 78, 84, 86, 88, 90–91, 93, 94, 103, 105, 110, 115, 121, 125, 128, 130, 131, 136, 142, 143, 146, 151, 158, 167, 170, 173, 179, 180, 183
Hungary Bonds: described, 58; mentioned, 83, 133, 166
Hunter, R. M. T.: as Douglas's vice-presidential choice, 115

Inalienable homesteads, 12
Impending Crisis of the South: How to Meet It, The: mentioned, 96
"Intervention for Non-Intervention": meaning of, 53; mentioned, 56, 89, 107, 116
Irving House, 8

Jackson, Andrew: mentioned, 19, 49, 58, 94
Jackson Democratic Association: banquet for Kossuth, 113–16; mentioned, 120
Jefferson, Thomas: recognition policy of, 34, 136; mentioned, 58
"Jenny Lindism," 98
Jesuits: attacked by Kossuth, 129
Johnson, Andrew, 175
Joel and Company, 61
Jones, James C.: criticizes Lewis Cass, 143–44; mentioned, 100

Kennedy, John Pendleton, 97
Kingsland, Ambrose C., 7

Klapka, General, 55
Knox, John, 126
Kossuth Bonds. See Hungary Bonds
"Kossuth hats," 60–61
Kossuth, Theresa, 2, 8

Lafayette, Marquis de, 8, 47, 52, 90
Lane, Joe: as presidential darkhorse, 113
Latin American Independence, 32
Liberator, The, 67, 68, 78, 122
Liberty Party, 73
Lincoln, Abraham: supports Kossuth, 24; sanctions Hungarian secession, 110; mentioned, 144
Lind, Jenny, 59
London Leader, 45
London Times. See Times, The (London)
Long, John C.: warned about Kossuth, 3
Longfellow, Henry Wadsworth, 156
López, Narciso: condemned by Fillmore, 86; endorsed by Stephen A. Douglas, 116
Louisiana Purchase, 13
Luther, Martin: mentioned, 126, 127

Macon Telegraph: quoted, 101
Maine legislature: supports interventionism, 109
Mallory, Senator, 129
Manifest destiny: defined, 13; mentioned, 13n, 178
Mann, A. Dudley: mission to Austria and Hungary, 25–27, 38
Mann, Horace: compares U. S. and Austria, 69; condemns South, 102; mentioned, 182
Mann, Mrs. Horace, 157
Marcy, William, 175
Marsh, George Perkins: quoted, 2–3; instructed to secure Kossuth's release, 36
Marx, Karl, 98
Massachusetts General Court: invites Kossuth to visit, 109
Mazzini, Giuseppe: in London, 173
Merk, Frederick: on Southern attitudes toward foreign policy, 99
Mexican War: mentioned, 15, 178, 180
Miller, Jacob: described, 141; rejects Young

America, 141–42; criticizes Lewis Cass, 143; mentioned, 144

Mirriam, George, 154

"Mission": described, 13–14, 177–78

Mississippi, U. S. S., 2, 3–4, 44

Mississippi Free Trader: identifies Kossuth as "fugitive slave," 103–4; quoted, 148

Monroe Doctrine: Lewis Cass on, 20; attacked by Kossuth, 52–53; mentioned, 13

Monroe, James: mentioned, 13

"Moral Force": Lewis Cass's theory of, 19–20

Morgan, Charles W.: criticizes Kossuth, 3

Napoleon, Louis: Kossuth's threat against, 4; mentioned, 17, 131

National Anti-Slavery Standard, 80

National Era, The, 24, 69, 108

New Doctrine of Intervention, Tried by The Teachings of Washington, The: quoted, 146

New England: Kossuth visits, 154–58

New Orleans Bulletin: identifies Kossuth with abolitionism, 103

New Orleans *Daily Picayune. See Daily Picayune* (New Orleans)

New Rome: The United States of the World, The: summarized, 171

New York *Courier and Enquirer. See Courier and Enquirer* (New York)

New York Herald, 14, 76, 91, 170

New York Times, The, 5, 47, 75, 170, 173

New York Tribune, 15, 91, 108, 170, 174

Nicholas, Czar: intervenes in Hungary, 24; censured by Americans, 30; mentioned, 24, 64, 77, 130, 132, 144

North American Review: quoted, 43, 172

Olds, Edson B.: to sponsor Kossuth citizenship, 47

O'Reilly, Henry C.: gives land to Kossuth, 57

O'Sullivan, John L.: and manifest destiny, 13n; and Central Hungarian Committee, 58; pressures Pierce to support Kossuth, 163

Pacifism: mentioned, 22, 46

Parker, Theodore, 156

Parkman, Francis: quoted, 172

Pennsylvanian, The, 119

Perry, Matthew C.: sent to Japan, 86

Peuples, Les, 4

Phillips, Wendell: condemns Kossuth, 79

Phrenology, 12

Pickett, John C.: as would-be filibusterer, 167–68

Pierce, Franklin: as presidential candidate, 113; nominated, 160; reputation of, 160; ignores Kossuth, 163, 165; pressured to support Kossuth, 163–65; asked for money by Kossuth, 167; criticized by Kossuth, 173–74

Polk, James K.: resurrects Monroe Doctrine, 13

"Progress," 11–14, 16, 178

Pulszky, Francis, 55–56

Pulszky, Theresa, 56

Quincy, Edmund: disillusioned with Kossuth, 80

Quincy, Josiah, 155

Reed, W. B., 80

Reid, Mayne: tries to join Kossuth, 23

Religion and Kossuth, 124–29

Revolutions of 1848, 14–18, 178

Rhey (Speaker of the House), 122

Richmond Guards: protect Kossuth, 6

Ritchie, Thomas: mentioned, 36, 158

Roman Catholic Church: and Kossuth, 126–29, 157

Romanoff, Nicholas. *See* Nicholas, Czar

Root and Company, 62

Russia: intervenes in Hungary, 1, 2; criticized by Americans, 8, 108, 109–10, 115, 129–33, 136–37; Jeremiah Clemens on, 140; in Crimean War, 173; as stereotype, 179–80; mentioned, 2, 26, 30, 36, 53, 94, 102, 114–15, 131, 132, 139, 140, 144, 174

Sanders, George Nicholas: supports Kossuth, 105; described, 116–17; and 1852 campaign, 117–20; rebuked by Douglas,

118–19; pressures Pierce to support Kossuth, 164–65; Kossuth asks loan from, 167; as Consul to England, 173; mentioned, 162–63, 173
Schwarzenberg, Felix: obtains A. Dudley Mann's instructions, 38; orders Hülsemann protest, 39
Scioto Gazette: quoted on progress, 12
Scott, Winfield: nominated, 160
Sedgwick, Theodore: and Central Hungarian Committee, 58
Seward, William H.: quoted, viii; supports Webb appointment, 35; sponsors bill for Hungarians, 49; and welcome to Kossuth, 75; hosts Kossuth, 88; at congressional banquet, 90; donates to Kossuth, 109; quoted on interventionism, 136–37; mentioned, 84, 103, 144, 151, 161
Shields, Senator, 88, 129, 151
Slavery: centrality of, 65; Kossuth on, 70, 76–77, 80, 148–49; effect on South, 95–100
Slavery As It Is: copy of, given to Kossuth, 71
Soulé, Pierre: supports Kossuth, 44n, 105, 163; described, 137; endorses interventionism, 137–39; pressures Pierce to support Kossuth, 163, 164
Soulouque, Faustin Elié, 167
South: backwardness of, 95–99; prevalent diplomacy theory in, 99–102; condemnation of Kossuth in, 100–102, 181–82
South Carolina College, 11
Southern Advocate: quoted opposing "progress," 97; quoted opposing interventionism, 102–3; mentioned, 99
Sparks, Jared: mentioned, 51
Spengler, Oswald: historical theory of, 11
Stephens, Major: quoted, 114–15
Stockton, Robert Field: described, 139; endorses interventionism, 139–40
Stowe, Harriet Beecher: mentioned, 97n
Strong, George Templeton: quoted, 54, 61
Sturdevant, Oscar W.: and Central Hungarian Committee, 58
Sultan of Turkey: "arrests" Kossuth, 2; interns Kossuth, 36–37; releases Kossuth, 44; mentioned, 67, 173

Sumner, Charles: supports European crusade, 46; compares Kossuth to slave, 68; first Senate speech of, 104; mentioned, 109, 156
Sun, Baltimore. See Baltimore Sun
Szcmere, Bartholomaeus: criticizes Kossuth, 147

Tammany Hall: supports interventionism, 45, 104
Taylor, Zachary: hopes to recognize Hungary, 24–26; appoints Webb, 35; offers Kossuth asylum, 36; sends Mann documents to Congress, 39; death of, 39; mentioned, 24, 27, 117
Temperance movement, 12
Thompson, Jacob: quoted, 165
Ticknor, George: mentioned, 41–42
Times, The (London): quoted, 63, 127; mentioned, 146
Times (New York). See New York Times, The
Tocqueville, Alexis de, 180
Tribune (New York). See New York Tribune, The
True Democrat (Cleveland): quoted, 79, 124, 175
Turkey: mentioned, 1, 156. See also Sultan of Turkey
Tyler, John: anti-Austrianism of, 31
Tyler, Robert: sympathy for Kossuth, 23

Underwood, Joseph: quoted opposing intervention, 101; mentioned, 100
Union, The. See Daily Union
United States Democratic Review. See Democratic Review
Universal public education, 12

Van Buren, Martin: as presidential hopeful, 113; attacked by Democratic Review, 118; mentioned, 114, 133
Vanderbilt, 6
Vicksburg Weekly Whig: quoted, 150

Walker, Isaac B., 21, 112–13
War of Ormuzd and Ahriman in the Nine-

teenth Century: summarized, 131–33; mentioned, 180

Ware, William, 56–57

Washington, George: Kossuth compared to, 8, 50; mentioned, 100

Washington's Farewell Address: summarized, 50–51; attacked by Kossuth, 51–52; used against Young America, 145–46, 160–61, 172; mentioned, 157

Watson, Nathan Bird, 69

Webb, James Watson: appointment as chargé to Austria unpopular, 35; opposes Kossuth, 54, 63

Webster, Daniel: quoted on power of public opinion, 22; censures Czar, 30; Hülsemann's opinion of, 37; correspondence with Hülsemann, 39–42, 89; fears interventionism, 46; meets Kossuth, 87; ambivalence of, toward Young America, 89–91; predicts decline of interventionism, 107; mentioned, 85, 87, 92, 178, 183

Weed, Thurlow, 84

Weld, Theodore Dwight, 71

Wheeling Conference, 170–71

Whig Central Committee (New York), 57

Whig convention (1852), 160–61; mentioned, 163

Whitney, Eli: gives Kossuth guns, 155

Whittier, John Greenleaf, 69, 70

Wigfall, Lewis T.: quoted, on Southern uniqueness, 97; mentioned, 99

Wilmot Proviso, 22

Winthrop, Robert: quoted, 171–72

Wool, John E.: warns of Kossuth's eloquence, 150

Wright, Henry C.: quoted on Kossuth and slavery, 68

Young America: defined, 11–14, 21–22; definition summarized, 177–78; compared to Christianity, 138–39; and slavery, 180–82

Young America! (New York): mentioned, 14

Zoroastrianism: symbolism of, borrowed by Henry Winter Davis, 132, 180

Library of Congress Cataloging in Publication Data
Spencer, Donald S   1945–
     Louis Kossuth and young America.

     Bibliography: p.
     Includes index.
     1. Kossuth, Lajos, 1802–1894. 2. Heads of state—
Hungary—Biography. 3. United States—Politics and
government—1849–1861. 4. United States—Foreign
relations—1849–1853. I. Title.
DB937.3.S66   301.29'73'0439   77-2123
ISBN 0–8262–0223–3

The illustrations on the following pages first appeared in the sources listed:

p. v, *The Illustrated London News* 15:406 (29 December 1849): 448.

p. vi, *The Illustrated London News* 19:527 (1 November 1851): 544.

p. xi, *The Illustrated London News* 19:527 (1 November 1851): 549.

p. xii, *The Illustrated London News* 19:527 (1 November 1851): 544.

p. 5, *The Illustrated London News* 19:527 (1 November 1851): 549.

pp. 7, 9, 46, *Kossuth in America, 1851–1852*, John Komlos (Buffalo, N.Y., 1973).

pp. 18, 23, 24, 41, 45, 72, 85, 132, 138, *Dictionary of American Portraits* (New York, 1967).

p. 29, *The Illustrated London News* 15:385 (11 August 1849): 97.

p. 31, *The Illustrated London News* 15:382 (28 July 1849): 57.

p. 60, Collection of Allen S. Davenport.